The Character of Class Struggle: Essays in Canadian Working-Class History, 1850-1985

The Character of Class Struggle: Essays in Canadian Working-Class History, 1850-1985

edited by

Bryan D. Palmer

M&S

Canadian Cataloguing in Publication Data
Main entry under title:
The Character of class struggle: essays in Canadian working-class history,
1850-1985

Includes bibliographical references.
(Canadian social history series)

ISBN 0-7710-6946-4

1. Labour and labouring classes – Canada – History – Addresses, essays, lectures.
2. Social conflict – Canada – History – Addresses, essays, lectures.
I. Palmer, Bryan D., 1951-   II. Series.

HD8104.C45 1986   331.11'0971   C86-093342-3

Printed and bound in Canada by Webcom Ltd.

McClelland and Stewart
The Canadian Publishers
481 University Avenue
Toronto, Ontario
M5G 2E9

Contents

Acknowledgements

Ian McKay, "Class Struggle and Merchant Capital: Craftsmen and Labourers on the Halifax Waterfront, 1850-1900," is an extensively revised version of an essay that appeared originally in Gerald Panting and Rosemary Ommer, eds., *Workingmen Who Got Wet* (St. John's, 1980).

Gregory S. Kealey and Bryan D. Palmer, "The Bonds of Unity: The Knights of Labor in Ontario, 1880-1900," is an abridged version of an essay that appeared in *Histoire sociale/Social History*, 14 (November, 1981), pp. 369-411, and appears with permission of the editors of that journal.

Craig Heron, "Hamilton Steelworkers and the Rise of Mass Production," is an abridged version of an essay that appeared in Canadian Historical Association, *Papers* (1982), pp. 103-131, and appears with permission of the Canadian Historical Association.

Gregory S. Kealey, "1919: The Canadian Labour Revolt," is an abridged version of an essay that appeared in *Labour/Le Travail*, 13 (Spring, 1984), pp. 11-44, and appears with permission of the editor of that journal.

Gail Cuthbert Brandt's "The Transformation of Women's Work in the Quebec Cotton Industry, 1920-1950" is an original essay appearing for the first time in this volume.

Jeremy Webber, "The Malaise of Compulsory Conciliation: Strike Prevention in Canada during World War II," is an abridged and edited version of an essay that appeared in *Labour/Le Travail*, 15 (Spring, 1985), pp. 57-88, and appears with permission of the editor of that journal.

Heather Jon Maroney, "Feminism at Work," is an abridged and edited version of an essay that appeared in *New Left Review*, 141 (September-October, 1983), pp. 51-71, and appears with permission of the editors of that journal.

Bryan D. Palmer's "The Rise and Fall of British Columbia's Solidarity" is an original essay produced for this volume. It is based on a larger, book-length study to be published late in 1986 by New Star Books.

Contributors

Gail Cuthbert Brandt teaches at Glendon College, York University, and has published a number of articles on women in twentieth-century Canada.

Craig Heron is co-editor of *On the Job: Confronting the Labour Process in Canada* and teaches at York University.

Gregory S. Kealey edits *Labour/Le Travail*, teaches at Memorial University of Newfoundland, and has published extensively in the field of Canadian working-class history. He is the author of *Toronto Workers Respond to Industrial Capitalism* and co-author of *Dreaming of What Might Be: The Knights of Labor in Ontario*.

Ian McKay lives in Halifax, works closely with *New Maritimes*, and has produced a number of studies of labour in the Atlantic Canada region.

Heather Jon Maroney is working on a study of women and trade unionism in modern Canada and Quebec while teaching at Trent University.

Bryan D. Palmer is the author of *Working-Class Experience: The Rise and Reconstitution of Canadian Labour* and co-author of *Dreaming of What Might Be: The Knights of Labor in Ontario*. He now teaches at Queen's University, although during 1983 he was teaching in British Columbia and involved in the Solidarity movement.

Jeremy Webber is a Vancouver lawyer/writer. In 1982 he was associated with a research project initiated by Alan B. Gold, a justice of the Quebec Superior Court.

For Herbert G. Gutman (1928-1985)
and what he did for all of us

Introduction

"The history of all hitherto existing society," wrote Marx and Engels, "is the history of class struggles." For these early advocates of class struggle, history was not so much a long march of progress as it was a perpetual contest between "oppressor and oppressed," who "carried on an uninterrupted, now hidden, now open fight."[1] These were words of propaganda, currently dismissed easily by sophisticates, sceptics, and scholastics. And they are right to insist that there has been more to history than class war.

But it would nevertheless be wrong to ignore the essential insight of Marx and Engels.[2] Much recent writing on the social history of Canadian labour, for instance, underscores the extent to which aspects of working-class life seemingly far removed from overt struggle have been structured around the harsh realities of class as a lived experience. Basic and mundane features of everyday existence – sustaining a family, sitting in a tavern, settling into a home – have been shown to be expressions of the very same polarization of classes that periodically erupts in episodic confrontation.[3]

This does not mean, of course, that workers have everywhere, at all times and places, been conscious of themselves as part of a class united against another class. It does suggest, however, that in the Canadian context in the period this book concerns itself with (1850-1985), those who worked for wages could never escape entirely their class place. To be sure, other identifications, especially those of region, ethnic group, craft, or gender, may well have blurred workers' consciousness of a common class experience, although it needs to be stressed that this has seldom occurred as decisively as some commentators imply.[4] Moreover, this was always a historically rooted phenomenon, subject to change and determined by the developing sets of possibilities emerging out of the transformation of productive life and the consequent character of class struggle.[5] In short, while workers' consciousness may well have been circumscribed historically by a host of competing identifications, dependency on wage labour has rooted workers in common experiences that have often resulted in class confrontations pitting labour against capital. When such overt instances of class struggle arise, the ways in which other identifications (ethnicity or gender, for instance) can reinforce and strengthen the bonds of class often reveal themselves, just as values and ideologies forged outside of working-class circles (respectability, temperance, or religion) can be seen to be turned toward the defence of working-class well-being.[6]

This collection of essays concerns itself with such instances of overt confrontation in an attempt to present a coherent picture of the changing character of class struggle in Canada from the mid-nineteenth century to the present. These 135 years encompass the sweep of industrial-capitalist development in Canadian history, a history marked by crucial changes and departures in the organization of productive relations and the utilization of political power. Such economic and political transformation has created the contexts in which class struggle has been embedded. These essays in Canadian working-class history may thus be read as an attempt to situate the character of class struggle within particular political economies.

Canadian capitalist development and class struggle could be divided by the historian into various historical periods, none of which would solve all interpretive dilemmas, overcome the essential untidiness of the historical process, or establish uncontestable chronological and regional boundaries within which change occurred.[7] These essays are structured around an elementary concern with three distinct, if overlapping, contexts: the nineteenth-century experience; monopoly capitalism from 1900 to 1950; and the attempts of advanced capitalism and the state to accommodate the class struggle from the post-World War II years to the present. If these contexts should not be substituted for a more rigorous and well-developed sense of periodization, they at least alert us to important aspects of Canadian class struggle.

The essays by McKay and by Kealey and Palmer focus on the late nineteenth-century years, exploring how varieties of capitalism (the one dominated by mercantile capital, the other by industrial capital) produced very different forms of class struggle. Where mercantile capital in the port of Halifax necessarily fostered highly fragmented and unstable relations of production, with casual labour markets and overwhelming dependence on shipping enterprises that were as volatile technologically as they were mobile geographically, industrial capital in the Ontario of the 1880's was tending to homogenize productive relations in an emerging factory system. Specific regional economies, then, gave rise to quite distinct types of class relations. The character of class struggle was consequently different in the port city than it was in the developing industrial heartland of the country: the bonds of unity were understandably weaker in a metropolitan centre of Maritime Canada. As McKay's later writing suggests, a close look at the decade of greatest working-class upheaval, the 1880's, might well serve to highlight some common features in the class struggles of East Coast and central Canadian workers.[8] But the remarkably dissimilar economies of the Victorian port and industrial cities of these two articles remind us that the class struggle is not solely the product of human will; it erupts within particular determined limitations.

Between 1900 and 1950, the old limitations of nineteenth-century capital – mercantile and industrial – were overcome. An age of entrepreneurial initiative, be it deployed in sustaining the patriarchal family-based firm of small-town Ontario or the transatlantic trade of the waterfront merchants, gave way to an epoch of corporate concentration, orchestrated by an alliance of industrial and finance capital. Centred in Montreal and Toronto, this budding partnership restructured productive and regional relations, stimulating business mergers and central Canadian take-overs of essential regional economic activities. The end product was an age of concentrated economic power unprecedented in the nineteenth century, a period of monopoly capitalism in which huge corporations overshadowed the still numerically dominant smaller firms. These vital new centres of production controlled entire economic sectors and consciously developed and cultivated specific markets and regions at the same time that they failed to develop other parts of the country.[9]

Class struggle in these years thus exhibited an essential schizo-phrenia. On the one hand, the emergence of national labour markets, the growing impersonality of workplace relations, and the relentless pursuit of corporate profit and productivity held out the potential, especially in the midst of moments of generalized crisis, for previously unanticipated labour revolt.[10] Kealey's dis-cussion of the national contours of the 1919 working-class agi-tation explores this aspect of class struggle within the age of monopoly. Situated within the post-war crisis of reconstruction and an international mobilization of working-class forces gal-vanized by wartime inflation, heightened bargaining power, and the example of revolutionary Russia, 1919 was a year of explosive class struggle. On the other hand, capital's newly created power circumscribed class struggle: it eroded old crafts and their long-standing workplace powers, forcing sectors of the labour movement into business unionism and aristocratic defences of their superior station; it recruited entire new labour forces from abroad and used them in ways that undercut resistance to its hegemony; and it created labour markets segmented by gender or ethnicity and ordered hierarchically along lines of socially constructed notions of "skill," where the English-speaking or the male worker was set above the immigrant, the francophone, or the woman. All of these developments, as well as many others, erected barriers in the path of working-class unity and limited the capacity of labour to resist capital's persistent assaults. The Heron and Brandt articles in this collection elaborate on this side of the class struggle in the age of mass production. Monopoly capitalism thus created the conditions for large-scale labour revolt at the same time as it pursued practices that aimed to stifle such upheaval. Class struggle was therefore a highly uneven phenomenon in the years 1900-1950.

The making of monopoly capitalism in Canada was also inseparable from the entry of the state into class relations. Indeed, the twentieth century marks an abrupt exit from the piecemeal, *ad hoc* manner in which an incompletely formed nineteenth-century state responded to the workers' movement.[11] As we enter the first decade of the twentieth century we are on the ground of the interventionist state, personalized in the figure of William Lyon Mackenzie King. He was a man who would chart the first paths the state would follow in its efforts to mediate class struggle, paths where both coercion and consent would accompany Canadian workers.[12]

In the World War II and immediate post-World War II years, however, an advanced capitalism finally reconciled itself to the need to use state power and one of its options, compulsory conciliation of labour-capital conflict, to accommodate the class struggle, minimizing its impact by instituting means to promote and regulate the resolution of fundamental class antagonisms. This development was itself a product of escalating class struggle during the war and post-war years, as Webber's article and other writings show.[13] But with the legitimation of trade unionism and the legal protection of workers' rights to bargain collectively secured through the passage of the 1948 Industrial Relations and Disputes

Investigation Act, the state was now a central participant in accommodating class struggle.

There would be other vehicles of accommodation, including the ways the trade union movement defined its own project of emancipation. As the article by Maroney reveals, the labour movement has been insufficiently attentive to the particular oppressions faced by working women, a shortcoming that necessarily feeds into capital's capacity to exploit all workers and further deepen the pit of inequality that women have found themselves mired in. Hardly confined to the post-war years, this arena has become an important sphere of struggle precisely because of the emergence of a women's movement that persists in raising challenges to long-standing trade union practices. Nor is the state uninvolved in this structured oppression of women, as recent developments reveal.

With the new right ascendant politically, the 1980's are a decade of restructuring class relations, of undermining the post-war legitimation of trade union rights, of curtailing and cutting back the welfare state's protections, however inadequate. Women are now paying a series of prices for such developments, as are organized labour generally and public-sector workers, overwhelmingly female, in particular. The rise and fall of British Columbia's Solidarity, a 1983 movement of opposition challenging such developments on the West Coast, illuminates how the state's initiatives can lead to invigorated forms of class struggle in the epoch of advanced capitalism. But Palmer's assessment also reveals how deeply a bureaucratized leadership is entrenched within the workers' movement, and how capable it is of terminating the class struggle should it threaten to break through other structures of accommodation, uniting men and women in a battle against capital, the state, and business as usual. The post-war period cannot, of course, be seen simply as a period of increasingly sophisticated accommodation of the class struggle, for new sectors of workers are becoming involved in class actions and Quebec, especially, has been the scene of impressive mass strikes throughout the 1970's and 1980's.[14] Yet neither is it possible to ignore the ways the accommodationist forces of the post-World War II years have worked to tame, at least partially, the character of class struggle in Canada.[15]

This is not to imply that the class struggle is now terminated, never to reappear. The following articles do not bid farewell to the working class, as do so many fashionable academic projects.[16] Rather, this closing stress on accommodation merely draws attention to the new structures and limitations that currently inhibit class struggle at the very point that it inevitably appears. Needless to say, no collection can adequately convey the full extent and diversity of the class struggle in Canada over the course of the last 135 years. But in trying to attend to regional difference, changing political and economic contexts, local circumstance and national development, the particular experiences of gender and ethnicity, and the ways in which labour's own containment is enhanced by a small but powerful layer of trade union leaders, these essays are intended to introduce readers to the changing and complex character of class struggle in Canada. If it has not consumed all of our history, it has at least occupied the centre of one of the stages on which our past has been acted out.

Part I

Varieties of Capitalism, Varieties of Struggle: The Nineteenth-Century Experience

Before 1850 the working class in British North America was weak and its struggles rarely broke out of the confines of particular occupational groupings and specific regional locales. In the years from 1850-1900, however, significant parts of Canada went through vast economic transformations. In south-central Canada the factory system emerged, while peripheral regions, once outposts of the fur trade or sophisticated trading economies linked to the mercantile centres of transatlantic commerce, became more integrated into and dominated by central Canadian financial and industrial interests. Economic development was linked to state formation and policy through major events and aspects of the 1860's and 1870's, such as Confederation and the National Policy. But development was not uniform and, as Canadian historians have long emphasized, regional peculiarities consolidated on the bedrock of these late nineteenth-century features of political and economic life.

Studies of class struggle in this period have focused on particular regions and have, for the most part, avoided explicit comparison of working-class activity in one region with that of another. In this section, essays by Ian McKay and by Gregory S. Kealey and Bryan D. Palmer provide an implicit contrast between the class struggles of a port city and those of a region where industrial-capitalist forms of production prevailed. Productive life in late nineteenth-century Ontario was increasingly structured around factories and expanding workshops, and the Knights of Labor led a series of battles that attempted to bring skilled and unskilled, men and women, and immigrant and Canadian workers together. The industrial revolution that swept across south-central Canada in the years immediately preceding the rise of the Noble and Holy Order, obliterating many past distinctions among workers and places, provided the foundations on which a mass movement of working-class resistance could be built. As McKay shows, however, no such foundations emerged in Halifax in the same period, where merchants attempted to secure some small measure of stability in an increasingly chaotic and industrialized world. The class struggles on the waterfront thus took a different direction than those of industrial Ontario, based as they were on a formal and enduring organization of work rooted in the separation of craft worker and unskilled labourer. Varieties of capitalism led to varieties of struggle.

1

Class Struggle and Merchant Capital: Craftsmen and Labourers on the Halifax Waterfront, 1850-1900

Ian McKay

They formed a powerful and worried group, the men who gathered at the Halifax YMCA on May 8, 1884.[1] Hon. A.G. Jones, Hon. L.G. Power, Messrs. George E. Francklyn, F.D. Corbett, W.C. Silver, J.C. Mackintosh, George E. Boak, W.E. West: these gentlemen comprised much of the Halifax merchant class and, not coincidentally, many of the city's past and future political leaders. As the city's Chamber of Commerce, they championed the port's interests in the ancient, languishing West Indies trade; and in the new and uncertain world of the National Policy, they had tried to win for Halifax a secure commercial niche as the winter port of the Dominion.[2] Neither campaign had borne fruit, and this class, now represented in this anxious forum, was in deep crisis.

Three related problems – competition of foreign steamers, the decline of the inshore fishery, and disappearing markets – coalesced in the overwhelming problem facing traditional Halifax merchants: plunging freights. Rules of trade that had guided several generations of merchants on the Halifax waterfront no longer applied. Better means of communication meant that buyers of West India produce were less at the mercy of carriers, who could now be played off one against another; the gradual triumph of the steamer upset traditional pricing mechanisms and drove sailing vessels into an ever-declining number of trades. Sail was being marginalized by steam even in those bulk trades in which it ought to have had an advantage. Internationally, sail in the late nineteenth century enjoyed advantages over steam as a cheap coal carrier. But even in this sphere, Maritime shipowners were complaining by 1888 that they were being discriminated against by coal companies: "A sailing vessel may be half or three-quarters loaded or even may only require a few tons to complete her loading," one shipowner argued, "but the moment a steamer comes in the sailing vessel has to lay off and the steamer, whatever she may be, is put in the berth and loaded."[3]

From the mid-1870's to the mid-1880's the bourgeoisie of Halifax was squeezed between two massive consolidations of capital: one on land, as the industries based on import substitution grew under the National Policy, and one at sea, as the capitalist world-system consolidated financial power and centralized shipping in a few great centres, and, in order to provide larger and faster vessels to transport goods and raw materials to all corners of the globe, replaced sail with steam. "There is no shipping in the province at the present time," exclaimed a man who had manufactured metal accessories for sailing vessels: it was hyperbole, but it drove home an obvious point.[4]

This sense of long-term structural crisis permeated the Chamber's meeting that day in 1884, but dominating the agenda was a more immediate problem: the militant eruption of the waterfront work force. Two days before, an important notice from the Laborers' Union of Halifax had appeared in the city's press threatening the "Merchants, Stevedores and Other Employers of Transient Labor in the City of Halifax" with a strike if the wage and other demands were not met.[5] Challenged from without by massive structural change in the capitalist world-system, the Halifax merchants were for the first time threatened from within their private waterfront world of wharves, sail-lofts, store-houses, shops, and ships by their own rebellious workers. It was this second, novel challenge to their power that the merchants were determined to crush when they met in May, 1884.

Mr. W.C. Silver, a well-known philanthropist and one of the wealthiest of the city's merchants, was perplexed that workers were not grateful for the social improvements of the past half-century: "At one time he could remember the majority of the laboring people could not read and did not know what was going on in the other centres of trade. . . . In old times mechanics and laborers used to go about in poor and patched clothing, though neat and clean, and worked for small wages, yet were happy and contented. Now they dressed in tweeds and cloths and with additional comforts in the homes and living not dearer yet they were discontented." Workers had scant appreciation for the merchants' lot in life: "They did not consider the difficulties of the merchant in successfully carrying on a business to employ men. They were too apt to consider all employers of labor as wealthy aristocrats who lived luxuriously in palatial residences. They seldom thought that men who became successful merchants had to work very hard for it."

Inspired by such sentiments, the Chamber of Commerce resolved that it learned "with regret" that the labourers and stevedores had made a demand for increased wages "at a time when all branches of trade and commerce are exceptionally dull," adding that in its opinion "any increase in wages such as is demanded will not in the end act to the advantage of the laborers themselves." Mayor J.C. Mackintosh – a noted financier and investor – read into this resolution a broad social program. It was vitally important to resist the union's demand, he urged, because "There was a great deal of latent communism in the city, and in his opinion it was not well to recognize the men's demands to too great an extent."[6]

The 1884 strike is important as an event, a moment of the awakening of the working class of the Maritimes in the 1880's, but it is even more important as a window on a little-explored world, that of social relations in the era of merchant capital. It brought to the level of discourse the two invisible axes of the waterfront world, its two overriding structural tendencies: technical obsolescence and casualism; and it dramatized the consequences of these two structures for the two main groups of waterfront workers: craftsmen, defending their obsolete trades as best they could in a rapidly changing world, and longshoremen, divided and immobilized by a casual labour system. Workers no less than merchants faced a huge transition as steamers replaced sail and the world trading system was centralized; but, ironically, this transition, generally so negative in its consequences for the Maritime region, enabled them to transcend a century-old tradition of fragmentation and dependence – those bitter fruits of merchant capital – and begin to organize as a class.

What follows is in three parts. In the first, the nineteenth-century waterfront craftsmen – the riggers, blockmakers, coopers, sailmakers, shipwrights, and caulkers – will be presented as a defensive "labour aristocracy" protecting their own immediate interests but structurally incapable of a more all-inclusive class consciousness.

In the second, the position of the longshoremen from mid-century to 1902 will be studied as an example of the class fragmentation and dependence caused by surplus labour pools and the casual labour system. A third and concluding section will place these two intertwined stories in a more general context.

I

A labour aristocracy emerged among the craftsmen of the Halifax waterfront because they feared, with reason, the encroachments of other craftsmen, both rural and urban, and the competition of unskilled labourers. Confronted with large surplus labour pools, they defended their craft privileges in the only way open to them: by creating an artificial labour scarcity through the devices of the restriction of numbers and of the common rule.[7]

The transition from sail to steam was a protracted affair, and from 1850 to 1895 the two technologies coexisted, although with steam gaining inexorably on sail. The Pickford and Black registers, listing vessels calling Halifax, show sailing vessels outnumbering steamers in 1881 by two to one, but a reversal by 1901 so that steamships outnumbered sailing vessels by a ratio of approximately three to two.[8] The owners of wooden fleets did not hold a "fire sale" to sell off their depreciating vessels; they fought instead to wrench the last penny of profit from them, paying for fast passages through loss of gear, masts, spars, sails, and men.[9] This meant that until the mid-1890's traditional waterfront craftsmen found employment in Halifax repairing rather than building wooden vessels. Riggers, blockmakers, mastmakers, coopers, sailmakers, shipwrights, caulkers: such maritime craftsmen were indispensable in the building and maintenance of the large softwood fleets of the Maritimes, with their daunting repair costs.[10] Nor did sail suddenly disappear from the strategies of Halifax businessmen. Halifax dreamed of becoming the major repair port on the East Coast. Labour, businessmen urged, should not stand in the way of this important development. In 1886, two prominent ship repair firms passed along to the caulkers' union allegations from marine insurance companies "stating that the Port of Halifax was one of the most expensive Ports for repairing Vessels now existing," and that, as a consequence, "they were obliged to send Vessels to other places which might have been repaired in Halifax."[11] The episode suggested that the traditional craftsmen still occupied a strategic position in Halifax's tenacious struggle to survive in the new maritime world. As wooden shipbuilding virtually vanished and steamers pushed out sailing vessels from the most lucrative routes, there was continuing demand for the services of traditional waterfront craftsmen in the repair of the aging fleets.

Maritime crafts represented bodies of skilled knowledge and technique that took years to acquire. Riggers, blockmakers, and mastmakers, the three smallest crafts, attended to the highly intricate work of fitting out the vessels with articles vital for their sails. Such men, few in numbers and highly specialized, were tied closely to the ship chandleries that dotted the waterfront; they were never sufficiently numerous to allow the development of an overt division between masters and journeymen.[12] Divisions did emerge in the four large crafts. Coopers played an important role throughout industrializing North America in such spheres as flour-milling, distilling, and oil, but in Halifax their craft had a maritime complexion and centred on two vital commodities: sugar and fish. One large cooperage, which imported its staves and hoops from Ontario, operated immediately opposite the Nova Scotia Sugar Refinery; other coopers were employed directly by sugar refineries, subcontracting for the sugar barrels and paying journeymen coopers by the piece.[13] More found work on the wharves, and the rhythm of their labour was set by the fishery, as was suggested by the journeymen coopers in a description of their trade in 1903: "The favourable season of our branch of the trade and the prevailing prosperity that should be looked for turns out to be a disappointment in the fishery which leads to a dull season also for the coopers of Halifax. The catch of bank fish is very small in quantity and the quantity of casks used is very small in comparison to former years, so some of the boys are not very busy at the present time."[14] Although manufactories had emerged in cooperage, the application of steam supplemented rather than replaced the work of the coopers.

Sailmaking was another essential craft within the mercantile economy. Often sailmakers were employed on voyages, repairing damaged sails; and of the waterfront craftsmen, they were apt to be the most peripatetic, travelling with their very portable kits up and down the coast. The making of sails required judgement and experience, as well as precision and strength. Using a roping palm or (if need be) a mallet, a sailmaker had to force large needles through tough canvas and measure expensive sail cloth exactly to the rigging plan, strengthening those parts of the canvas likely to chafe against masts, yards, and ropes; he enlarged holes in the edges of the canvas with a "fid," a cone made of wood or bone, and inside the holes sewed "grommets," rings that prevented the rope from cutting into the canvas. Once these and other tasks in the sail loft were completed, the sailmaker would deliver the sail to the master rigger, proud of his artisanal accomplishment.[15]

The two remaining groups of waterfront craftsmen, shipwrights and caulkers, also believed the skill demanded by their work separated them out from other manual labourers. Shipbuilding entailed all the skills demanded by general carpentry,[16] complicated by the need to work with a wider range of angles, to lay the plank in complex patterns requiring skill and forethought, and to use joints peculiarly adapted for shipbuilding. No matter how graceful the model, botched work by the shipwrights would ruin the vessel.[17] Caulking, the process by which the ship was made watertight, seems at first glance a far less intricate art, but it required specialized tools (the caulking-iron and caulking-mallet), physical stamina, and experienced judgement. Caulkers worked with oakum, tarred hemp, or manila fibres made from old and condemned ropes. (This is why apprentices in this trade were sometimes called "oakum-boys.") Although "picking oakum," the tedious and unpleasant job of unpicking old rope and reworking it into threads running from forty to seventy feet to the pound, was elsewhere assigned to inmates of prisons and workhouses, in Halifax it was the preserve of the caulkers. After it had been "picked," the oakum was then rammed down between the seams with the chisel-like caulking-iron and the mallet, and hot pitch was poured along the seams. A poorly caulked vessel would not be seaworthy, and marine insurance companies laid down rules governing how these tasks were to be performed, specifying that the bottom of every ship was to be caulked once in every five years. It was a musical craft: the ring of the caulkers' mallets provided the unofficial economic index of the health of the port, and the caulkers themselves required good ears to listen carefully for the sound of a solidly filled seam.[18]

Here, then, were the crafts of the waterfront, each one indispensable, each one based on time-honoured and critical skills. Together these craftsmen constituted a large and important component of the Halifax working class.[19] With the partial exception of the coopers, a minority of whom were assembled in somewhat larger groups in steam-powered manufactories, none of these craftsmen faced a change in modes of production that had prevailed for decades along the waterfront. So entrenched were the small workshop and the small master artisan along the waterfront that when the *Census of Canada* raised the qualifications of "manufactures" to a minimum of five employees in 1901, the number of Halifax County cooperages fell from ninety-six in 1891 to six in 1901, the number of sail-lofts from four to two, and the number of shipbuilders from seven to two.[20] The small, often precariously marginal producer clearly continued to dominate these trades, and they never truly became industries. Craftsmen clearly faced no revolution in production that would have suddenly undermined their status.

But together they did face two structural problems that weakened their position: competition from other workers and the obsolescence of their trades in the new world of steam. These two structures determined the outlook of the waterfront craftsmen and consequently the nature of their trade unionism.

To organize a craft means to establish boundaries, most commonly determined by apprenticeship regulations, marking the craft off from "common, unskilled labour" and from other crafts. Each one of the four major crafts felt threatened by other workers. Halifax coopers serving the fishing industry were unable to compete with rural, self-employed artisans whose costs of production were far lower. Local sailmakers found their sphere invaded by the work of merchant seamen trained in sailmaking: in a strike in 1874 these craftsmen complained that "The employers have resorted to all sorts of means to fill the places left vacant by the strike. One shop . . . has two discharged soldiers as apprentices, and merchant sailors, to do the work of sailmakers, which they are not competent to do. Merchants and Insurance Agents should notice these facts."[21] Halifax shipwrights found themselves confronted with the hundreds of rural "hatchet and saw" men who streamed out of rural Nova Scotia as the age of shipbuilding came to a close.[22] When Dartmouth shipbuilder Ebenezer Moseley attempted to replace resident shipwrights on the Chebucto Marine Railway with rural newcomers in 1874, he was denounced by one indignant worker:

Since the large increase of Shipbuilding throughout the Province, employing as it does about 50 per cent of unskilled labour, we have had numerous applications for admission from persons who, having acquired the alphabet of a mechanical education, attracted to the city by cash payments, travelling like birds of passage from place to place, with an abundance of assurance and a moiety of modesty, who would as readily engage to construct a locomotive or a watch, as a ship, provided they had some persons to show them how, have now taken refuge at Mr. Moseley's Shipyard, a veritable cave of adullam for them, from whence he now trots them out and introduces them to the mercantile community as Shipwrights and Caulkers.[23]

The problem of these alarmingly versatile rural craftsmen persisted into the next century, and their distinctive outlook was echoed in the words of M.L. Oliver, a crusty old shipbuilder in Digby: "I am an old ship builder, built ships in U.S.A. before the civil war & have never struck a Labour Union. *I hate the name.*"[24]

There were equally intractable problems of demarcating the turf of the shipwright from that of other crafts. The union's rulebook established, on its very first page, precise criteria for separating the work of the shipwright from that of the joiner: members were exempt from penalty while working with joiners at such work as "fitting up cabins, houses, and forecastles; planing up deck planks, putting on bulwarks, except such as requires [sic] caulking, finishing and moulding rails, &c.," but it was stressed that joiners were "to put in no piece that requires caulking." Jurisdictional friction between joiners and shipwrights became more common in the late nineteenth century, as land-based carpenters came to do an increasing amount of joiners' work on steamers and adamantly refused to accept shipwrights as members unless they left the shipwrights' association.[25] Similar patterns of competition can be found in the relationship between the shipwrights and the caulkers. Caulkers were often lumped together with the shipwrights and the two trades overlapped; when the caulkers organized to form a separate union in 1882 they spoke of their reasons for creating a distinct caulkers' body:

. . . the Secretary read a clause showing how the Caulkers feeling themselves infringed upon by Carpenters in many ways as regards their work, thought it a benifit [sic] to have a Caulkers Society and had Called this meeting for the purpose of organizing themselves into a Caulkers Association.[26]

On May 11, 1885, a resolution passed stating that "no members of the Association shall work with anyone employed on the same job painting or scraping who are in the habit of doing Caulking or other wise interfering with the interest of the Association Under a penalty of $5.00 Dollars fine for each offense."[27] Sydney and Beatrice Webb argued that this spirit of "local monopoly" and the resulting fierce jurisdictional battles were especially characteristic of shipbuilding and other port trades, and E.J. Hobsbawm has underlined the intense localism of British waterside unionism, operating in ports that were competitive with each other.[28] Halifax bears out their analyses completely.

Craft unionism on the Halifax waterfront was thus profoundly marked by pressures within the labour market. The Shipwrights' and Caulkers' Association of Halifax and Dartmouth (1863-c.1914), the Caulkers' Association of Halifax and Dartmouth (1882-1908), the Sailmakers' Union Club (1871-c.1888), the Coopers' Union (1870-c.1878, 1884-1901), and Local 140, the first Canadian local of the revived Coopers' International Union (1901-1903), while participating in some of the general debates of the Halifax labour movement (such as denouncing the highly suspect "workingman's candidate" who sought labour support for the Tories in 1874), were never progressive, outward-looking bodies. Significantly, with the exception of the short-lived coopers' local, none was affiliated with a larger labour organization. Only rarely did any of these bodies take a clear political initiative.

What one finds, instead, is the adamant defence of craft privileges through restrictive devices, the most important of which was the limitation of numbers through skill qualifications and apprenticeship. The 1867 *Supplementary Rules* of the Shipwrights' and Caulkers' Association stated that "The term of apprenticeship shall not be less than five years or exceed seven." No member of the society was to work for any employer having more than three apprentices, and journeymen shipwrights and caulkers were forbidden to keep them. Apprentices out of their time were to pay an initiation fee of $4, which was $3 more than the initial sum.[29] Other crafts followed similar practices, often defending such limitations by strikes.[30] Restricting the number of apprentices closed the gates of the craft to the vast majority of the unskilled as well as limited the dilution of skills by the employers.

Besides apprentice restriction, such craft unions could employ other means to limit entry to crafts, including paying off rural craftsmen who came to the city. The caulkers, with a separate union after 1882, likewise survived by using the device of the limitation of numbers and the practice of the common rule. On November 11, 1884, the union simply closed entry to caulking by deciding it would receive no applications for membership for the next three months.[31] In 1886, its ability to control the hiring of caulkers was severely tested. The trouble began in mid-January when the barque *Chignecto*, carrying oil from New York to Rotterdam, put in to Halifax in distress. She was scheduled to undergo repairs at the Marine Slip in Dartmouth on January 28, but the Dartmouth caulkers refused to work at $2.40 per day and held out for ten cents more. Country men began work on the *Chignecto* the next day, with special constables sworn in to prevent rioting; at least one caulker was arrested. But after a delegation of unionists waited on the country men most of them were "persuaded" to return to their homes with sums ranging from $5 to $20. The records of the caulkers' union report that it borrowed $135.06 (far greater than the association's total assets) to rid itself of the rural craftsmen, a cost that was supposed to be divided evenly between the shipwrights' and the caulkers' unions. It appears that the *Chignecto* was repaired slowly with a few remaining non-unionists, but such merchant revolts against the association's rule were not repeated, and shipbuilders and shipowners had learned the difficulties they would encounter in any frontal assault on its monopoly.[32]

Rivalling the importance of restricting entry to the crafts in the strategies of these unions were various controls exerted over work. Information on this topic is plentiful only for the shipwrights and caulkers. The Shipwrights' and Caulkers' Association from its inception sought control over both new (i.e., shipbuilding) and old (ship repair) work; meeting staunch resistance from the dockyard in 1864, it reduced its jurisdiction to ship repair alone. While its *public* founding documents emphasize the association's benevolent and "improving" activities,[33] its *private* documents, most notably the remarkable *Supplementary Rules*, sound like a reveille for militants. The very first rule candidly outlines what should be done when conflict breaks out in the shipyards:

> SHOULD any cause of disagreements arise between masters or employers and this association . . . the members working on the job shall then meet to consider and decide on the most desirable method of arrangement. They shall then appoint a committee from their number to carry out such instructions as may be agreed on by two-thirds of their members present, and should such persons neglect or refuse to carry out such instructions they shall be liable to a fine not exceeding five dollars . . . and any member refusing to act in accordance

with the decision of the aforesaid majority of two-thirds of the members, shall be fined one dollar, unless it be clearly shown that he would violate the rules of this association by so doing.[34]

These eminently practical (and, by mid-Victorian standards, unusually candid) measures for job control soon made an impact. The stridently anti-union *Evening Express* found them outrageous:

> To give the public some idea of the effect of incorporating Trades' Unions, we may mention the fact that a few days ago one of our Merchants employed a Ship Carpenter to do some repairs to a vessel. It seems the person engaged was only a short time in business and could not afford to employ a large number of hands, so as usual with many a poor Master Mechanic, was obliged to take off his coat and work himself. But what think you reader, he worked one day, and on the next was coolly told by his employees that if he worked the second day they would quit work, and he was obliged to yield.[35]

Galled by such actions, some merchants applied pressure on the legislature to outlaw the association, and harsh criticisms were aired in the House of Assembly of the association's attempt "to create monopoly and prevent men coming to the city and engaging in work," but the effort to reverse the 1864 legalization of trade unionism came to nought. Attempts to organize a rival, more compliant union, the Dartmouth-based "Union Society of Shipwrights and Caulkers" founded by shipbuilder Ebenezer Moseley, also proved ineffectual, and the association exercised a quiet control over hiring until the turn of the century, sending for "country men" when they were required and arranging employment for its members in shipyards as distant as those of Honolulu.[36]

The Caulkers' Association was particularly noted for its tough working rules. Perhaps the most brazen and monopolistic was the constitutional provision that only oakum prepared by the caulkers themselves was to be used on any vessel. No one seriously maintained that caulkers deserved to prepare the oakum because it was "skilled work," nor that the article they produced was superior; the only rationale for such a rule was to bring under the control of the Caulkers' Association an important branch of maritime work for the relief of its underemployed members. At their anti-strike meeting in 1884 the aggrieved merchants protested that they were forced to use oakum spun by the caulkers themselves, which, at fifty cents per pound, was five times more expensive than the ready-spun article.[37] Far from being swayed by such appeals to liberal economics, the association tightened its grip. In 1886, "The Secretary asked if there could not be something done to stop one or two members from spinning Oakum when the rest of the members were walking about or not employed causing a large amount of illfeeling and Dissatisfaction," and the discussion ended by reaffirming the clause in the constitution that "no member should drive any Oakum except [of] his own spinning." On July 17, 1886, a member was charged with violating this decision by driving oakum not spun by himself; although he was not fined, the association passed the drastic resolution "That after this date no member be allowed to spin Oakum if he can be employed elsewhere at Caulking & Coopering or while any members are non employed," which meant giving the union exclusive control over the basic raw material of the craft. Even by the standards of Canadian craft unionism in the nineteenth century, the caulkers' control was remarkable.[38]

There were less contentious and "monopolist" aspects to the device of the common rule, although from an employers' viewpoint they were no less coercive. Both shipwrights and caulkers imposed conditions of hours and wages well in advance of other trades. From its foundation in 1863 to 1872, the association struggled for the $2.50 day; such was its strength that by 1872 it successfully negotiated on behalf of its eighty-eight members not only this advanced rate of wages but the nine-hour day from May 1 to October 1. The wage rates established in 1872 seem to have held up remarkably well as the century progressed and business slowed down; even a rough sort of eight-hour day was in effect in the winter months by 1888, although this appears only to have applied to shipwrights.[39] On the basis of such conditions (which were denounced as extravagant and unusual by the merchants) the shipwrights and caulkers were able to sustain a reasonable standard of living. Michael O'Brien (1847-1912), the association's secretary from 1864 to 1894 and a native of Killarney, Ireland, told the Labour Commission in 1888 that half of the shipwrights owned their own homes; he himself, estimating his pay at $800 per year for the last seven years, had managed to accumulate a half-dozen houses, which he rented out to other working-class families. O'Brien's thirty-year stint as secretary suggests the stability, not to say immobility, of the Shipwrights' and Caulkers' Association and of waterfront craft unionism in general.[40] Unless provoked, these small unions (never totalling more than 200 members, approximately one-fifth of the waterfront work force) defended themselves quietly, patiently, effectively. The turning point in their fortunes appears to have come in 1895 - "the worst year in the history of the craft," it was remarked in Dartmouth - after which these craftsmen lapsed into a profound silence, culminating in their disappearance as an organized force, probably shortly before World War I.[41]

The achievements of these waterfront craft unions were impressive. They made the most of their difficult situation within a context of dying crafts and diminishing possibilities. But these achievements were only possible on the basis of deliberately fostered labour scarcity and monopoly control over minute details of the work process. Craft achievement demanded a policy of exclusion toward labourers and rural craftsmen. In all the published and manuscript records left by these unions, there is no mention of craftsmen making common cause with the labourers who worked on the same waterfront with them, nor of them extending their organizations to their brother craftsmen in the country. Perhaps the most telling indications of the narrow structural limits of the craftsmen's achievements and their "labour aristocratic" mentality are the symptomatic silences: the silence in 1884 when the longshore labourers struggled for their rights; the silence in 1885 when the union's battle was lost; the silence in the minute books of the caulkers' union, where the most significant of all the disturbances along the Halifax waterfront did not merit a single word.

II

One of Halifax's first labour historians, regrettably anonymous, summed up the history of unskilled labour on the Halifax waterfront this way: "The history of the labor movement on the Port of Halifax would make interesting reading. Its earlier record has been a succession of failures. The workmen realizing the necessity of banding themselves together for common good, would form a union, and a large amount of enthusiasm would be generated, the men crowding into line, and for a time everything would go along successfully, but the reaction would set in and the membership gradually dwindle away again."[42] This first historian of longshoremen in Halifax described the situation exactly, but the explanation for it eluded him. The relative failure of nineteenth-century Halifax longshoremen appears all the more puzzling when set beside the examples of militant ship labourers in Quebec City and Saint John, who organized massive unions and successfully struggled for better hours and wages.[43]

The answer lies in the structure of work in the port, which, unlike Saint John or Quebec City, did not have as its vital nucleus the heavy, collective, highly seasonal labour demanded by a bulky staple trade, timber, but rather the lighter, more individualized, and less seasonal tasks of an entrepôt and fishing port. Occupational structures – notably the role of the stevedore – defined quite sharply in Saint John by the 1870's, were much less so in Halifax. An 1842 visitor to Halifax from Saint John remarked upon the difference in hiring customs in the two cities: "[Y]esterday I passed along the head of the market wharf [Halifax], and I counted 20 labourers standing with their hands in their pockets, shoved down to the elbows. I at once recognized them as having come from your market [Saint John] – for in Halifax the labourers do not take up their position at the head of the wharf, as in Saint John. They scatter themselves about, as if ashamed to be seen in one another's company."[44] In Halifax, hiring practices varied from wharf to wharf. Some stevedores were permanently stationed on specific wharves; others managed several wharves and might specialize in various kinds of loading operations. (The loading of deals at Richmond was handled by one particular such master stevedore.) On other wharves, men who were normally considered longshoremen might contract to unload a given cargo and employ fellow workers to do the job. On West India wharves, labourers worked in good weather, drying fish and placing it in barrels by means of a "screw." Some were hired directly by the merchants; others worked under master coopers who supervised the process by which the fish was dried and secured in barrels. The most advanced wharf, Cunard's, employed clerks, a wharfinger, a timekeeper, a storekeeper, truckmen, cargo checkers, and forty-two permanent employees.[45]

Such an array of hiring practices and conditions did not give labourers the same unity they had in the timber ports, and the potential for united action was further undermined by the casual (or "transient") labour system. The distinction between permanent and casual labourers was crucial. Permanent employees worked a regular nine- or ten-hour day, were paid by the week, and were steadily employed through the year; casual employees worked the hours demanded (up to twenty at a stretch), were paid by the hour or by the day, and enjoyed no security of employment. Longshore work was frequently resorted to by other workers, even craftsmen, when times were hard, and by "foreigners" from laid-up schooners, who were said to take twice as long to do the work of "skilled" longshoremen.[46] But many of the men mainly dependent on longshore work would themselves rely part-time on the fishery or take up marginal occupations (such as pawn-broking) in the city. The transient workers who prepared fish were even less secure because whenever it rained – as it is apt to do in Halifax – they would be paid only for the number of quarters of the day they had worked. This policy of placing the unavoidable risks of fish-drying on the shoulders of the workers had aroused violent antipathy at least as early as 1856, but it was still the system in 1884.[47] Estimates in 1884 of annual earnings suggest that labourers who worked steadily could aspire to earn about $350 in the year, about half the pay of the shipwrights. Not surprisingly, the longshoremen were among the most wretched workers of the city. They were described as living in "attics and in the cheapest sort of way" and forced to place their barefoot children at work on the waterfront for fifty or sixty cents per day.[48] Sporadic strikes against such evils in 1854, the mid-1860's, 1873, and 1880 brought some short-term successes but no structural change.[49]

The steamer changed this rather desolate picture. It arrived in Halifax before any attempt had been made to alter loading or unloading techniques by using the steam winch or the donkey engine.[50] The steamer brought an entirely different tempo to longshore work. When a large steamer came into port, between 200 and 500 men might be employed in loading, discharging, or coaling. Not only was this work more collective, it was also more intensive.[51] Only if the heavy investment in the new technology was rewarded with greater speed and economy, and hence a short turn-around time in port, would it pay off. The results for labour were ambiguous. New employment was undeniably created – especially in Halifax with its advantages as a coaling centre for European steamers – and labourers were able to work in the winter to a greater extent. But in the short term, the initial consequence was the intensification of casualism, because the requirement for masses of men to be available at a moment's notice created a large surplus labour pool.[52] In the long term, nevertheless, the industrial revolution in shipping made effective trade unionism a genuine possibility, since it alone could create a sudden scarcity of labour in ports that did not otherwise have this structural characteristic.

The Laborers' Union of Halifax (often also called the "Longshore Laborers' Association") was founded on April 13, 1882, and united casual and permanent wharf labourers into a well-organized body. According to its constitution, it was open to male persons aged sixteen to sixty, "provided that they be in good health and of moral character." It provided a fund from which its members could receive assistance (based on monthly dues of twenty-five cents) and urged the necessity of a "uniform price for labour, per day and by the hour," for discharging and loading vessels and for other labour. After three months in existence the union had 325 members, an eight-man executive, and a twelve-man council. This was Halifax's first mass union. By 1883 it had 518 members and worked to give them a sense of solidarity and pride. There were marches through the streets with a fife and drum corps, picnics to McNab's Island, and an important new cohesiveness between men who worked on the wharves and those who worked on vessels.[53]

The leader of the union was John A. Mackasey (1840-1919), who for years was a commission merchant on Water Street and who represented many of the Gloucester fishing vessels when they called at Halifax.[54] A middle-class recruit to labour's cause, Mackasey became disillusioned with the impact of the National Policy on the staple trades of the Maritimes and penned a compelling analysis of the regional imbalance of the tariff in a critique of federal timber policy in 1883.[55] Although one of his motivations in entering the longshoremen's struggle was his desire to wean the labourers from drink,[56] he was plainly outraged by the vast gap between the wealthy merchants and their wretched labourers. Mackasey had a well-developed critique of the Halifax merchants, who, he argued, had ignored the trading opportunities at their doorstep.[57] And, above all, he was an effective labour leader. When the merchants alleged that Halifax labourers earned more than their counterparts in Portland, Maine, Mackasey telegraphed a Portland merchant and proved the allegation false; when the merchants alleged that they provided labourers with work drying fish as a benevolent gesture, Mackasey detailed the profit margins involved in curing; when merchants argued that the labourers' living standards had improved remarkably, Mackasey simply led reporters through the hovels and attics housing the longshoremen's families. He used his contacts with the Gloucester fishing fleet to ship out some strikers for the Greenland fishery at $190 a trip, making sure to tell the merchants that, given the great demand for fishermen, they stood to lose the services of the labourers for the season. He was careful to distance himself from the militant model of Saint John trade unionism, which Halifax merchants loved to cite as a horrible example of mob rule, and he instructed union members to be respectful of their employers. In a port that had traditionally revered its merchant princes, however, Mackasey's critique and actions were genuinely radical. Workingmen, he warned, would never submit to having the city develop at their expense. The longshoremen's desire for a better life, he said sardonically, "had been taught them by the merchants themselves. The merchants of twenty years ago, mostly lived over their stores. Now they live in palaces on the banks of the North West Arm."[58]

Mackasey's efforts lay behind the 1884 demand that labourers be paid $1.50 per day for store work, seventy-five cents for a half-day, and twenty cents per hour for work after 5 p.m. (This represented a 20 per cent increase.) There were to be no more quarter or three-quarter days, and Sunday work was to be paid at a rate of fifty cents per hour. Stevedore work was to be paid $2 per day on sailing vessels and twenty-five cents per hour on steamships, barges, lighters, and tugboats. These demands, for all their modesty, were precisely calculated reforms, aimed at the casual labour system and low wages alike. The Laborers' Union, now representing what Mackasey called "the whole laboring class of the city," adopted new methods of mass unionism: badges were issued to identify members, marked with "L.U." for Laborers' Union, with the member's number as recorded in the union's rolls. This tactic would allow the swift identification of strikebreakers and allow permanent longshoremen not directly involved in the strike to identify and avoid non-union gangs.[59]

The strike began on May 12, 1884, a rainy day on which no fish-drying would take place in any event; many of the independent master stevedores caved in immediately. As the week progressed, they were joined by some master coopers. Everyone waited for the crucial test: the arrival of the first steamer. The unloading of the steamer *Caspian* on May 16 by union men at the union rate was a day of jubilation for the union. The remaining master coopers now gave the advanced rate and paid their labourers a full day's pay even if they had been able to work only three-quarters of the day. Union men coaling the steamer *Faraday* earned the high wage of fifty cents per hour; some cleared ten dollars each. The victory of Mackasey and the union was complete.[60]

It was also short-lived. By May 27, merchants were planning to employ regular hands in drying fish instead of casual labour. Some employers were also insisting on removal of the badges as a condition of going to work. The return of fine fish-drying weather precipitated a crisis and the union, successful on the vessels, met defeat on the shore. By July 9, Hart's, Butler's, and Boak's wharves were all reported to be employing non-union men exclusively. The union was forced to pass a resolution allowing union men to deliver to non-union men on the shore, provided that all gangs were "on one side and the other." These defeats paved the way for the biggest defeat of them all, in January, 1885. When the *S.S. Newcastle City* was docked at Pickford and Black's, it was not unloaded by the usual labourers, who stood about demanding the union rate of twenty-five cents an hour. Instead, unemployed schooner men had taken the work away from the Halifax labourers. By 1886 casual labourers were accepting twenty cents an hour for steamer work (five cents less than the 1884 demand).[61] The Laborer's Union survived these defeats and endured until 1899 (probably largely on the strength of its death and sickness benefits). But it did not strike again for the rights of the longshoremen. Sporadic, doomed strikes for higher wages in the 1890's were without union backing.[62]

The causes of this brave failure were to be found in the structure of the port labour market. Mackasey backed away from the creation of a coercive labour monopoly on the Saint John model (and, because of Halifax's distinctively fragmented character, there were reasons to doubt such a monopoly could have been imposed). But without such power – without union domination over port hiring – the reforms wrested in 1884 were bound to be eroded by the merchants. Badges were not enough. And as the steamers called at Halifax less and less frequently, and as some lines withdrew altogether in the late 1880's and early 1890's, the structural conditions favouring united trade union action had largely dissipated.

In February, 1900, the longshoremen, reorganized as the Port Workers Union of Halifax, refused *en masse* to work a mail steamer on Sunday unless the steamship companies guaranteed their fines for working on the Sabbath. By 1902, two locals of the International Longshoremen's Association had been formed. On April 2, the longshoremen went on strike for a twelve-point program, which included such demands as the exclusive employment of union labour, where possible, recognized holidays, a day scale of twenty-five cents, and a night scale of thirty cents an hour. They settled for twenty cents and twenty-five cents, after a successful mediation by Mackenzie King, but their union was effectively broken in the struggle.[63]

The same cycle of failure had returned, despite the intervention of an international union and impressive support from a united Halifax labour movement. There was no mystery to this failure. Once again the inability of the men to control the labour market meant that they faced the threat of submission or replacement. As James Hall, manager of the Furness-Withy line of steamers, remarked, "There are thousands of men all along the coasts of Nova Scotia and Newfoundland seeking work. And they will be only too glad to come to Halifax and get work at twenty cents an hour." The logic of the union's demand for exclusive hiring lay precisely here as well: the building of a union could not occur in a context of uncontrolled casualism.[64] Only in 1907, in the context of an acute scarcity of labour, were the longshoremen able to build a more secure union; and a genuine structural response to waterfront casualism was left until World War II. For all its brilliance, 1884 had turned out to be a false dawn for the port workers.

III

Every day in the last quarter of the nineteenth century, a thousand or so men – more than would find work at one of the larger provincial coal mines – gathered for work on the Halifax water-front. Like coal miners, they worked in a very distinctive milieu, with their own customs and traditions, taverns and neighbour-hoods.[65] Unlike the coal miners, however, these workers never built large, strong unions. Craftsmen, threatened by rural migrants and urban labourers, built small, exclusivist unions that defended their particular privileges. Labourers, fragmented by the casual labour system and the diffuse character of the port, built much larger unions that failed either to change the system or to achieve a secure status on the waterfront. The indispensable coal miners wrested major political and social reforms from the government and large wage increases from the coal companies; the equally indispensable port workers won no such victories.

The difference stemmed from the stratification of waterfront labour under the aegis of merchant capital. Although nineteenth-century Canadian labour historiography has seen the struggles of skilled workers as the profoundly progressive elaboration of a "culture of control" and such men as leading a more general struggle for working-class rights, the Halifax case calls such interpretations sharply into question.[66] There is simply no evidence to suggest that skilled workers were concerned to extend their workplace controls to the unskilled, or saw their battles as parts of a more general social struggle. Had they done so, we would find them leading (or, at the very least, enthusiastically supporting) the longshoremen in 1884. They did not, and for a perfectly good reason: their whole style of trade unionism was based on excluding others from their obsolescent crafts. They were not artisans enunciating a doctrine of workers' control that could inspire all workers but labour aristocrats understandably anxious to preserve their status in a rapidly changing world. Only further research will ascertain whether this narrowly based craft unionism in Halifax or the radical, progressive, class-conscious craft unionism described in Hamilton and Toronto is the more general pattern in Canada.

With the industrialization of the port of Halifax in the twentieth century these patterns of casualism and exclusivism would change. The coming of monopoly capitalism is rightly associated with the breaking down of crafts; certainly the consolidation of world shipping capital slowly destroyed the intricate and specialized skills of the Halifax waterfront. But it should also be associated with an improvement in the conditions of labourers, for it was only within this new structure that longshoremen joined the ranks of "respectable" labour and made Halifax trade unionism a broadly based movement of workers.[67] And this was part of a regional pattern. Merchant capital was conservative. It created fragmented and fragmenting structures, from the debt bondage of the fishermen and the archaic quasi-serfdom of merchant seamen, to the isolation and pervasive paternalism of mercantile coal villages. Such fragmentation made unified opposition impossible and confined dissent to movements, which were often tremendously courageous and forceful, but which were also tragically isolated, short-lived, and non-cumulative.[68] The new possibilities opened up by the era of large-scale capital included those of linking up masses of workers in a far more aggressive search for political and social alternatives. This change would decisively mark off the eras of mercantile and competitive industrial capitalism in the Maritimes from that of monopoly capitalism. Only within this new structure could merchant capital's legacy of social fragmentation be addressed and partially overcome.

2

The Bonds of Unity: The Knights of Labor in Ontario, 1880–1900

Gregory S. Kealey and Bryan D. Palmer

The nineteenth century was the crucible from which Canada would emerge as a capitalist economy and society. It is indisputable that the latter half of the nineteenth century saw the creation of a sophisticated transportation network, the articulation of a strategy of industrial development that pinned the hopes of Canada's rising capitalists on political consolidation, tariff protections and settlement, and the evolution of a diversified manufacturing sector in central Canada. All this, to be sure, developed in the context of a social order wracked by major depressions and frequent recessionary downturns. Nevertheless, as early as the 1860's the transforming power of capital had become visible in the rise of factories in Ontario and Montreal, the increasing use of steam power, and the mechanization of important industries such as tailoring and boot and shoe production. For the *People's Journal* these were the hallmarks of momentous change, factors that had "set agoing an industrial revolution."[1]

Ontario stood at the very centre of this process of capitalist development. Aggregate data begin to tell the story. Capital invested more than doubled in each decade between 1870 and 1890, while the number of hands employed increased 90 per cent over the twenty-year period. These aggregate data can give us an imprecise measure of the character of social and productive relations, the setting within which a major movement of class struggle – the Knights of Labor – unfolded and one which this workers' movement of the 1880's undoubtedly influenced (Table 1).

Table 1
Aggregate Ontario Data, 1871-1911

Year	Capital Invested ($)	Hands Employed	Yearly Wages ($)
1871	37,874,010	87,281	21,415,710
1881	80,950,847	118,308	30,604,031
1891	175,972,021	166,326	49,733,359
1901	214,972,275	151,081	44,656,032
1911	595,394,608	216,362	95,674,743

Year	Value Raw Material ($)	Value Product ($)	Value Added ($)
1871	65,114,804	114,706,799	49,591,995
1881	91,164,156	157,889,870	66,825,714
1891	128,142,371	231,781,926	111,639,555
1901	138,230,400	241,533,486	103,303,086
1911	297,580,125	579,810,225	282,230,100

SOURCE: *Census of Canada*, 1871-1911. Note that the 1901 and 1911 figures are unadjusted in light of the changing criterion employed by the census in enumerating manufacturing establishments. All firms were considered for 1871-91, while only those firms employing five or more hands were considered in 1901 and 1911. The capital invested figures for 1901 and 1911 are computed by adding together the figures for fixed and working capital. There had been no distinction between these realms in the earlier period.

Table 2 illuminates trends within the aggregate data for the years 1871-1911. If, for instance, we take capital invested as a percentage of value added, we note a steady increase over the years 1871-1901, with the rate of that increase dropping precipitously in the opening years of the twentieth century. Wages, however, exhibit a different trend, and as a percentage of value added were relatively stable until they fell dramatically in the 1901-11 years. When we take capital invested and wages as a percentage of the total product value other trends emerge: capital as a percentage of product value rises steadily over the entire period, while wages as a percentage of value decline only in those years of most pronounced economic growth, the 1880's and 1900's.

Such rough calculations gesture toward essential processes in the sphere of social and productive relations. First, we note that

Table 2
Trends within the Aggregate Ontario Data, 1871-1911

Year	Capital as % of Value Added	Wages as % of Value Added	Capital as % of Product Value	Wages as % of Product Value	Per Capita Yearly Wages ($)	Capital Invested Yearly per Worker ($)	Yearly National Growth Rates in Manufacturing Output (%)
1871	76	43	33	18	245	433	
							4.4
1881	121	45	51	19	257	684	
							4.8
1891	157	44	73	18	287	1,057	
							2.4
1901	208	43	89	18	295	1,422	
							6.0
1911	210	33	102	16	441	2,751	

SOURCES: Our calculations from census data. Same reservations as in source note to Table 1. Yearly national growth rates in manufacturing output are taken from Gordon W. Bertram, "Historical Statistics on Growth and Structure of Manufacturing Canada, 1870-1957," in J. Henripin and A. Asimakopulos, eds., *C.P.S.A. Conference on Statistics, 1962 and 1963* (Toronto, 1964), pp. 93-146.

wages declined as a percentage of product value precisely in those years – 1881-91 and 1901-11 – that the growth rates in national manufacturing output soared. This suggests a growing intensification of labour. That these periods, then, saw increasing organization among Ontario workers – first, in the Knights of Labor, and second in the craft unions during the upheaval of 1898-1904 – should cause no surprise. But to study the character of exploitation we must probe the relationship of wages to value added, considering the capital input. This leads us to our second speculative hypothesis: it would appear that the social cost of labour was relatively high throughout the late nineteenth century. This was a period, after all, that pre-dated Taylorism, an attempt to manage work and simplify tasks that was premised on a supposedly scientific analysis of all jobs within a workplace, and other efficiency-conscious managerial innovations. It is not until the turn of the century that wages as a percentage of value added plunged, even in the face of soaring per capita yearly wages (largely a consequence of inflation, for real wages declined).[2] These turn-of-the-century years also witness a virtual doubling of the capital invested yearly per worker, and leave behind the more modest decadal increases in this relationship characteristic of the 1871-1901 years. And yet, even given this mammoth dose of capital in the years associated with the beginnings of Canada's century, capital as a percentage of value added makes only a marginal, clearly insignificant, gain. Thus, although both the 1880's and 1900's are years of economic growth and increasing intensification of labour, it is not until the 1901-11 years that one sees the actual rationalization of productive relations, a shift in the character of exploitation, and the probable degradation of labour. Before that the social costs of labour remained high.[3] What gains in output that did occur late in the century were probably more a consequence of capital input than of extraction of surplus from the hide of labour, although these spheres are ultimately impossible to separate analytically.

If this was indeed the trend, then it becomes important to ask what forces kept the social cost of labour high in this period. The lack of a managerial strategy at the workplace, "scientifically" conceived, was no doubt one aspect, as was the technological foundation of production, weak in the 1880's compared to the post-1900 years. However, the mass character of the Knights of Labor, as a movement aimed at uniting all workers, probably played a considerable role in resisting capital's quest to increase output and reduce labour costs through wage reductions or increasing the pace of work. Looking at the yearly per capita wage figures confirms this picture. While yearly wages rose only $12 in the 1870's and only $8 throughout the 1890's, the increase for the 1881-91 years was at least two and one-half times as great, or $30. The social relations of production, in which worker stood counterposed to employer and in which the nature and extent of organization was of vital importance, must have contributed to this outcome. And these social relations of production during the 1880's were inseparable from the explosive growth of the Knights of Labor. In whatever area one wants to consider – economic, social, political, cultural – the Noble and Holy Order of the Knights of Labor voiced the need to go beyond the social relations of production as then constituted.

I

"To write the history of the Knights of Labor is an impossibility," warned Terence V. Powderly. The much-maligned leader of the Order was aware that "some young men fresh from college have tried to write the history of the organization," but he argued that they had failed: "They applied logic and scientific research; they divided the emotions, the passions, and feelings of the members into groups, they dissected and vivisected the groups; they used logarithms, algebraic formulas, and everything known to the young ambitious graduate of a university." Powderly's words of warning are worth remembering. Yet, in spite of our recognition of the importance of his sceptical assessment of a history premised on impersonal data and mere quantities, we commence with numbers. They, too, were part of what the Noble and Holy Order was all about.[4]

Organizationally, the Knights drew workers into their ranks through a relatively simple procedure and institutional apparatus. Individual members joined local assemblies, either in mixed (diverse occupational affiliations) or trade (adhering more rigidly to specific craft categories) assemblies. Normally those who were part of a specific trade assembly followed a particular skilled calling, but occasionally the trade assembly was merely an organization of all workers employed in the same plant, shop, or factory. For a local assembly to be organized formally a minimum of ten members was required, and once established local assemblies were known to swell in membership to over a thousand. If a specific geographical region or trade contained five or more assemblies a district assembly could be formed. District assemblies were of two types: the national trade district, representing the interests of all assemblies of a specific craft, such as the window glass workers or the telegraph operatives; or the mixed district assembly, in which diverse interests of many mixed and trade assemblies were represented. In Canada this latter mixed district assembly was pre-eminent, and in Ontario the various district assemblies were always mixed in form and representative of specific geographical/territorial units. Local assemblies were allowed one delegate in the district assembly for each hundred members they had enrolled, and one for each additional hundred or fraction thereof. Presiding over all these bodies were a series of leading elected officials: the master workman of the local assembly; the district master workman; and many lesser figures. Each district elected delegates to the annual convention of the Order, the general assembly, and at this gathering, in turn, were elected the national officers and the general executive board. The Order, then, was a highly centralized body, with a well-defined hierarchy and structure; yet it was also egalitarian, and the local assemblies had a large measure of autonomy, with their own courts to prosecute those who transgressed the discipline and regulations of knighthood.

Although strongest in Ontario's rapidly expanding industrial cities like Toronto and Hamilton, the Knights also penetrated the province's towns, villages, and tiny hamlets. In its approximately thirty-year lifespan (1875-1907), the Order organized locals in eighty-two towns from Amherstburg in the west to Cornwall in the east, and from Port Colborne in the south to Sudbury in the north. These eighty-two towns contained a total of at least 249 local assemblies, which in turn formed ten district assemblies. Toronto, Hamilton, and Ottawa led the way with fifty-eight, thirty, and twelve local assemblies respectively, but the Knights were also active in eight communities of less than 1,000 people, and there were thirty-one local assemblies in places with populations of under 3,000. Ontario's five largest cities in the 1880's (Toronto, Hamilton, Ottawa, London, and Kingston) contained 46 per cent of all Knights of Labor assemblies, but the range and dispersal of the Order were perhaps most significant: of the forty-seven Ontario towns with a population of at least 3,000 in the 1880's, fully thirty-eight, or 81 per cent, witnessed the formation of a local assembly.[5]

How many members were drawn into the ranks of the Knights of Labor? This is a difficult question. In the United States, at their peak, the Knights were said to have enrolled between 700,000 and 1,000,000 members, but this is a static count taken in the spring months of 1886. The data are questionable and tend to underestimate the membership. Moreover, the central problem is the timing of influx into the Order, for the Knights peaked at different moments in different regions. Thus, Jonathan Garlock has estimated that if one looks beyond peak membership the American Order may well have enrolled over 3,000,000 workers in its assemblies over the course of its history. As in the United

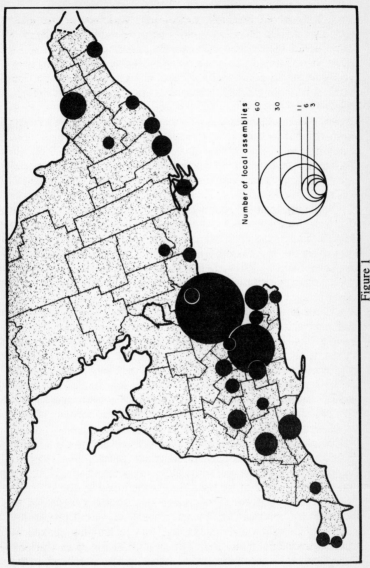

Figure 1

Concentrations of Knights of Labor Local Assemblies in Southern Ontario, 1880–1902

States, the Ontario Knights did not peak until 1886, a year that saw the founding of ninety-nine local assemblies, and even then the dating of the upsurge varied from region to region within Ontario. Across south-central Ontario the Knights of Labor climbed to their highest membership point in 1886 and then deteriorated, rapidly in some places, more slowly in others. Thus, any attempt to address the numerical significance of the Order will founder if it is reduced to a count of peak membership at any given point.

We can, nevertheless, start with peak official membership at single points in time for some specific locales. Toronto DA 125's forty-one local assemblies had 5,000 members in 1886, while Hamilton DA 61's 2,200 workers were organized in thirty local assemblies. District Assembly 6, of Ottawa, had 2,000 affiliated in 1892. The London-St. Thomas DA 138 reported a membership of 4,435 in 1886-87, enrolled in thirty-six assemblies in such western Ontario towns as Aylmer, Ingersoll, Listowell, and Wyoming. St. Catharines DA 207 encompassed some 2,000 advocates in twenty-two local assemblies. Other district assembly peaks were Windsor DA 174's 616, Belleville DA 235's 1,548, Uxbridge DA 236's 523, and Berlin DA 241's 348. Perhaps more striking still are some of the individual town reports: Brockville's Franklin LA 2311 with 430 members in November, 1883; Gananoque's 700-800 members in 1887; Gravenhurst LA 10669's 300 lumber workers in June, 1888; the 500 cotton workers in Merritton's Maple Leaf LA 5933 in 1886; Petrolia's Reliable LA 4570 with 500 members in 1886; LA 6722's 200 workers at the Frost and Woods agricultural implements works in Smiths Falls in August, 1887; and the 500 workers of Woodstock's Unity and Concord LAs 3151 and 4922 in 1886. The Knights were strong wherever a particular industrial activity predominated: among Cornwall's cotton workers, Hamilton's iron and steel workers, and St. Thomas's railway workers the Order had many advocates.

Available data do not allow us to make any firm calculations on the percentage of the work force organized by the Order, nor would the official membership figures necessarily reveal the true impact: the tendency is always to under-represent the strength, and the volatility of the rank and file further compounds this problem of undercounting. The case is made strongly in the instance of Toronto's LA 2305, which reported a mere twenty-nine members in July, 1885, swelled to 550 in the following months, and then fell back to forty-five within a year. To appreciate fully the numerical significance of the Order we need to understand not a static cross-sectional profile but a process and flow determined in part by the movement's vitality and particular events, developments in the economic realm, and social relations. But the figures do not readily allow this, and we are forced to consider the Knights in the context of peak membership figures that defy all this, a problem further exacerbated by the problems of reliance on census data that correspond only to decadal points and that mask local situations in larger county calculations.

We can begin with the larger picture. If we take the total peak memberships (at specific points in time with no account taken of volatility) across the province and add them together we see that over the course of their history the Knights organized a minimum of 21,800 members. This represented 18.4 per cent of the hands employed in manufacturing in 1881 and 13.1 per cent of those so employed in 1891. These aggregate data, of course, distort the facts dramatically, for they include all workers with no regard to region, sex, or age. Some but not all of this distortion can be eliminated by looking at particular places, presented in Table 3. The limitations of the census impose themselves here, for in attempting to focus on the percentage of the organized manufacturing work force we are handcuffed to the 1881 and 1891 figures: the former are problematic because the Knights were not even on the scene at that early date, while the latter are equally flawed because the Order was, by that time, in the throes of decline. Moreover, such data are often available only on a county basis. Locales like St. Thomas get buried in the total county employment figures. Nevertheless, the figures are an indication of the impressive numbers of workers drawn to the Order, and in places like St. Thomas, Kingston, and the Lincoln, Niagara, and Welland region there is no doubt that the Knights of Labor organized an absolute majority of the people employed in manufacturing. The inclusion of people outside of manufacturing, but still working-class in their occupations, would understate these figures but not dramatically enough to alter the impressive record of organizational achievement.[6]

The census, moreover, did not report on those employed in such small towns as Merritton, Chatham, and Gananoque. Yet we know from many sources that the Order was actively engaged in such places. To attempt a crude estimate of the percentage of the work force organized we have taken our figures on membership and compared them to rough calculations of the

Table 3
**Knights of Labor Membership as Percentage of Hands Employed, 1881
and 1891**

City or County	1881	1891
Essex (Windsor)	30.0	22.2
London	29.3	22.5
Elgin East (St. Thomas)	80.0	58.6
Hamilton	33.8	22.8
Toronto	39.3	20.4
Brockville	44.9	31.9
Kingston	101.8	56.0
Cornwall	32.3	14.8
Lanark South (Perth, Smiths Falls, Carleton Place)	21.1	18.1
Ottawa	–	31.7
Lincoln, Niagara, and Welland (St. Catharines, Welland, Merritton, Thorold)	–	50.5
Perth North (Stratford, Listowell)	36.0	30.5

SOURCES: *Census of Canada*, 1881, 1891; Knights of Labor, General Assembly, *Proceedings*; Ontario Bureau of Industry, *Annual Reports*.

number of people employed. This latter figure was obtained by taking the total population for 1881. In no case would the work force have been more than 40 per cent of the population, and it is unlikely that it would have even reached 20 per cent in these years, but we have taken these poles as our gauge. Table 4 reveals how thoroughly the Order penetrated these small Ontario manufacturing towns, organizing an extremely high percentage of the work force.

What all this means, we would argue, is that the Knights of Labor represented the most important moment in the history of Ontario labour until the 1919 upheaval or the coming of the Congress of Industrial Organizations in the late 1930's. But if the Knights of Labor represented a quantitative breakthrough for Ontario's workers, they also represented a crucial qualitative shift in the orientation of the working class. The Order took the raw material of a class culture – ambiguous, fragmented, and unfocused – and moulded it into a movement culture of opposition and alternative.

Table 4
Knights of Labor Membership as Percentage of Work Force
(estimated at between 20 and 40 per cent of 1881 population)

Town	20% of 1881 Population	40% of 1881 Population
Chatham	25.4	12.7
Woodstock	46.5	23.2
Petrolia	72.0	36.0
Merritton	139.0	69.5
St. Catharines	51.8	25.9
Guelph	17.6	8.8
Hespeler	71.4	35.7
Oshawa	52.0	26.0
Gananoque	87.0	43.5
Smiths Falls	47.9	23.9

SOURCES: Same as in Table 3.

II

This movement culture was formed in the process of daily life, both on and off the job, and it was tempered in the political and workplace struggles that we will examine shortly. It began with the workers' initiation into the Knights of Labor assembly, where a whole series of symbolic and ritualistic practices rooted the member in the movement, reinforcing traditions of collectivity and solidarity in an age of hostile, individualistic pieties. Each new initiate vowed to defend the interest and reputation of all true members of the Order, be they employed or unemployed, fortunate or distressed, and was instructed that "Labor is noble and holy." Upon admission to the Order, the recently christened Knight was informed that "open and public associations have failed, after a struggle of centuries, to protect or advance the interest of labor," and that the Knights of Labor merely imitated "the example of capital," endeavouring "to secure the just rewards of our toil." To counteract this distressing tendency of the modern age, the Order asserted: "We mean to uphold the dignity of labor, to affirm the nobility of all who earn their bread by the sweat of their brow." In these ritualized incantations, which resounded in local assembly halls across south-central Canada, lay much of the promise and potential of the Knights of Labor.[7]

That promise and potential reared its head in many cultural events: the picnics, parades, demonstrations, dances, hops, and balls that the Knights organized across the province in the heady days of the upheaval of the 1880's. These occasions were no doubt moments of recreation, diversions that moved people away from the concerns of the next day's work, the next week's groceries, and the n??? :month's rent – the range of insecurities the next year could bring. But they were also exhilarating reminders of self-worth and class strength. They were prominent in Toronto and Hamilton, as we would expect, but places like London, Woodstock, Ingersoll, Chatham, Thorold, Gananoque, and Belleville were also the sites of such cultural activities, and the Order was capable of drawing anywhere from 1,000 to 5,000 people to these "monster" gatherings. After an 1887 Gananoque Knights of Labor picnic, the local newspaper commented: "Probably no gathering anywhere near the size ever took place here, where there was such good order. . . . They have shown that they are a power in the community, able to command respect."[8]

An understanding of class place and pride stood at the core of this culture, as well as individual longing for a better world. Forging a multitude of diverse, often contradictory, ideals into a collective assertion was the movement itself. As a strikingly creative effort, the Knights of Labor was the very embodiment of human striving that evolved out of residual components of a class culture, nudged toward new, or emergent, purpose by those who embraced the causes of labour's rights, men and women who, in advocating reform, did much to create a culture of "democratic promise." The difficulty we ourselves experience in comprehending their vision and their striving is a measure of significant failures – theirs *and* ours.[9]

But in the 1880's that failure was not a settled fact, embedded in the historical record in indisputable concreteness; the sharp clarity of defeat was not yet there for all to see. Thousands of Ontario workers took Richard Trevellick's words to heart when he promised that the Knights of Labor would "make Labor respectable by having men and women respect themselves, and while courteous and kind, refuse to bow and cringe to others because they possess wealth and social position." Certainly Thomas J. O'Neill, of Napanee's Courage Assembly (LA 9216), regarded such proclamations with appropriate seriousness, writing to Powderly that "this section of the country is sadly in need of organization, but fear of the money kings [the Rathbuns] keep the working class in slavery." Railroad men, organized in Headlight Assembly (LA 4069) of St. Thomas, acted on Trevellick's words in 1885. They conducted their own statistical survey of their town of 11,000 with the intention of using "all lawful means of obtaining their rights, also to educate those of our members who heretofore have permitted others to do their thinking, thereby allowing themselves to be used as mere machines in the hands of unscrupulous men." The *Labor Union* proclaimed its mission in mid-January, 1883: "To Spread the Light; to expose the inequalities of the many. To call things by their right names, and to point out to workingmen how these inequities could be redressed and the workingman secure the full reward of his toil."[10] Employers found much to dislike in the words of Trevellick, O'Neill, LA 4069, and the *Labor Union*. Their actions throughout the 1880's spoke loudly of their fears and antagonisms. They regarded the increasing consciousness of class, and threat of active opposition, as a dangerous development. By 1891 the business community was convinced that "the spirit of trades unionism is strangling honest endeavour, and the hard-working, fearless thorough artisan of ten years ago is degenerating into the shiftless, lazy, half-hearted fellow who, with unconscious irony, styles himself a knight of labor." The culture had, as well as advocates, staunch opponents.[11]

In the midst of a virtual war between these contending forces (in which battles were both practical and intellectual), the labour reform cause gained hard-won adherents. And in this context the "educational" thrust so prominent in the Order's own priorities was consolidated. Local assemblies became, in the parlance of the 1880's, "schools of instruction" in which the lessons learned turned on the principles of labour reform, reaching a mass audience in literally hundreds of reading rooms, Knights of Labor libraries, and assembly halls. In the words of Trevellick, members first learned "their duties and their rights" in the "schoolroom" of the local assembly.[12]

Providing much of the text of instruction were a handful of committed publishers/editors. Often themselves practical printers, these men struggled through the 1880's and 1890's, working into the early morning hours to put out their weekly journals, devoted, as in the case of the *Palladium of Labor*, "to the Interests of the Workingmen and Workingwomen." Always on the brink of financial ruin, these papers occupied an unenviable position in the often gloomy world of the nineteenth-century press. Small wonder that the men who kept them going were often ill-tempered and indiscriminately combative, like Hamilton's William H. Rowe or St. Thomas's George Wrigley, or constantly manoeuvring to attain economic ends, like the notorious but resourceful A.W. Wright. But whatever their personal idiosyncrasies these men attempted to move the class beyond economism, striving "to take a broader and more comprehensive view of the entire subject of Labor Reform than is embodied in mere unionism, and to grasp and apply those great underlying principles of equity and justice between men which alone can permanently and satisfactorily solve the issues between Labor and Capital." This was an important component of what Frank Watt has referred to as the "freely germinating" radicalism of the 1880's, a phenomenon spawned by the presence of the Knights of Labor.[13]

This radicalism was popularized by a group of brainworkers and local advocates – men like Toronto's Phillips Thompson – as well as more obscure, but highly talented and committed local figures. Among these were Joseph Marks of London, who began as a Knight, organized the Industrial Brotherhood in the 1890's, and edited the *Industrial Banner* well into the twentieth century; Galt's J.L. Blain, a lecturer who described himself to Powderly as a well-educated "rat from the sinking ship of aristocracy"; a Hamilton coppersmith, George Collis, who boomed the Order under the nickname "Sandy the Tinker," travelling to Oshawa, London, and other southern Ontario towns; poets like the carpenter Thomas Towers and Listowel's blind and deaf Walter A. Ratcliffe; or anonymous supporters – St. Thomas's "Knight of the Brush" and "True Reformer"; Brantford's "Drawbar"; or "Pete Rolea" from the oil-producing region of western Ontario. Individuals like these helped the Order to establish itself in countless communities and made the cause of reform a popular and lasting one. From virtually every corner of the province anonymous correspondents informed labour newspapers of the local state of reform agitation.[14]

This agitation contributed much to the attainment of class cohesion, strengthening the bonds of unity. Education became, not the responsibility of the schools, the press, and the elite, but the duty of all. "L.C.S." of Gananoque argued that the Knights were "engaged in solving the greatest problem of the age," urging all wage labourers to drink at the fountain of labour reform, rather than from the cesspool of the "capitalistic press," which consistently suppressed facts, failed to consider just causes, and aligned itself with "upper anarchy," money, and monopoly. "Educate yourself and you will be in a position to enlighten others," he wrote. That accomplished, working people had only to "obey the laws of knighthood, be loyal to self and manhood, defend the interest of the Order, and labor for the new era until it dawns upon the toilers of our country, until the weary men and women chained by the wage-system can see justice enthroned, and this, the land of the free." As Albert V. Cross reported to Powderly from Hamilton's LA 2481 in 1887:

> When we entered the Order we were taught that in the home of labor there would be no distinctions of Country, Creed & Color because all were of the Earth and with equal rights to Earth, when we understood this great truth that all men are brothers we rejoiced, and we solomly [sic] resolved that we would do all in our power to strengthen the bonds of unity between the workers of the world.[15]

Perhaps the most significant aspect of this strengthening of the bonds of unity was the Order's role in overcoming past deficiencies of workers' organizations. Nowhere was this more visible than in the Knights of Labor effort to draw *all* workers into one large movement. Across the province skilled and unskilled workers, craftsmen, factory operatives, and labourers united in local assemblies to oppose a common enemy and to cultivate common ties. Unlike virtually every previous chapter in the history of Ontario workers' rebellion, the Knights of Labor stamped the 1880's with concern for those whose status in the working-class community ill-suited them to wear the badge of respectability, a consensual cultural norm that the Order recast to express class antagonisms. Premised on the fundamental rejection of exclusion (tarnished only by the Order's stand on the Chinese), the Knights of Labor, most often led by skilled workers, offered their ideals and their strengths as a force protecting and speaking for all of those "below" them.[16]

Indeed, the introduction of women into the mass struggles of the 1880's shattered decades of complacency and effected a fundamental shift in attitude. To be sure, the Knights acted out of chivalrous intent, and did not abandon age-old conceptions of hearth and home, domesticity and place. But they could turn all this to new purpose and strike out at forces they felt to be undermining all that was good and proper in such traditional practices. Thus, at a London speech by the popular and well-travelled Knight, Richard Trevellick, members of the Order raised "their hands to heaven and pledged themselves that wherever women were employed, they would demand equal pay for equal work without regard to sex whatsoever." It is difficult to see in such action only a retrogressive glance over one's shoulder to a pre-industrial arcadia: the language is unmistakably that of an industrial society, and the problem has yet to be resolved. Finally, the Knights did not stop and settle comfortably in this niche but attacked those who would define women's rights in some circumscribed way. In such Knights of Labor centres as Belleville, Brantford, London, Stratford, St. Thomas, Thorold, Hamilton, and Toronto, where "the ladies" joined the Order in assemblies named "Advance" and "Hope" and attended musical and literary entertainments as "Goddesses of Liberty," the possibility forged in the 1880's was on many women workers' lips.[17]

This notion of possibility, this movement toward alternative social relations, is central to an understanding of the Knights of Labor in the 1880's. In the words of Phillips Thompson, member of Toronto's Victor Hugo LA 7814, the Order taught men and women to "dream of what might be." By doing their part in "spreading the light," Thompson argued, labour reformers were bringing close to realization the "beautiful ideal of universal democracy and co-operation."[18] To explore the strengths and weaknesses of this reform crusade we now turn to the political and workplace struggles in which the Knights of Labor both thrived and foundered.

III

Not only in Toronto and Hamilton but throughout the southwestern Ontario manufacturing belt and even penetrating into eastern Ontario, the Knights created a political movement that demanded attention. Prime Minister Macdonald, in assessing the political climate in the summer of 1886, worried that the Conservative Party was "not in a flourishing state." The "rocks ahead" that threatened the Tory "ship" were "Riel, Home Rule, the Knights of Labor and the Scott Act."[19] The Knights thus specifically merited the old chieftain's close attention and two of the three other threatening reefs were movements intimately tied to the Order and its ideals, namely the Irish question and temperance.[20]

From the moment of their entrance into Canada the Knights actively engaged in politics. December, 1882, saw the first stirrings of these activities when labour in Hamilton helped elect two aldermen;[21] meanwhile, in Toronto, the Labour Council played a prominent role in defeating a candidate identified as particularly anti-labour.[22] Those initial successes propelled labour reformers in both cities into independent campaigns in the 1883 provincial election. In Hamilton locomotive engineer and prominent Knight Ed Williams, an English immigrant and the epitome of the respectable workingman, ran and won a solid 23.4 per cent of the vote in a three-way race.[23] In Toronto, where partisan politics had flared during the nominating process, the campaign results were more mixed. Painter John Carter, a labour leader of the 1870's and a member of Toronto's Excelsior LA 2305, ran in Toronto West and won 48 per cent of the vote. His candidacy, however, had gained the unstated support of the Reform Party, which ran no candidate against him. In Toronto East, carpenter Samuel R. Heakes faced nominees from both old-line parties and finished a distant third with only 7 per cent of the vote.[24]

Despite the relative success of these campaigns, partisan recriminations followed and were to re-emerge in subsequent campaigns. In both cities disgruntled Tory workingmen accused the Grits of double-dealing.[25] In Hamilton these charges died down, however, and labour reformers created the Hamilton Labor Political Association to continue the thrust for an independent working-class party. In subsequent municipal elections in 1883 and 1884 the association, under the leadership of Knights' activist Robert Coulter, enjoyed some success in electing Knights as aldermen. The best-known of these figures was Irish carter Thomas Brick, who provided Hamilton workers with a colourful and bombastic leader.[26]

In Toronto, Excelsior LA 2305's leadership core of old labour reformers, led by Daniel J. O'Donoghue with the able support of Charles March and Alfred Jury, consolidated the position of the Knights of Labor first in the newly created Trades and Labor Congress of Canada (which met originally in 1883) and subsequently in the Toronto Trades and Labour Council (TTLC). Once entrenched there they proceeded to make good use of both bodies as effective lobbying agencies, especially against the federal Tory government.[27] Their success in attracting political attention was evident in T.V. Powderly's 1884 Toronto visit. The stage at his major address was graced by the presence of Edward Blake, Timothy Anglin, Toronto Tory Mayor Boswell, and numerous Tory aldermen.[28] In the ensuing 1884 municipal election Toronto workers threw a considerable scare into the Tory machine although it held the mayoralty by a slim margin.[29] In 1885, however, this hold was broken with the sweeping victory of W.H. Howland, who enjoyed the united support of both the Knights of Labor and the TTLC.[30] His victory led to considerable soul-searching on the part of the Tories both in Toronto and in Ottawa. The results of this re-evaluation manifested themselves in a remarkable labour settlement at the *Mail* newspaper, where an ironclad contract had caused many former Tory workingmen to defect,[31] and later in the equally striking creation of the Royal Commission on the Relations of Labor and Capital.[32]

These quite considerable concessions to the political strength of the working-class movement did not prevent it from contesting the December, 1886, Ontario provincial election and the February, 1887, federal election. In December seven labour candidates took the field. One could be described as Lib-Lab, two as Tory-Labour; the other four were independents who faced candidates from the other two parties. St. Thomas brakeman and leading Knight Andy Ingram won West Elgin,[33] while in Lincoln Lib-Lab candidate William Garson succeeded.[34] In Lambton A.W. Wright, running as a Conservative-Labour candidate, caused considerable controversy when many of the Knights repudiated him. Not surprisingly, he did not run strongly.[35] In London, however, cabinetmaker and Knight Samuel Peddle, running with temperance support, gave Tory Opposition Leader W.R. Meredith a considerable scare before going down to a narrow defeat. In the previous election Meredith had gained his seat by acclamation.[36]

Toronto witnessed a confused race owing to the extraordinary gerrymandering of Oliver Mowat. Toronto had gained a third seat in a redistribution, but the three MPPs were to be elected at large for a city-wide riding, *and* each voter would be allowed to vote for only two candidates. The logic of this tactic was, of course, to ensure that at least one Grit would be returned from Tory Toronto. Knights' organizer Charles March finished fourth overall, while his Knight running mate, temperance advocate and evangelical Christian John Roney, finished fifth. Statistical calculations in this anomalous electoral situation are complex but March did win over 4,000 votes and Roney some 3,400. (Tory E.F. Clarke, an Orange printer, topped the poll with 7,000.)[37]

In Hamilton complications also arose when the Tories nominated a leading moulder, John Burns, as their candidate and then called on Labour to endorse him. The Labour convention refused, however, roundly condemning Burns and the Tories. Instead they nominated Grand Trunk machinist and Knight Hamilton Racey. In the bitter three-way race that followed Racey finished third with 17.2 per cent of the vote, a total that fell short of Ed Williams' 1883 vote.[38] This result did not prevent Hamilton workers from trying again in the federal election in which moulder Fred Walters ran as a Lib-Lab candidate in the two-seat constituency. He outpolled his Liberal running mate but nevertheless trailed the two victorious Tories, although his 48.8 per cent was a respectable showing.[39]

In Toronto E.E. Sheppard, the controversial editor of the *News*, campaigned in West Toronto for labour, while in East Toronto Knights' leader Alfred Jury ran. Neither was opposed by a Liberal although Sheppard's previous ties were Tory, if anything. Sheppard won 47 per cent and Jury 35 per cent, but expectations of victory had been so high that this was viewed as a significant setback. Fierce factional fighting ensued, which pitted D.J. O'Donoghue and his *Labor Record* against A.W. Wright and the *Canadian Labor Reformer*. The charges back and forth only confirmed for many the growing fear that independent labour politics was a diversion from the Knights' major tasks.[40]

Workers had entered politics with considerable scepticism and their failure to make a quick and decisive breakthrough led to much discouragement, especially since it appeared that their leaders were still intriguing in partisan politics. Nevertheless, throughout the late 1880's municipal politics continued to gain much attention from the Order and victories ranging from Brantford and Chatham to Brockville and Ottawa were recorded.[41] In Cornwall, for example, the Knights helped defeat a municipal railroad bonus in the 1888 municipal election and two years later were reported to have elected nine of thirteen aldermen and the mayor and reeve. Moreover, the Order was particularly prominent in lobbying activities in Ottawa after the creation of a Canadian Knights of Labor Legislative Committee.[42]

The Knights thus made significant political efforts and enjoyed some success, but they certainly did not overcome all the tensions in the working-class world. Partisan politics had established a deep hold on Canadian workers and the battle to create an independent working-class party was sharp and difficult. Yet on the local level tangible gains were made – early closing, union wages and jobs in corporation work, just assessment rates, more responsible public transit. But the Knights had never regarded the political arena as their major battlefield. It was only one campaign in a war on many fronts. This war was perhaps sharpest at the workplace.

IV

Much of the previous literature on the Knights of Labor has focused on their dislike of strikes. Frequent citation of major Knights' leaders such as T.V. Powderly and lengthy consideration of splits within the Order, such as the expulsion of general executive board member T.B. Barry in 1888, lead to the image of an organization committed to class co-operation through the vehicle of arbitration. Like most long-propounded views, these arguments contain a kernel of truth but they also disguise much that is central to an understanding of the Knights of Labor. In Ontario the Knights either led or were involved in almost all the major strikes of the 1880's and early 1890's.

In the Order's earliest years in Canada it grew owing to its willingness to organize the larger class forces on behalf of localized trade or industrial struggles. Thus, in Toronto the Order emerged from the coalition of forces knit together by experienced trade union militants to support the striking female boot and shoe operatives in the spring of 1882. This was apparent again the following summer when DA 45 (Brotherhood of Telegraphers) engaged in a continent-wide strike against the monopolistic telegraph companies. Although DA 45 had done little preparatory work within the Order before its epic struggle, as a bitter Powderly would argue again and again, it did appear to have established sufficient local contacts so that organized labour, and especially the Knights, rallied to its cause. In Hamilton and Toronto, for example, support came from union contributions to the strike fund, benefit concerts, lectures, and theatricals. Meanwhile, the first wave of massive Labour Day demonstrations organized by the Knights, but involving all organized labour, took place in Toronto, Hamilton, and Oshawa. In each case, support for the telegraphers played a prominent role in the speeches and provided a compelling symbol for the necessity of labour solidarity. The ultimate failure of the telegraphers' strike and its bitter aftermath, which saw DA 45 withdraw from the Knights of Labor, appear to have been less important than the solidarity expressed in its course. As the *Palladium of Labor* declared: "The telegraphers' strike is over. The People's Strike is now in order."[43]

"The People's Strike" took many forms in the following few years. At its most dramatic it involved mass strikes that crippled whole industries or communities. Examples of struggles of this magnitude included the two Toronto Street Railway strikes of the spring and summer of 1886, a Chatham town-wide strike of December, 1886, the cotton strikes in Merritton (1886 and 1889) and Cornwall (1887, 1888, and 1889), and the massive lumber strikes in Gravenhurst in 1888 and in Ottawa-Hull in 1891.[44] Each of these struggles rocked the communities with previously unmatched levels of class conflict and involved workers previously untouched by trade union organization. Yet the Knights of Labor also led or took part in conflicts far less riveting. In the early 1880's this often meant coming to the support of striking craftsmen, as with Toronto female shoe operatives in 1882 and their Hamilton sisters in 1884, or Toronto printers in 1884.[45] In these cases and in countless others, the Order proved its mettle by practising what it preached and aiding all workers' struggles. This type of activity initially helped to break down entrenched conservative craft suspicions of the Order. Then, as craft unionists and craft unions flooded into the Order in 1885-86, the Knights continued to fight their battles. These struggles, often involving issues of control, represent the second major type of Knights' strike activity, exemplified in the case of the close relations of the Order and organized craftsmen in the iron-moulding trade.

Moulders had their own international craft union that dated from the late 1850's in Ontario. The Iron Molders International Union (IMIU) had strong locals in Hamilton (No. 26) and Toronto (No. 28) and after 1887 had an Ontario-wide district organization.[46] The relationship between the IMIU and the Knights cannot be plotted with mathematical certainty but in Brantford (Standard LA 3811), Hamilton (Library LA 1864), Kingston (Frontenac LA 10539), and Oshawa (Tylers LA 4279) there existed trade assemblies identified as moulders. In addition, however, we know from scattered sources that Toronto (Maple Leaf LA 2622), Brockville (Franklin LA 2311), Smiths Falls (LA 6772), Lindsay (LA 5402), and Oshawa (Aetna LA 2355 and LA 4428) all contained moulders and other metal workers as well. Finally, we have considerable reason to suspect that Cobourg (LA 2598), Toronto (LAs 5254 and 5650), Woodstock (LAs 3151 and 4992), Galt (LA 6112), and Peterborough (LA 6952) might also have had moulder members.

Organized throughout Ontario in stove foundries and in the

agricultural implements industry, the moulders played a significant role in one of Ontario's most successful industries. This prominence and their skill, which resisted mechanical innovation throughout this period, gave them a high degree of workplace control they fought vigorously to maintain.[47] These issues led to at least twenty-five strikes between 1880 and 1893.[48] The major strikes in 1887, 1890, and 1892 in Toronto and Hamilton have already received historical attention,[49] but much smaller Ontario centres such as Brockville, Oshawa, and London also saw frequent struggles in their foundries throughout the 1880's. These smaller centres demonstrate well the interrelationship of IMIU members and Knights.

Brockville, a railroad and manufacturing centre on the St. Lawrence in eastern Ontario, illustrates these themes. The James Smart Manufacturing Co. (est. 1854) dominated the local economy of the 1880's and employed 200 workers in the production of stoves and lawn mowers by 1890.[50] The IMIU first organized in Brockville in 1868 or 1869 and had a spasmodic existence there throughout the 1870's, which included work stoppages in 1875, 1879, 1880, and 1881 – the last three of which appear to have resulted in union victories.[51] The last two struggles took place after Robert Gill replaced James Smart as the manager of the works and tried to break the union by demanding the workers abandon it. After this failed, there was a single year of peace at the foundry – a year in which the Knights established themselves strongly in Brockville. In August, 1882, Ogdensburg Knights' leader Archer Baker organized Franklin LA 2311, which grew rapidly. By the following summer the assembly numbered in the hundreds and contained many of the most prominent moulders' leaders in town, including Samuel Miller, a former IMIU international convention delegate and a perennial member of the moulders' local executive.[52] The year of peace ended in June, 1883, when Gill refused the moulders' demand for a wage increase. The ensuing eleven-week strike was eventually lost but the polarization of the community continued to increase. During the strike Brockville's working class demonstrated its solidarity when the corpse of twenty-eight-year-old moulder William Hutcheson, murdered by a scab in a strike in Troy, New York, was returned to his native town for burial.[53] The delegation of Troy Knights and moulders that accompanied the body joined with the Brockville Knights in commemorating his death with "one of the largest funerals" ever seen in the city. Building on this solidarity, the

Knights grew rapidly that summer, enrolling over 100 members in one week shortly after Hutcheson's funeral. The town also had telegraphers' LA 2335 with about forty members, which struck solidly and with "manifest public sympathy" during the continent-wide strike. In the early fall Franklin Assembly held a picnic that attracted 500 to 800 and by November the assembly reported a membership of 430.[54]

The stage was set for the next bitter conflict between Gill and his moulders, which began in January, 1884. Seven months later, in late July, the moulders returned to work, their union crushed and their vestiges of craft control destroyed, at least for the moment. This time Gill ignored community sentiment and engaged in active union-smashing. He recruited scabs from Connecticut, housed them in the foundry, and ignored the public discontent that labelled the company managers "the enemies of Brockville." When forced to defend his position, Gill explained simply:

> The question at issue is simply one of 'control.' It is a fact, however humiliating the acknowledgement, that during the past three years of the company's existence, the business has been practically controlled by the Moulder's Union. . . . If the conditions are such that 'control' cannot be gained by the proprietors, then Brockville will lose the industry which we are trying to carry on.

In Brockville the owners won back their control but only after a long history of struggle in which the Knights helped to provide the opposition. The intimacy of Knights and moulders in Brockville was evident in the latter stages of the 1884 strike when Franklin Assembly selected moulders' leader Sam Miller as its general assembly delegate and when John S. McClelland of the general executive board arrived in Brockville to investigate the strike. McClelland's visit resulted in a $500 grant from the Order's assistance fund.[55]

Oshawa, west of Brockville on Lake Ontario, witnessed an analogous set of struggles in the 1880's and a very similar organic relationship between IMIU Local No. 136 and the Knights. The IMIU, which dated from 1866, was joined in Oshawa by the Knights on August 12, 1882, when Aetna LA 2355 was organized by a Buffalo Knight. This large assembly, with nearly 300 members in 1883, was entrenched in the local iron and agricultural implements industry. Co-operating closely with the IMIU, the Oshawa Knights hosted nearly 2,000 workers at their August,

1883, labour demonstration. Members of IMIU Local 136 marched in uniforms of "gray shirts, black hats and black neckties" and were joined by their brother moulders from Toronto (Nos. 28 and 140) and Cobourg (No. 189) and over 1,500 Knights of Labor. Local 136 provided the "main feature of our procession," "the moulding, melting, and casting of iron in the line of march," reported LA 2355 and IMIU No. 36 Recording Secretary Joseph Brockman. The commemorative coins that they struck during the procession were distributed to the participants.[56] Two months later the labourers at the Malleable Iron Works, members of Aetna LA 2355, struck against a wage reduction. The moulders, out in support of the labourers and facing a similar wage cut, were warned that if they did not return, the shop would "be permanently closed against them." Six weeks into the strike the Oshawa Stove Works and the Mason Agricultural Implements Works locked out their moulders to create a solid employer block against the workers. Even then it was only after the Oshawa moulders' sister unions in Hamilton (No. 26) and Toronto (No. 28) accepted 10 per cent wage cuts in December without striking, that Oshawa No. 136 felt compelled to concede defeat. Earlier in December the labourers had returned on the advice of the LA 2355 executive, which argued that "it would have broke Jay Gould with his seventy-three millions of stolen money to have kept labourers and immigrants away from here."[57]

By the next fall, however, the union had reasserted itself and another of its leaders (and a charter member of LA 2355), Lewis Allchin, wrote Powderly seeking his support for a profit-sharing plan at the Oshawa Stove Works. He also mentioned that they had "affected every Reform obtained in the shop, one for instance, piece workers used to work almost all noonhour, and not later than last spring, we managed to institute a rigid observance of noonhour, we also limited the wages to $2.50 per day."[58] The new success of the moulders probably made another struggle almost inevitable; it came two years later, in late January, 1886, when the Malleable Iron Works again tried to force the union out of its foundry. This time the issue was simply the question of a closed shop. John Cowan, the manager of the works, insisted on continuing to employ two non-union moulders; IMIU No. 36 and Tylers LA 4279 (Moulders) refused to work with them. After a bitter two-month strike in the depths of a severe winter that witnessed alleged incendiarism, a "surprise party" (charivari?), a widespread sending to Coventry of the non-union moulders, and considerable public support for the men, the company finally caved in and recognized the closed shop. The concession came at the end of March when the union and LA 4279 began to call for a total boycott of the foundry's goods.[59]

Similar events involving moulders and Knights occurred in Lindsay in 1886,[60] in Kingston in 1887,[61] in London in 1882 and 1886,[62] and in Ayr, Galt, and Smiths Falls later in the decade.[63] Success varied dramatically, but in all these cases the principles of the Knights, of craft control and of labour reform, were carried on. Lewis Allchin, Oshawa moulder-Knight and the author of "Sketches of our Organization" (a serialized history of the IMIU from its founding to 1890 published in the *Iron Molders Journal*), summed up the close intertwining of these themes: "The object, in brief, is the *complete emancipation of labor*, and the inauguration of a higher and nobler industrial system than this of the present, under which one human being is dependent upon another for the means of living." Denying at the outset later historians' views of the Knights, he emphasized: "We cannot turn back if we would; we cannot return to a primitive system of working, however much we might desire it." Trusts and syndicates he viewed as "an inevitable phase" of "an excessive and pernicious competitive system," but they would not "be the *finale* of the whole question." They "contained within themselves the germs of their own dissolution," since "selfishness and greed were but foundations of sand to build upon." The future he would not predict, but he hazarded one final conclusion:

> That no system which does not recognize the right of labor to a first and just share of its products, which refuses each and every toiler a voice in the business transactions of the enterprise, that does not establish a just and relative measure of standard of value for all services rendered, labor performed, products manufactured, and commodities exchanged, will ever be a just or permanent one.[64]

Here, quite clearly, we can see that the values and ideas of the late nineteenth-century working-class world were shared by its articulate leadership, be they Knights or craft unionists, and, as was so often the case, the personnel overlapped. For our chosen group of skilled workers, the moulders, this unity demonstrated itself most clearly in the streets of London in the late summer of 1886 when the IMIU held its seventeenth convention. The city's first labour demonstration "of 4000 unionists in line" was held to honour the assembled moulders and was witnessed by crowds estimated at between 8,000 and 10,000.[65] Addressed by Captain Richard Trevellick, the Knights' chief itinerant lecturer, the convention also considered at length a motion to amalgamate the IMIU with the Knights of Labor. After a full day of debate the resolution was soundly defeated but it did win support from militant moulders' strongholds such as Albany and Troy, New York. In registering his opposition, the IMIU president made clear his support "for always remaining on the most friendly terms with the Knights of Labor, and rendering them all the assistance that our organization can possibly give them in all legitimate undertakings in the interest of labour."[66] This solidarity began to disintegrate the following year during the vicious war between the Founders Association and the moulders in the Bridge and Beach strike.[67]

The solidarity so evident in the London streets in July, 1886, had also spread far beyond the moulders and their skilled brethren. The Knights also successfully organized the unskilled – women factory workers, male operatives, and large numbers of labourers both in Ontario's cities and towns and in her resource hinterland. These workers, organized for the first time under the banner of the Knights of Labor, also engaged in militant struggles in the 1880's and early 1890's. Strikes to gain the right either to organize or to win modest economic advances occurred in these sectors as opposed to the struggles for control of the skilled workers. Ranging in size from minor affairs to massive, almost general strikes that polarized single-industry communities, these struggles were most prominent in the mill towns of eastern and western Ontario.

Cotton mill struggles hit Merritton in 1886 and 1889 and Cornwall in three successive years, 1887, 1888, and 1889. The Merritton mill, which remained totally organized as late as 1892, witnessed numerous work stoppages led by the Knights in 1886. Three years later a week-long strike over a wage reduction won a compromise settlement. None of these represented major victories, but in an industry known for its exploitation and anti-unionism Maple Leaf LA 5933's 500 workers were more successful than most. Their achievement may well have been one of the factors that led Canadian Coloured Cottons to shut down the plant after the merger of 1892.[68]

Cornwall's cotton workers joined the Knights of Labor in 1886 in LAs 6582 and 6583. The first test of the Order came in the summer of 1887 when eighteen dyers demanded that their hours be reduced from ten to nine. Although the Order provided $400 in financial assistance to its striking members, they still lost the strike.[69] In February, 1888, wage reductions at both the Canada and Stormont mills precipitated strikes involving from 1,300 to 1,500 employees. After a few weeks the workers returned with a compromise settlement. The wages were still cut but by an estimated 10 per cent instead of the alleged 20 to 23 per cent originally imposed. This settlement held at the Stormont mill, but the Canada mill was struck again when workers accused the company of not living up to the agreement. After another month these workers again returned.[70] One year later, in the spring of 1889, the Stormont mill workers struck once again. After five weeks the 600 operatives returned when the company agreed to honour the weavers' demands.[71]

The lumber industry, another long holdout against trade unionism, also experienced two major strikes led by the Knights of Labor. Gravenhurst LA 10669 was organized in 1887 under the leadership of Uxbridge DA 236 after a short lumber strike in which the hours of work in the mills on Muskoka Bay had been reduced from eleven to ten-and-a-half with a promise that in 1888 they would be further shortened to ten. In 1888, however, a province-wide agreement was signed by the Muskoka, Georgian Bay, and Ottawa River lumber barons preventing a further reduction of hours under pain of forfeiting a bond. The angry workers of LA 10669 consulted the DA 236 leadership, which counselled caution and urged the assembly to strengthen its ranks. By June, 300 of the 375 workers had joined the Order and they then appointed a committee to meet with the mill owners. This met with a blanket refusal from the employers and the workers again sought aid from DA 236. Although reluctant, the district assembly had no choice but to sanction a strike, which began on July 3, 1888. A few mills acceded but the majority held out. Aylesworth of the Knights' general executive board responded to an emergency call from DA 236, but his efforts were unsuccessful and by September the men had returned to work with no gains.[72]

In the Chaudière region of the Ottawa-Hull area, another lumber workers' strike erupted in September, 1891.[73] The Knights' success in the Ottawa Valley came late: only in the fall of 1890 had they gained a foothold in the mills with the creation of Chaudière LA 2966. As three years earlier in Gravenhurst, a particularly harsh winter created the situation that would lead to that fall's huge mill strike. Already late returning to work because of the weather, the workers were informed of a fifty-cents-a-week wage cut. In return for the reduction, the owners offered the ten-hour day but soon violated their own concession. With hours again extended to eleven and twelve the workers sought the aid of the Knights of Labor in May. When informed that the Order would not sanction a strike until they had been in the organization for at least six months, the workers remained on the job. By fall, however, their tempers had worn thin and on Saturday, September 12, 1891, the outside workers at Perley and Pattee demanded that their wages be reinstated to the 1890 rate. Denied this, the workers met on the Sunday and agreed to repeat their demand the next day. Again rebuffed, they proceeded to march from mill to mill pulling all the workers out. Over 2,400 workers left their jobs and the Knights quickly took over the strike leadership. The mill workers were subsequently enrolled in Chaudière LA 2966 and Hull's Canadienne LA 2676.

Over the next few weeks some of the smaller mills conceded to the workers' demands of the previous year's rate and a ten-hour day, but the larger mills stood firm. As community support for the workers stiffened, massive meetings of 3,000 to 10,000 people were held. Meanwhile, incidents of violence occurred, the militia was mobilized, and workers responded with a charivari and with their own security force. Over $1,500 was raised by the Order and an extensive relief system was established. By the end of September, however, strike leaders urged their followers to seek employment elsewhere and by early October the relief system began to break down. By October 12 the workers were back with their 1890 wage but with the same long hours of work. Two hundred of Bronson's workers promptly struck again on October 14 when they claimed he had reneged on his agreement, but by the end of the month work was back to normal. Although not an unmitigated success, the Order had won a limited victory and the millmen stayed with the Knights. The next year Ottawa DA 6 was created with an impressive 2,000 workers, largely from the lumber industry. These workers finally won the ten-hour day in 1895.

Turbulence, strikes, and class conflict thus played an important role in the history of the Knights of Labor in Ontario. The oft-invoked image of an organization interested in avoiding strikes at all cost and the implicit projection of a class-co-operative, if not collaborationist, body begin to dissipate under more careful scrutiny.

V

The 1880's were a critical decade in Canadian history – a decade that witnessed the fulfilment of the National Policy industrial strategy with a rapid expansion in central Canadian manufacturing, especially in textiles. Yet these years also saw the breakdown of the previous consensus on industrial development, as Canadian workers, especially in the country's industrial heartland, began to raise their voices in an unfamiliar, concerted fashion to join the growing debate about the nation's future. Ontario's mainly British and Canadian workers, many with previous trade union and industrial experience, provided leadership to the emerging working-class movement that found its most articulate expression in the Knights of Labor. The challenge this movement mounted in all realms of Ontario society – the cultural, intellectual, and political as well as the economic – engendered in turn a class response from employers and from the state. The employers engaged in a virulent, open warfare with their worker-Knights, especially in the period of economic decline after 1886. In the 1890's they began as well to turn to the ever-increasing concentration and centralization of capital and later to the modern management devices of a rampant Taylorism in their battle with labour. Meanwhile, the state and the political parties responded in a more conciliatory fashion. Mowat and, to a lesser degree, Macdonald interceded to provide workers with many of the protections they demanded – factory acts, bureaus of labour statistics, arbitration measures, suffrage extension, employers' liability acts, and improved mechanics' lien acts. The political parties proved even more flexible and managed through patronage and promises to contain much of the oppositional sentiment that flared in the 1880's. Thus the Canadian political system functioned effectively to mediate the fiery class conflict of the 1880's.

In the following decade, with the exception of eastern Ontario, the Knights were moribund. Yet the heritage of the Order lived on. Its major contributions to working-class memory centred on its oppositional success as a movement that for the first time provided *all* workers with an organizational vehicle and, further, for a moment at least, overcame the splintering forces that so often divided the working class.

Part II

Monopoly Capitalism and the Unevenness of Class Struggle

Economic historians have long emphasized the tremendous growth and development associated with the early years of the twentieth century and the war-induced boom of the 1940's. While a post-war recession in the early 1920's and the depression collapse of the 1930's did indeed represent serious years of economic downturn, and while few would argue that the fruits of economic expansion were distributed equitably among all Canadians, there is no denying the sustained advance of the economy in the years 1900-1950. Canada emerged as an advanced industrial-capitalist nation in this period as the city replaced the country as the home of most Canadians; workers, rather than small independent producers, began to predominate in the social structure. Corporate power grew ever more concentrated as waves of business mergers brought smaller firms under the control of larger entities such as the Steel Company of Canada. New technologies eroded old craft skills and created whole new semi-skilled work forces; so, too, did a willingness to recruit labour previously shunned, including women.

How did the class struggle develop in this context of change? The question is not easily answered. On the one hand, because the increasingly monopolistic form of capitalist development clarified the extent of corporate power and the close ties between capital and the state, thus creating both national labour markets and policies, it stimulated the first large-scale national labour revolts, first in 1919 and then in 1943-48. On the other hand, with corporate power so enhanced and so capable of cultivating new divisions among workers, there is no doubt that while the episodic contours of class struggle might reveal moments of massive revolt, the underlying continuities of class relations often inhibited struggle and fragmented workers. The character of class struggle in this period was thus uneven. If 1919, as Kealey shows, was a remarkable year of national labour revolt, the class struggle in specific sectors, such as the steel and textile industries studied by Heron and Brandt, was far more subdued, for reasons that the essays in this section try to explain.

3

Hamilton Steelworkers and the Rise of Mass Production

Craig Heron

Industrial capitalism came to Canada, as it did to most Western nations, in two distinct phases. The so-called "First" Industrial Revolution, based on coal, iron, steam, and for the most part relatively simple technology, took root in Canada in the 1850's and 1860's and blossomed in the National Policy hot house of the 1880's. The momentum for the "Second" Industrial Revolution, which took off at the close of the nineteenth century within the emergent monopoly capitalist economy, came from the complex new technology and production processes of corporate giants in steel, auto, chemicals, pulp and paper, electrical goods, meat packing, and so on. This paper attempts to tell the part of that story that unfolded in one of Canada's three leading steel-producing centres, Hamilton, Ontario.

The decade before World War I brought the first major managerial innovations in the steel industry – new machines, new industrial recruits, and new labour policies – to create the now familiar world of high-speed mass production. The workers drawn into this new factory environment initially tended to pass through it quickly, enduring the harsh, unfamiliar work routines only long enough to earn some ready cash. Gradually, however, this "floating" labour force developed some experience with this kind of industry, as well as an increasing commitment to their jobs that would encourage them to challenge the company's employment policies. A series of sporadic revolts before the war evolved into the first effort to organize an industry-wide union in 1919-20. This first experiment in industrial unionism raised the human concerns being ignored in the new industry but did not succeed in shaking the steelmasters' firm control over their production processes.

I

An exuberant crowd of several hundred visitors cheered the lighting ("blowing in") of the new furnace of the Hamilton Blast Furnace Company on December 30, 1895, and production of pig iron began within a few weeks. In 1899, as part of the trend toward integration of all the stages of iron and steel production within a single firm, the company amalgamated with a twenty-year-old Hamilton enterprise, the Ontario Rolling Mills Company. The next year the new company, now known as the Hamilton Steel and Iron Company, opened a small steel plant.

Over the next decade expansion was cautious; as a company executive recalled, "so limited was the market at this time that it was found impossible to keep both [open-hearth] furnaces running continuously. Even one furnace running at its capacity for over a month made more steel than could be sold." Two more open-hearth furnaces and facilities to produce railway spikes were eventually added, and in 1907 a second blast furnace, but the firm's great leap forward came in 1910. That year the Hamilton Steel and Iron Company merged with the local Canadian Screw Company and a string of iron and steel finishing plants in Montreal, Belleville, Gananoque, Swansea, and Brantford. The new corporation, the Steel Company of Canada, included facilities to produce a wide range of metal products – screws, nuts and bolts, wire, nails, pipes, and much more – and in order to supply these plants with steel, a massive expansion of the corporation's production facilities in Hamilton followed the merger: two new open-hearth furnaces and large new rolling mills capable of producing blooms, billets, rods, and bars. The demand for munitions in World War I brought a further increase in capacity and the addition of by-product coke ovens and a mill for the production of sheet metal, as well as vertical integration into iron-ore and coal-mining operations in the United States. By the 1920's the Steel Company's strategy of relying on diversified markets and its central location in the heartland of Canadian manufacturing had brought the corporation to a leadership role in the country's steel industry, surpassing its crisis-ridden competitors in Sault Ste. Marie and Sydney.[1]

The Hamilton iron and steel complex emerged later and more cautiously than its principal counterparts in the United States, but, like all other Canadian firms, its production processes were nonetheless modelled on American practices. The inventive American steelmakers were producing the world's cheapest steel by the 1890's,[2] and, in order to survive in the face of this competition with minimal tariff protection, Hamilton's steel men had to match the American standards of efficiency. When a careful eye was therefore trained on production costs, the cost of labour inevitably received particular attention. Increased productivity would necessitate speeding up production, increasing output, and securing more predictability within a large, integrated corporation.

What were the labour requirements of iron and steel production at the end of the nineteenth century? The Bessemer converter and later the open-hearth furnace had been introduced into the American industry over the previous three decades to get around the slow, independent routines of the iron puddler, who had combined muscular prowess and an unschooled knowledge of metallurgical science to transform pig iron into wrought iron. The Ontario Rolling Mills and, for a time, the Hamilton Blast Furnace Company employed a few puddlers, but by the turn of the century the market for this metal was dwindling and Hamilton's puddling furnaces were idle after 1907.[3] Aside from a small number of specialized workmen not directly involved in iron and steel production – moulders, machinists, carpenters, steamfitters, operating engineers, and so on – the only other significant group of operatives with some valuable skills were the heaters and rollers in the rolling-mill plants, the men who manipulated the steel ingots through each set of rolls.[4] The general decline of the skilled workingman in the American industry had been registered by the crushing of his craft union, the Amalgamated Association of Iron and Steel Workers, first at Homestead, Pa., in 1892, and then throughout most of the United States Steel Corporation's operations in 1901. A Hamilton lodge of the association had been defeated by the Ontario Rolling Mills management in the 1880's, and this craft union did not revive in the city before World War I.[5] The Hamilton steelmasters would therefore face few problems with independent-minded craftsmen defending their traditional modes of work.

Iron and steel production did, however, continue to rely on large numbers of unskilled labourers for some of the hottest, heaviest, dirtiest, least appealing jobs available to any worker. In 1926 W.A. Child, an executive of the Ontario Rolling Mills in its early days, recalled the use of brute labour for the countless tasks of handling materials, whether lifting, carrying, pushing, hauling, loading and unloading, or manoeuvring the ubiquitous wheelbarrow. Years later an elderly Hamilton steelworker remembered that "There wasn't one derrick on the property when I started in 1905."[6] The Hamilton iron and steel plants would still need the brawn of unskilled labourers well into the early 1900's.

Faced with these labour requirements and the intense competition in the market for their products, Hamilton's steelmasters gradually initiated managerial policies that would alter the work routines around their plants. Probably the most striking change was the substitution of machines for men wherever possible – a process that gave the industry the characteristic shape we have come to know as "mass production." Skilled workers, of course, normally exercised a degree of independence on the job, which often irked company supervisors, but even the labourers presented annoying problems for corporate planners. Not only, as we will see, were they surprisingly prone to striking and raising the spectre of higher labour costs, but they provided an element of unpredictability in the work process, by slowing down according to the dictates of human endurance or quitting frequently. "Workmen find it bad enough to be forced to handle frozen pig and scrap iron in winter," the *Canadian Foundryman* lamented, "but when the summer heat comes beating down the men become inefficient and discontented. Many of them leave." In fact, North America's unskilled work force in the early twentieth century was a footloose lot. In 1907 the Hamilton *Times* described "a large roving element in the labor market" that was disturbing employers:

> They complain that there is a considerable element of a floating nature, composed in part of foreigners and in part of young men from the country, who come to the city as soon as the fall work is over and expect to go back when spring plowing begins. . . . They are not the class that the manufacturers want, because men coming and going upset organization in the shops and have an unsettling effect upon the regular hands.

After conducting preliminary social surveys in Hamilton and five other Canadian cities for the Methodist and Presbyterian churches,

Bryce Stewart noted in 1913: "Tired of 13 hours night shift in the steel plant at Sydney, the immigrant tries railroad construction out of Fort William, and when winter comes presses on to tend a coke oven or 'work a face' in one of the coal mines of Crow's Nest, or returns east to 'The Soo,' or Hamilton or Montreal or back to the Sydneys."[7] This transiency and instability could create plenty of corporate headaches for iron and steel executives – especially in prosperous periods when labour became scarce.[8] By the end of World War I industrial relations experts would have coined the term "labour turnover" for this informal form of working-class protest.[9]

As competition intensified in the decade before World War I, steel managers became ever more anxious about obstacles to increased productivity. The limited assistance of the bounty system ended in 1910, and all Canadian steel companies recognized the need for "reducing costs in order to keep up the measure of profits."[10] The new Steel Company of Canada initially faced this situation with small, relatively labour-intensive facilities for the production of steel, but the years before the war saw the first wave of a great expansion of productive capacity with the most up-to-date steel-making equipment, virtually all of it American in origin.[11] A key feature of this new technology, trumpeted through all the trade journals, was its "labour-saving" quality; that is, the new machines reduced the need for manual work and in the process speeded up and streamlined production by eliminating many of the bottlenecks that human labour created. It consequently provided managers with more effective control over the flow and pace of production in their plants. The results were evident by early 1913 when the Steel Company president, Charles S. Wilcox, reported to the shareholders the reasons for the firm's increased earnings: "we have greatly improved our plants and increased the efficiency of our operations, and thereby reduced the cost of production."[12]

This transformation can best be traced by considering the evolving work process in each of the three main departments of primary steel production at the Steel Company of Canada and its predecessors – the blast-furnace, open-hearth, and rolling-mill departments. Blast-furnace work was quite primitive in the 1890's when the Hamilton company erected its plant on the outskirts of the city. The furnace had to be charged regularly with iron ore, limestone, and coke, and at intervals it was tapped to let the molten pig iron flow out into sand moulds on the casting floor, forming blocks of iron known as "pigs." At the turn of the century coal for various heating purposes would be unloaded from sailing ships by gangs of men assisted by a work horse. Other raw materials arrived by train from Lake Erie and were shovelled out of the railway cars by hand.[13] Labourers then wheeled the stock to the back of the furnace in large two-wheeled barrows, each holding about 1,200 pounds; after weighing them, another set of men pushed the barrows into an elevator that carried them up the side of the seventy-five-foot furnace. On a platform at the top, half a dozen "top-fillers" emptied the ore, limestone, and coke into the mouth of the furnace – a potentially dangerous job that cost one worker his life in the first year of the furnace's operations.[14]

About every four hours in normal production, the furnace would be tapped. The slag that had formed on top of the molten iron would be run off onto the ground outside the casting house. Visitors to the plant in February, 1896, saw "men with crowbars and sledge hammers . . . on the outer edges of the greyish mass in the yard breaking the cooled parts of a former discharge into handleable chunks, which were carted away to be used as refuse in filling up the waterfront of the property." Meanwhile, back on the casting floor, the hot metal had flowed out of the bottom of the furnace into a network of channels in the sand to set in the "pigs." Men scurried along the little rivers of fire "like the demons in a Kirafly spectacular theatrical hell, poking about with their flaming wooden poles and seeing that each individual piglet was duly 'fed'." Then sand was shovelled over the molten iron until it cooled. Since each pig was still connected to a central cord of iron, labourers had to smash the blocks apart with hammers. The men then loaded them into wheelbarrows, carted them out to a railway car, and heaved them in by hand.[15]

These work routines around the blast furnace began to change in 1907 when the Hamilton Steel and Iron Company added its second blast furnace, which was equipped with new, mechanized devices for moving the raw materials from storage and depositing them in the furnace. On arrival at the plant the stock would be dropped from high trestles through the bottom of railway hopper cars or else unloaded with "whirlie cranes equipped with grab buckets" onto piles in the storage yard. The same mechanical shovel would be used to load the stock, as needed, into the drop-bottom cars, which would then unload their cargoes into a series of stock bins behind the blast furnaces. Out of the bottom of these bins could be released the desired amount of raw materials onto a small, electrically driven car, mounted on railway tracks. This vehicle, in turn, automatically weighed the stock and emptied it into an elevating device known as a "skip hoist," which lifted and dumped the stock into the top of the furnace with no manual assistance. Gone were all the shovels, wheelbarrows, and brawny labourers, and in their place were a handful of men who manipulated gears.[16]

Work on the front of the furnace, where the casting of pig iron took place, changed more slowly. Eventually the slag was drained into large pots on railway cars and hauled away for dumping. In 1907 the process of breaking up the pigs was mechanized: an overhead electric crane carried the hardened iron to a "hydraulic pig breaker" at the lower end of the casting house, where, as it was broken, the iron dropped into chutes conveying it to railway cars. The expansion of steel production before the war also meant that much more of the molten iron was swept away in giant ladles by electric cranes for use in the open-hearth department, rather than being allowed to harden and broken apart. By the end of World War I the annual output per man in the company's blast furnace department had consequently increased enormously.[17]

Only in 1920, following wartime labour shortages and wage gains, did the Steel Company finally move to full mechanization of its blast-furnace production. That year it installed a pig-casting machine to replace the more primitive method of casting in sand. Now the molten iron was poured into a slowly moving belt of iron moulds, which cooled the metal quickly, dropped the solid pig iron into a railway car, and then returned under the machine to receive another load of hot metal. The backbreaking labour of the early years had thus been almost completely eliminated, and the number of workers in the company's most strike-prone department could be greatly reduced. "Under the old style it took 150 men per 24 hours to operate a 200 ton furnace and the output was 1.33 tons per man turn," a trade publication reported in 1924. "Under the modern style it takes only 60 men per 24 hours to operate a 550 ton furnace, and the output is 9.17 tons per man turn."

In the second stage of steel production, the metal was moved to the open-hearth department, where the pig iron was transformed into steel. This had been the arena of the industry's greatest technological changes in the late nineteenth century, when the patient craftsmen at small puddling furnaces were replaced by a new, more mechanized process for refining pig iron into a tough, resilient steel. In a long row of open-hearth furnaces, molten pig iron and a quantity of scrap metal were exposed to the intense heat of a gas flame to remove impurities and were combined with certain chemical agents to provide the carbon necessary for hardness. For charging pig iron and scrap into the furnaces, the company had the material loaded into steel boxes on a train that ran through the stockyard. An "electric charging machine" picked up the boxes, emptied the contents into the furnace, and returned them to the train for refilling. Before the adoption of these charging machines, six to eight men would have taken nearly six times as long to charge each furnace by hand. The first two furnaces at the Hamilton Steel and Iron Company were tilting models that poured the molten steel directly into small ingots. By 1908 giant ladles suspended from travelling cranes were being used to catch the fiery stream of molten steel from the now stationary furnaces and were drained into the ingot moulds (in the jargon of the industry, these two steps were known as "tapping the heat" and "teeming the ingots"). In the post-merger expansion of the Steel Company's open-hearth facilities, a specially designed crane was also installed for stripping the moulds from the ingots, a process that eliminated the difficulty and hazards of loosening by hand any moulds that stuck. With the effective use of all of this machinery, the annual output per man in the open-hearth department rose from an average of 156 tons between 1901 and 1904 to 996 in 1919.[18]

In the third main arena of Hamilton's iron and steel production, the rolling-mill department, the steel ingots were passed several times through mills of various sizes to create a variety of usable shapes. Large, bulky "blooms" were reduced to smaller "billets" and then to bars, channels, rods, and so on. Before the major post-merger innovations, the rolling-mill facilities of the Hamilton Steel and Iron Company remained much as they had in the last decades of the nineteenth century. The old Ontario Rolling Mills lacked the large rolls for blooms and billets, and its four trains of rolls were smaller "merchant" and "guide" mills producing mostly iron bars that were then refined into bolts, nails, axles, horseshoes, and many other articles. The two new sets of rolls incorporated into the new steel plant in 1900 were similarly small and turned out steel bars.[19] The men who worked on these rolls used muscle and skill in wielding their tongs, as they pulled the hot bars from the reheating furnaces and thrust them into the successive sets of rolls.[20] The job of pushing the sizzling hot metal bars by hand along a set of rollers to the giant shears that trimmed their length was particularly tough.[21]

The new installations of 1912-13 diversified the range of rolled products and changed the company's rolling-mill work dramatically. They won international acclaim for the efficiency of the continuous, electrically driven system of production that eliminated all the heaving and shoving between rolls. As the *Canadian Foundryman* noted in surveying the new operations: "Modern rolling mills are really automatic machines on a large scale, one machine sometimes covering an acre or more of ground, and operated by a few men almost entirely without hard muscular labour." Robert Hobson, the Steel Company's president, boasted to the American Iron and Steel Institute in 1919 that the new electrically driven reversing blooming mill required only one easily trained operator per shift, who sat high on a platform, or "pulpit," overlooking the rolls and the automatic machinery.[22]

Did Hamilton's steelmasters introduce all this new technology purely to get a tighter rein on the work process in their plants, in a wilful assertion of authority? The question is complicated, since some of the innovations were within existing operations, while many were part of completely new installations, especially new rolling-mill facilities. In some instances the machinery undoubtedly solved long-standing management problems, but the prime impetus for its introduction undoubtedly came from market conditions, which demanded higher volume production at lower costs. Above all, the speed and reliability of all the charging and conveying devices promised a larger output of cheaper steel. Still, the modern American technology that the Hamilton steel men bought embodied many years of experimentation in American steel plants, aimed overtly at eliminating manual labour and reducing workers' shopfloor control over production processes. Consequently, whether or not the new technology was seen explicitly as a management tool for imposing order on an unstable work process, it did guarantee the company's managers more control over the pace and flow of production.

Technological change thus occurred in steel plants like those of the Steel Company of Canada not primarily to lighten the workers' burden but to serve corporate needs for greater predictability and productivity. So-called "labour-saving devices" were meant to save money, not sweat. The net result was the elimination of some of the most unpleasant, backbreaking work, but simultaneously the speeding up of production for the workers still needed in the plants. Predictably, these ever-present dangers produced appalling accident rates: in 1916, for example, the Steel Company's Hamilton plants produced 488 serious accidents requiring at least a week off work, one of which was fatal – amounting to nearly one worker in six on the firm's payroll.[23] Although production was fully integrated throughout the company's Hamilton operations by World War I and was normally continuous (hence a twelve-hour working day), its rhythms were erratic, requiring frenzied bursts of strenuous exertion from its workers as the metal was charged, heated, tapped, poured, or rolled into shape. It was a form of mass production that did not involve the monotonously repetitive tasks of an auto plant or a textile mill, but it was nonetheless physically demanding.[24]

As the Hamilton steelmasters turned to machines to replace men, they also undertook to make the fullest use of the workers they still needed. From the turn of the century they adopted the North American practice of intensifying the labour process by "driving" their workers, especially the common labourers, as hard as possible to extract the maximum effort from them in the gruelling twelve-hour days (eleven hours on the day shift, thirteen at night) that would last in Hamilton until 1930. To maintain this direct, authoritarian pressure, the Steel Company managers found that they had to restructure the ethnic composition of their work force. In part, the problem for the company was finding Anglo-Canadian workers who would tolerate the long hours and unpleasant labour in its plants. As early as 1901 the *Labour Gazette*'s correspondent reported the firm's difficulties in obtaining sufficient unskilled labour "owing to the opportunities for employment for such men elsewhere and the heavy nature of the work in and about the smelter." Two decades later, when returned soldiers were demanding jobs, the city's Ontario Employment Bureau found few of them willing to accept employment in the steel plants.[25] Equally important, however, were the testiness and independent-mindedness of English-speaking workmen.

The first major confrontation with these workers – and apparently a crucial turning point in the ethnic recomposition of the work force – came in the spring of 1902, when between sixty-five and seventy Anglo-Canadian labourers around the blast furnace struck for a 10 per cent wage increase. "We have a body of men second to none in the city," their spokesman insisted, "and we are paid the magnificent sum of 15, 16 and 16½ cents per hour for the work that only the strongest and most rugged men can do, and we have to work in all weathers and seven days a week. . . ." Rumours began to circulate that the men would like to abolish the twelve-hour day and were taking the first steps toward unionization. It was no doubt this stubborn aggressiveness that would prompt a Steel Company executive to blurt out a decade later, "the English workman is the cause of more labour troubles than any other nationality." To combat such a spirit of resistance among its labourers the company recruited strikebreakers, including a trainload of Italians from Buffalo, who were encouraged to camp in makeshift shacks on the company property. The strike was broken, and the shanties became permanent quarters for many of the company's labourers.[26]

The shift to European migrant labourers in blast-furnace work was so thorough within five years that the next strike in that department, in the spring of 1907, involved only "foreigners," mostly Italians, and by the war the newcomers comprised some three-fifths of the company's work force. By 1918 the superintendent of the Ontario Labour Department's Employment Bureau in Hamilton could report that the "foreigners" did "practically the whole of the heavy and laborious work" in the city's iron, steel, and metal-working plants. The city's ethnic mix similarly shifted, so that by the 1920's more than one male worker in ten was European born. For the Steel Company this new work force was cheap: between 1910 and 1920, for example, the company's wage bill for blast-furnace work stayed relatively constant at around $300,000, while the value of pig iron production doubled from just under $3 million to nearly $6 million and company profits quadrupled to some $2 million. "It would be a very serious matter to do away with foreign labour," a company official warned in 1919 during heated debates about deporting the "aliens." "If we expect returned soldiers to do the rough, rugged work, many of us would be out of business because we could not produce at anything like low enough cost."[27]

The needs of Hamilton's steelmakers actually meshed well with those of the migrant labourers from southern and eastern Europe who were flooding into North America in the early twentieth century. Driven by worsening under-employment, over-population, and agricultural depression, many men in Italy's *Mezzogiorno* and similar agricultural regions in eastern Europe had begun a process of seasonal migration to earn cash that might help to better the situation of themselves and their families in their homelands.[28] Ethnic intermediaries, especially labour agents, helped to funnel these men into available jobs, and, once a particular employer had developed an acknowledged preference for Europeans, informal networks of communication would carry the news back to the villages to direct future migrants to specific locations like Hamilton. "Each nationality has one or more citizens who keep their eyes open in the interest of their people," a Hamilton workingman noted in 1914, "and a very striking instance of this may be noted from the fact that one will often see a gang of Italians or Poles, etc., being led around to the various factories by one of their interpreters to help 'land a job'."[29]

The seasonal cycles were often extended into longer sojourns on this side of the Atlantic, especially if unemployment, accident, or ill health had eaten up the labourer's savings, but a large percentage still returned home. During their sojourn they shared cramped quarters in boarding houses with their fellow countrymen. The great majority of them were men in the prime of life; women comprised only 29 per cent of the city's foreign born in 1911 and still only 37 per cent twenty years later. In 1913 Methodist and Presbyterian investigators conducted a detailed survey of a block of immigrant housing near the Steel Company's east-end plant. In seventeen eight-roomed houses occupied by Italians, Bulgarians, Poles, Rumanians, and Macedonians, they found 232 men, nineteen women, and twelve children; 213 of the men were single, either boarding or living co-operatively. As a census-taker had discovered two years earlier, the men ate and slept in shifts and "the beds never grow cold." Such a lifestyle was, of course, quite cheap in comparison with that of Anglo-Canadian working-class families and allowed the European migrants both to accept lower wages and build up their savings.[30]

The transiency of these men seemed to make them willing to endure the unpleasant work at low wages, and their unfamiliarity with workplace routines in a city like Hamilton made them a pool of apparently docile, easily exploited labour. Their instrumental orientation to their jobs was particularly adaptable.[31] By using ethnic sub-foremen known as "straw bosses" to organize and discipline the work groups in their plants, steel companies got the strict authoritarian style of management they sought. The tyrannical rule of the foreman in Hamilton became notorious, and a company executive admitted in 1919 that "we have more trouble through workmen and foremen than anywhere else."[32]

The additional advantage of this new work force for the steelmasters was the cultural gulf that set them apart from the rest of the city's working class and inhibited class-conscious activity. These were men from peasant backgrounds whose ties were usually stronger with family and village across the Atlantic than with fellow workers a few blocks away. Their presence, moreover, was deeply resented by many of Hamilton's Anglo-Canadian workers, who feared that the newcomers could bring about the degradation of work and living standards in Canada. In 1910, when hundreds of Europeans organized the city's biggest steel strike of the period, the English-speaking workers remained aloof. In 1912 the Steel Company precipitated an unsuccessful strike by its wire-drawers when it put two Poles to work in their shop. By the end of World War I the "anti-alien" sentiment had reached hysterical proportions, and in February, 1919, a boisterous crowd of 10,000 in which "returned soldiers and working men seemed to predominate," demanded the deportation of "enemy aliens and other undesirables." In 1910, in a moment of unusual candour, the Hamilton *Herald* had summarized the special advantages of immigrant labour for the city's steel company:

> The fact that almost all of the steel and iron workers are foreigners and single men who have no real place in the life of the city, who know nothing about our civic and national affairs, and who are here only for the money they make and will be away once they have saved a sufficiency, and whose standard of living is below that of the average English-speaking workman, makes the public comparatively indifferent to their claims. Thus the great manufacturing corporations serve a double purpose when they import cheap labour from continental Europe. They get work done at a cost less than the cost of getting it done by English-speaking workmen, and they prevent the enlistment of public opinion on the side of the workers when troubles arise with their foreign employees.

Thus, the efforts to revamp the work process in Hamilton's steel industry brought hundreds of European labourers inside the factory walls to be driven by relentless foremen for twelve hours a day at the lowest wage rates in the city – jobs made bearable only by the expectation of imminent departure. By 1910 the fierce heat, smoke, noise, and heavy labour had won for steel plant jobs a reputation among the city's labourers as "the lowest on the scale."[33]

HAMILTON STEELWORKERS 81

The whole work force in the steel industry, however, could not be flooded with transient labourers. Some work in a steel plant still required a degree of skill or at least familiarity with the job. The company's approach to this small skilled portion of its workers revealed a desire to keep them in their jobs and to promote a quiescent loyalty to the firm and its managers. Primarily the company appealed to steelworkers' concern for economic security. In the first place, it made promotions to higher-paying jobs from within its own work force and thus increased the more ambitious workers' dependence on the corporation for advancement. Second, it initiated a range of welfare programs that tied workers to long-term benefit schemes and encouraged them to identify their economic security with the corporation. An employees' benefit society organized in 1902 provided insurance against sickness and death, and a limited stock-subscription plan and a pension fund were added in 1912 and 1918, respectively. The Steel Company's vice-president, F.H. Whitton, explained to a royal commission in 1919 that these welfare-capitalist measures were not acts of philanthropy toward the firm's employees but were intended "to give them a direct interest in the business, and promote continuity of effort and permanence of employment," since "continuous and contented service is an asset to any company." This "continuous and contented" faction of the work force nonetheless remained small and restricted: after seven years the stock-option plan had drawn only 629 subscribers out of more than 4,000 employees, and the exclusively Anglo-Canadian names on the executive of the benefit society indicated limited participation by the European-born steelworkers.[34]

In the Hamilton steel industry, therefore, we can see three processes in the organization of work and the management of labour aimed at strengthening management control: the increasing substitution of machinery for manual labour, both skilled and unskilled; the intensification of labour through the old-fashioned authoritarian management of a raw, inexperienced work force and through wage-incentive schemes; and the development of promotion and welfare policies to stabilize the more skilled elements among the workers. By the 1920's the incorporation of managerial control within new technology had probably become more important than pure authoritarian rule or welfare capitalism, but the tyranny of the foreman would nonetheless last until the consolidation of industrial unionism in the 1940's.[35]

A new industry thus gave birth to a new category of mass-production workers, the steelworkers. One striking characteristic of this new work force was its occupational homogeneity: old-time craftsmen had largely disappeared and labourers were needed in much smaller numbers. It would, of course, be an exaggeration to claim that mechanization completely eliminated manual labour, both skilled and unskilled, from the works. Yet surveying the work process in the Hamilton steel plants as a whole, what was striking was how drastically the new technology had reduced the need for both highly skilled men and a large unskilled labour force.[36] In fact, the old nineteenth-century dichotomy of craftsman and labourer had been replaced by a less sharply differentiated body of workers, a large percentage of whom were machine operators. The term that became current for this new work force in the early twentieth century was "semi-skilled," but this disguised how little skill was required in most jobs and how easily these workers could be replaced. These new steelworkers may have been required to exercise more responsibility for their machinery and its output than labourers, but their knowledge of the whole production process, their training, and their control over the form and pace of the work was not as great as was the case with the old craftsmen.

Several factors reduced the impact of this increasing homogeneity. Ethnic barriers between groups of steelworkers were no doubt the most important, especially in separating the more skilled English-speaking workers from the much larger number of Europeans. At the same time the company's widespread use of piece rates, instead of hourly wages, tended to encourage individual effort over broader identification with fellow workers across the plant (though the fact that workers usually worked in gangs that collectively earned the piece rates gave the system a somewhat more co-operative spirit). Such incentive schemes seem to have had the desired impact since most of the strikes at the steel plant in this period involved labourers paid by the hour, rather than pieceworkers. In 1923 the company's blast-furnace superintendent described "good incentive wages" as one of the keystones of the firm's industrial relations policies.[37] Its graduated job ladders were similarly designed to encourage individualism, with minute distinctions in pay between semi-skilled jobs. In 1916, for example, in the Steel Company's munitions department, men in shipping and pure labouring were paid twenty-six cents an hour, tongsmen, stackers, gaugers, stampers, wheelers, stamp carriers, annealers, annealing bedmen, chargers, and doormen got twenty-seven cents, heater helpers, swabbers, and press operators thirty and a half cents, punch setters thirty-three cents, and heaters thirty-eight cents.[38] Such a spread of pennies per hour could create new levels of competition for promotion to higher job categories.[39] It remains to ask how effectively workers with broadly similar occupational status overcame these fragmenting forces to act together in pursuit of their own interests.

II

As we have seen, mass-production processes in the steel industry grew up in a context of great geographic mobility among large numbers of Canadian workers – the so-called "floaters." "If a laboring man working in, say an ironworks, revolts at the conditions of life and labor," a socialist worker wrote in 1906, "well he may clear out and go west, or he may find other work, railroad building or in the mines. The demand for labor and constantly shifting habits of a large number of workers are a 'safety valve' which ward off the social revolution."[40] This kind of purposeful drifting reached a peak during World War I, when the Hamilton press noted "a floating population that keeps in constant circulation to those cities and towns where labor is scarce and wages good," and when one Hamilton plant normally employing 1,500 men had 2,300 quit in three months.[41] Large numbers of workers in steel and other mass-production industries, it seems, developed only casual, instrumental contact with the work processes that efficiency-conscious managers were introducing.

Any more collective resistance to intolerable working conditions was, of course, extremely difficult for workers with few skills who could usually be quickly replaced. The vigorous repression of the 1902 strike set the pattern of anti-unionism among Steel Company executives. By World War I, in fact, the company was using a spy system to keep track of troublemakers. A pervasive fear became a severe brake on working-class protest in Hamilton's steel plants.[42] Yet, despite workers' individualized strategies of survival and managers' authoritarian power, company officials did not run their plants unchallenged. Hamilton's steelworkers soon began to assert their own needs within the industry and to contest some basic tenets of their employers' management policies. The response of Hamilton's steelworkers to their evolving work environment fell into two phases, roughly divided by the war.

In contrast to other industries with a greater artisanal residue, the steel industry was not disrupted by beleaguered craftsmen.[43] Instead, pre-war collective action came in the form of spontaneous militancy among the hundreds of Europeans in the company's plants. Despite their transiency these men revealed a determination to fight for good wages during their sojourn in North America and thus challenged the steelmasters' low-wage strategy. In the tightly packed immigrant ghettoes the men cultivated ethnic solidarities in boarding houses, cafés, mutual benefit societies, and churches, which encouraged them to stand up to their employers. The Steel Company consequently had to deal with six large strikes by its immigrant employees before World War I and four more during the war. Although details of these confrontations were seldom fully recorded in the local press, it is clear that they were more than simply chaotic riots and showed evidence of careful timing and effective, if impromptu, organization. The most dramatic was a full-scale walkout in April, 1910.[44]

The workers, mostly Italians, with a sprinkling of Poles and Hungarians, had been agitating for a wage increase from their fifteen-cent-per-hour rate. To meet the rising cost of living, they wanted a new wage scale of seventeen, eighteen, and twenty cents per hour and decided to press their advantage in a situation of labour scarcity. On March 22 the company decided to announce a one-cent increase effective April 1 to head off any dispute, but the gesture could not halt the growing feeling for a strike. On the night of March 30 a mass meeting of "foreigners" alerted the company to trouble. The next morning the men arrived at work as usual, but ten minutes after starting up they threw down their tools and walked out of the company's plants. The firm estimated between 800 and 900 men were out, while the strikers set the figure at more than 1,200. "No union exists among the foreigners except the union of brotherhood," reported the *Spectator*, "and they realize that the union does not include English-speaking employees of the steel works, for so far as can be learned no attempts were made to get them to strike."[45]

The company had immediately put on a stern face, refusing to discuss any grievance or to take back certain of the strikers. It placed the blame for the walkout squarely on the "foreign agitators, so-called interpreters who do not work themselves." The *Spectator*, whose publisher, William Southam, was the company's largest shareholder, reported, "The trouble with the interpreters is that they incite the men to strike and riot, according

to some workmen at the plant, and the foreigners follow like sheep."
Perhaps this articulate leadership with valuable English-language
skills was spreading the word about the large organizing drive
that had begun in the American steel mills that winter under
American Federation of Labor auspices. In any case, the report
of their activities underlines the important leadership role of non-
proletarian elements in the ethnic ghettoes.[46]

Hamilton's polite society was stunned by this new alien force
rearing up in its midst. "The police fear," the local press announced,
"that the quiet manner in which the foreigners are going about
the strike at the present time will only be a calm preceding a
storm." The fear of impending violence was inflated by rumours
that the immigrants had been purchasing secondhand guns and
by police suggestions that "every foreigner on strike carries his
native weapon – a knife. . . ." The company quietly moved a stash
of dynamite used for blasting slag to a building half a mile from
the steel plant, and constables on duty made sure that "every
foreigner who turned up within half a mile of either the rolling
mill or smelter without a dinner pail and a satisfactory explanation,
was ordered to move on." An air of mystery and danger hung
over the "foreign colony" in those early spring days:

> Last night the strikers were holding secret meetings. The minute
> an English-speaking person begins to ask questions they become
> suspicious and shut up tighter than a clam. Around the district
> known as "Little Italy" little groups of foreigners were
> assembled, apparently discussing the situation, but directly a
> Britisher hove in sight not a word was heard until he had passed
> out of hearing distance.[47]

On the afternoon of the second day Robert Hobson, then the
company's vice-president and general manager, met a delegation
of foremen and convinced them to lead the strikers back to work
while a committee discussed their grievances. By the night of
April 2 the east-end steel plant was back to normal, and within
a few days the west-end rolling-mill plants had also resumed
production. The company had agreed to collect information on
wage rates in the Buffalo steel industry and to fire two foremen
who had been accused of extorting money from the immigrant
labourers for the privilege of working in their gangs. Ten days
later the firm announced an elaborate new wage scale with
increases of 5 to 10 per cent. In this short-lived eruption of anger
– the most serious disruption of the company's production in the

whole half-century before the 1946 steel strike – this new element in the Hamilton labour force had effectively challenged, though not eliminated, the company's authoritarian, low-wage policies.

No permanent organization ever appeared during these confrontations, although the role of ethnic societies remains a mystery that the period's English-language press never bothered to probe.[48] In 1919, however, the Hamilton steel industry encountered its first revival of formal unionization in nearly two decades. Having broadened its membership base to include virtually all steelworkers, the Amalgamated Association of Iron, Steel, and Tin Workers had begun an aggressive organizing campaign in the United States in 1918 and established a Hamilton lodge in October, 1919.[49] With the relatively skilled men from the Steel Company's new sheet mill as a backbone, membership quickly reached 1,300. For the first time unity was growing across ethnic divisions, and the union's organizer was able to report considerable success in recruiting "the foreign element in and around the various steel plants of the city." The company fought back with new efforts to promote corporate loyalty and employee welfare: wage increases, a new pension plan, and a new company magazine. But the severe depression of the early 1920's effectively crippled this first attempt at industrial unionism before any strikes or significant negotiations took place.[50] Not until the return of full employment and a more sympathetic attitude from the state during World War II would Hamilton's steelworkers be able to present a powerful collective front to their employer.[51]

What had prompted this first experiment in industrial unionism among Hamilton's steelworkers? The war had been the chief disruptive force in work relations in this and so many other industries. Not only did it generate discontent with rising living costs, profiteering, and government mismanagement and at the same time unleash a powerful new rhetoric of democracy and public service, but it also provided full employment at high wages, giving Hamilton workers a more secure economic base from which to struggle for better living and working conditions. A resurgence of craft unionism and the first efforts at industrial unionism in textiles, clothing, meat-packing, metal-working, and steel were matched by the new triumphs of the city's Independent Labour Party in 1919. The war had a special impact on Hamilton's European immigrant community. Movement across the Atlantic was curtailed, and, while mobility across the continent continued, the new job opportunities for Europeans in the steel plants must have encouraged more of them into a more settled position in the city. Moreover, the Russian Revolution had inspired a new militancy and radicalism among some ethnic groups, especially Russians and Ukrainians, and it was undoubtedly the oratory of these radicals at the steelworkers' organizational meeting that led a visiting Montreal organizer to express surprise that "the soviet idea was so rampant here among the foreign-speaking iron and steel workers." The cutting edge of activism among Hamilton's steelworkers, however, came from the relatively skilled rolling-mill hands in the Steel Company's new sheet mill plant, where technological change had been minimal and where manual labour was still essential. These men, imported by the company along with the new machinery, transplanted their considerable union experience to Hamilton soil and would form the core of renewed industrial-unionist efforts in the 1930's.[52]

Though hard evidence is lacking, it might be argued that the new work force in steel plants, filling the new specialized, semi-skilled jobs, were beginning to identify themselves as *steelworkers*, with distinct experience and steadier commitment to a specific industry in a specific community. Certainly more workers had now accumulated experience in mass-production plants, notably in the munitions industry, and the pre-war pattern of wide-ranging work experience that combined factory work with outdoor construction or agricultural work was giving way to more regular factory employment. Perhaps the reshaping of the work process and the workers' growing familiarity with the new workplace rhythms were gradually creating a more cohesive, more self-conscious work force. It was certainly becoming more settled; in 1935 the Steel Company was able to report that 88 per cent of its employees had been with the company at least five years.[53] The stability the Steel Company was trying to promote among its more skilled workers could thus become a double-edged phenomenon; under normal circumstances, a quiescence among steelworkers dependent on the company for their livelihood and for any advancement; or, under such exceptional circumstances as World War I and its immediate aftermath, which dispelled the fear of poverty and tarnished the legitimacy of capitalist control, a stubborn militancy from this increasingly entrenched work force. Such a dynamic within the consciousness of Hamilton steelworkers could only be in the formative stages by the end of World War I, but in the special conditions of the next war it could translate into successful industrial unionism.

In general, the collective activity of Hamilton's steelworkers in the early twentieth century did little to change fundamentally the distribution of power between workers and managers in the industry. Concerted working-class protest in the steel plants periodically brought slightly higher wages for a time, but the technological and managerial innovations that had created the distinctive work relations were never seriously threatened. The absence of any significant body of craftsmen with a wider perspective on the whole industry deprived the steelworkers of the kind of articulate critics of industrial transformation who could be found in foundries or machine shops, in print shops, or in the needle trades in the same period. The combination of a powerful and doggedly anti-union employer and an ethnically stratified work force further reduced the ability of Hamilton's steelworkers to act together. Their individual patterns of resistance, whether slowing down on the job or quitting altogether, probably created a greater impact, resulting in technological changes that attempted to circumvent this element of unpredictability in the production process.

III

Mass production thus came to the Hamilton steel industry as a result of two convergent social processes: the struggle of the owners and managers of the Steel Company of Canada and its predecessors to maintain a profit-making enterprise in the face of stiff American competition, and the migration of thousands of southern and eastern European peasants to North America in search of short-term employment. The standards of economical production set by the American steelmakers dictated the form that Canadian steel mills would have to take, and the availability of this new pool of labour allowed the Hamilton steelmasters to administer their plants and alter work routines with greater freedom than they might have enjoyed with a more settled Anglo-Canadian work force (such as British steel men confronted in this period).[54]

By the 1920's the Hamilton steel industry had passed through its formative phase. At its core was a large, powerful corporation presiding over a fully integrated system of production, from mining to nuts and bolts. Its technology had reached the perfection of a "gigantic automaton" and would change little over the next four decades. Its work force had also stabilized considerably from the pre-war days. Labour turnover would continue to be a problem for Steel Company managers, but a substantial group of steel-workers had settled down in the industry, with some commitment to their semi-skilled jobs.

The process of reaching this equilibrium had been harsh and turbulent. Raw industrial recruits with no experience had passed through the new industrial environment of the steel plants in huge numbers, looking only for quick earnings. The casualness of so many steelworkers' approach to their jobs, which was evident in absenteeism and labour turnover, indicated an ingrained resistance to the new rhythms of mass-production work. Wanderlust, however, did not prevent these men from turning into militant strikers whenever they sensed the opportunity to challenge their employer's labour policies. World War I was a catalyst in solidifying this spirit of resistance. By the end of the war the men in these plants were uniting across occupational and ethnic divisions to create the first spectre of industrial unionism – the first indication that a considerable number of steelworkers had begun to share a sense of common identity.

Hamilton's steelworkers, it seems, would not accept without question the terms of employment offered them in speeded-up, rigidly supervised, narrowly specialized jobs. Unlike many craftsmen in the metal trades, they never contested the fundamentals of workplace organization and authority – indeed, mass-production workers seldom did in the twentieth century – but their actions in pursuit of better remuneration for their work suggested that the administration of steel plants had to be altered to take account of their material needs as well as of profit margins. Only then could these workers begin to share in the benefits that mass production was supposed to bring to Canadian society.

4

1919: The Canadian Labour Revolt

Gregory S. Kealey

In late March, 1919, a worried Union government appointed a royal commission to "enquire into Industrial Relations in Canada." From April 26 to June 13 the commissioners toured industrial Canada, visiting twenty-eight cities from Victoria to Sydney and examining a total of 486 witnesses. Canadian workers appeared before the 1919 commission and defiantly challenged it.

British Columbia MLA J.H. Hawthornthwaite, a former Socialist Party of Canada stalwart and then Federated Labour Party leader, asserted in his appearance before the commission:

> Working men today understand these matters . . . and if you go into any socialistic bodies and listen to the discussion you would understand the grasp that these men have. I do not know any college man or university man who can for ten minutes hold their own in an argument among these people.[1]

Workers across the country more than lived up to Hawthornthwaite's boast. In city after city, the commissioners were regaled with Marxist-influenced histories of the development of industrial capitalism. A few of these lectures came from middle-class proponents of the workers' movement, such as Edmonton Mayor Joseph Clarke, or Social Gospel ministers William Irvine, A.E. Smith, William Ivens, Ernest Thomas, and Salem Bland. But more impressive were the many workers – some well-known leaders, but many not – who appeared to explain patiently to the commissioners, in the words of Edmonton Grand Trunk Railway machinist E.J. Thompson, "We are the producers and we are not getting what we produce." Like most other workers who appeared, Thompson was uninterested in the commission's extensive plans for industrial councils; only "complete ownership of the machines of production by the working class" would suffice, he asserted.[2]

Thompson's evidence is of interest for two reasons: first, he was not a front-line leader of western labour; second, he came directly out of the railway machine shops. In city after city, metal trades workers from the shipyards, from the railway shops, and from the more diversified contract shops came forward and talked socialism. Even James Somerville, the International Association of Machinists' (IAM) western representative, who predictably chose to distinguish himself from the radicals in his testimony and who worried about the workers having "gone so far that they do not recognize the authority even in their own organization," explained: "One of the things they want first is nothing short of a transfer of the means of production, wealth production, from that of private control to that of collective ownership, for they know that is the only solution."[3]

Lest there be any notion that this was a regional manifestation of class unrest, let us travel east to Sudbury, Ontario. There, Frederick Eldridge, a machinist and secretary of the local Trades and Labour Council, received "considerable handclapping, stamping of feet, and vocal enthusiasm" from the commission's working-class audience when he asserted:

> The workers do not get enough of that which they produce.
> ... I advocate government ownership of everything: mills, mines, factories, smelters, railroads, etc. That is the only solution of the problem and I am only one of hundreds of workmen in Sudbury that think the same thing.[4]

In Toronto, machinist James Ballantyne called for the nationalization of all industry.[5] In Hamilton, IAM District 24 representative Richard Riley more cautiously noted that "although a great many workers have not given the matter much thought, they are beginning to think that there must be a change of the system, that is to say the present competitive system."[6] When the commission reached Montreal, John D. Houston of IAM District 82 presented a prepared brief on the economic system, arguing in part:

> I believe that in the system of ownership lies all our social

problems. . . . For 300 years or over, while the businessman was consolidating his position as captain of industry, the institutions of autocracy provided, through the law, the machinery of force and fraud which was rigorously applied, to make the worker a proletarian with no means of livelihood except to work for wages or a salary. . . .

He closed with the familiar call for production for use, not for profit.[7]

By the time the commission arrived in the Maritimes, the commissioners' impatience was showing, no doubt increased by the mounting industrial crisis sweeping the nation. While the evidence of their sessions in Amherst, Nova Scotia, at the height of the General Strike there, has unfortunately been lost, evidence from New Glasgow and Sydney demonstrates the eastern manifestation of the workers' revolt.[8] While UMWA District 26 leaders such as Dan Livingstone, Robert Baxter, and Silby Barrett provided much of the fire, Alex T. Mackay, representing carmen and steelworkers, infuriated the commissioners by warning of an intensification of the struggle:

The way the fight in Winnipeg will be terminated, will very largely influence the attitude throughout Canada. I think if matters are allowed to run their course there will be no interference in this part of Canada, but if there is any attempt at coercion, the first shot fired in Winnipeg, will hit every labouring man in eastern and western Canada, and the result will be confusion from the Atlantic to the Pacific.[9]

A day earlier, in Halifax, Nova Scotia Federation of Labour organizer C.C. Dane had threatened a province-wide general strike for the eight-hour day and had added almost gratuitously: "Industrial unrest? Why, gentlemen, we have none to what we are going to have. I am a Bolshevist and I will warn these two governments that trouble is coming and the men will have what belongs to them."[10]

Machinists were not the only group of workers who testified in these terms. Indeed, most workers who appeared made similar points, although not always couched in a socialist framework. An additional important group of witnesses who echoed much of the above but who also added a new dimension to the workers' revolt were women witnesses, including representatives of retail clerks' unions, women's labour leagues, local councils of women, and consumer groups. Among them were then-prominent figures such as Montreal's Rose Henderson and later leading Communist militant Bella Hall, but also many women who enjoy no such historical fame. These women universally complained of bad housing, runaway inflation, high food prices, and the low wages paid to working women. Calgary's Mrs. Jean MacWilliams, who had organized laundry workers, asked rhetorically, "Are we in favour of a bloody revolution?" and answered, "Why any kind of revolution would be better than conditions as they are now."[11] Mrs. Resina Asals of the Regina Women's Labour League told the commission:

> There is only one thing that the workers have to thank the capitalists for, and that is that they have tightened the screw up so much that they are awakening the worker up to the fact that he is the most important factor and that until we produce for use instead of profit this unrest will still prevail. Let the workingman, the one who produced, have control and then we shall see the light of a new dawn.[12]

Rose Henderson simply advanced the proposition that "the real revolutionist is the mother – not the man. She says openly that there is nothing but Revolution."[13] Working-class women, both wage workers and unpaid domestic workers, had started to view the world in new ways in 1919.

These examples are intended simply to demonstrate that the revolt was national in character and that its seeds were not rooted in any unique regional fermentation. World War I, a profoundly national experience for Canadians, helped provide part of the cement for this nascent national working-class response.[14] Yet World War I, while providing specific sparks to light the flame of working-class struggle in 1919, should not be viewed as its cause. Underlying structural changes in capitalist organization, on both a national and international scale, must be viewed as providing the necessary fuel for this fire. Indeed, although the early war years 1914 to 1916 had seen little overt class conflict in Canada, the changes in the capitalist organization of production and the consequent "remaking" or reconstitution of the working class were well advanced before the outbreak of war. The years 1912 and 1913 should be seen as a prelude to the 1917-1920 conflagration. Tables 1, 2, and 3 demonstrate this continuity with pre-war class conflict.[15] This continuity extended, moreover, throughout the entire country.[16]

A more specific look at 1919, and especially at the months

Table 1
Strike Activity in Canada, 1912-1922

Year	Number of Strikes	Number of Workers Involved	Striker Days Lost
1912	242	43,104	1,136,345
1913	234	41,004	1,037,254
1914	99	9,911	491,358
1915	86	11,480	95,242
1916	168	26,971	241,306
1917	222	50,327	1,123,916
1918	305	82,573	657,152
1919	428	149,309	3,401,843
1920	459	76,624	814,457
1921	208	28,398	1,049,719

Table 2
Number of Disputes by Province

	1912	1913	1917	1918	1919	1920
N.S.	9	12	8	18	19	39
P.E.I.	1	–	2	–	–	1
N.B.	21	20	5	11	19	15
Que.	32	31	31	28	100	79
Ont.	100	114	68	112	158	122
Man.	13	6	18	20	16	5
Sask.	19	10	6	10	13	4
Alta.	23	15	24	53	29	39
B.C.	22	25	55	46	73	124
Interprov.	2	1	5	7	2	1
Total	242	234	222	305	428	459

of May, June, and July, helps to clarify some of these points. While these months generally figure high in the calendar of industrial conflict, clearly the summer of 1919 was not simply any year. Table 4 shows both the geographic and industrial range of the strikes and Table 5 highlights the central role of coal, the metal trades, shipbuilding, and, of course, the general strikes themselves in the wave of unrest.

Table 3
Number of Disputes by Selected Industry

	1912	1913	1917	1918	1919	1920
Logging	1	–	1	–	32	66
Coal-mining	6	5	22	49	22	48
Other mining	6	6	6	3	10	14
Metal manufac- turing	27	30	44	43	46	61
Shipbuilding	2	3	13	16	25	12
Steam railway	16	8	12	16	6	2
Electric railway	2	7	5	11	12	5
Service	12	18	11	30	39	38
General	–	–	–	1	12	–
Total	72	77	114	169	204	246
Total, all disputes	242	234	222	305	428	459
% Total	29.8	32.9	51.4	55.4	47.7	53.4

The summer strike wave consisted of three main types of strikes: first, local strikes contesting the normal range of issues; second, general strikes called in support of such local strikes as in Winnipeg, Amherst, and Toronto; and, third, general sympathy strikes called either in support of the Winnipeg General Strike or to protest its repression. Variants two and three have received some attention, although even here the focus on Winnipeg has tended to obscure these less well-known struggles. Local strikes, however, have received little study.

Table 5, while describing all industrial action in these three months of 1919, suggests how important the local or category-one conflicts were to the strike wave. Clearly these strikes cannot be described in this paper in any detail, but I will highlight a few to suggest the range of activity. Let us reverse the historiographic trend and travel across the country from east to west.[17] In Moncton, N.B., and Amherst, N.S., moulders won victories over iron founders. A lockout of 350 quarry workers in Sweet's Corner, N.S., lasted fifty-five working days and resulted in higher wages. Brief walkouts on the street railway systems in Halifax and Moncton also occurred. The most significant story in the Maritimes, however, focused on Amherst; we will return to it in our discussion of general strikes.

Major Quebec strikes occurred in the shipbuilding industry at

Table 4
Strikes: May, June, and July, 1919[1]

	Number of Strikes (total)	Number of Strikes (complete data)	Number of Workers Involved[2]	Duration in Worker Days[3]
A. By Month:				
May	110	96	68,606	742,506
June	101	89	84,054	1,274,998
July	84	75	71,121	555,802
Total	210[4]	178[4]	114,423[4]	2,573,306
B. By Province:				
Nova Scotia	11	9	3,461	85,135
New Brunswick	6	6	128	631
Quebec	57	50	25,988	395,285
Ontario	90	78	34,544	632,409
Manitoba	6	5	21,756	817,686
Saskatchewan	9	7	2,041	31,833
Alberta	9	8	9,271[5]	304,967[5]
British Columbia	23	16	17,234[5]	305,360[5]
Total	210[6]	178[6]	114,423	2,573,306

[1]Strikes in progress.
[2]Figures for strikes beginning before May or extending beyond the end of a month are not adjusted to account for strikers returning to work.
[3]Figures are adjusted to account for strikers returning to work.
[4]Totals are for strikes in progress over the three-month period.
[5]Includes provincial estimates for the District 18 coal-mining strike.
[6]District 18, UMWA strike counted once.

Lauzon and Trois-Rivières, and in the metal trades at Lachine and Sherbrooke. The brief metal strikes were both successful for the workers, and the Trois-Rivières shipyard strike won union recognition for the strikers. Montreal, however, was the centre of activity in Quebec, accounting for 82 per cent of all provincial strikes. Indeed, the Borden government was sufficiently alarmed about the conflicts in Montreal that the city was included on its

Table 5
Strikes: May-July, 1919, by Industry

	Number	%	Number of Workers Involved	%	Duration in Worker Days	%
Mining	11	5.2	10,216	8.9	340,216	13.2
Manufacturing						
(total)	101	48.1	43,495	38.0	922,117	35.8
Leather						
and textile	(20)	(9.5)	(9,505)	(8.3)	(204,897)	(8.0)
Metal						
and shipbldg.	(43)	(20.5)	(24,590)	(21.5)	(623.577)	(24.2)
Construction	32	15.2	9,829	8.6	185,488	7.2
Transportation and						
public utilities	21	10.0	4,772	4.2	68,964	2.7
Service and public						
administration	19	9.1	1,137	1.0	4,799	.2
Other industries	14	6.7	607	.5	18,036	.7
General	12	5.7	44,367	38.8	1,033,686	40.2
Total	210	100.0	114,423	100.0	2,573,306	100.0

emergency daily briefing list. Over 22,000 workers in Montreal struck during the three-month period, logging nearly 380,000 striker days lost. Again the metal trades and shipbuilding figured prominently. A metal trades strike at Canadian Car and Foundry in early May involving 4,000 workers ended in victory after only three days. In the shipyards, however, it took a one-day strike to force negotiations and then a five-week strike before the employers conceded to some of the demands of their 3,500 workers. This strike was led by a General Strike Committee, not by the union officials of the Marine Trades Federation. A major strike of 2,000 wire workers failed after three weeks. A series of skirmishes in the garment trades led to a number of worker victories, and a major battle involving over 3,500 workers at Dominion Textiles gained some employer concessions after nearly three months of struggle. Other industrial workers showed a new ability to organize as well. Over 1,400 rubber workers, for example, won a compromise settlement after a strike of three weeks, as did 350 sugar refinery employees, while 700 meat packers won a quick victory to match a settlement won earlier by Toronto workers. This militant activity on the part of industrial workers represented a new departure for Montreal's working class.[18] While the majority of the Montreal Trades and Labour Council (MTLC) opposed a general sympathetic strike, the tactic had proponents in Montreal. The machinists (IAM) and the engineers (ASE), true to national form, held a massive support rally in late May, which was addressed by Winnipeg strike leader R.J. Johns.[19] At their subsequent meeting in mid-June the arrests of the Winnipeg strike leaders were roundly condemned and Richard Kerrigan led a debate in which the Canadian Vickers General Strike Committee sought to gain the endorsation of the MTLC for a general sympathetic strike. In this, they failed.[20]

Ontario's ninety strikes involving 34,122 workers were not as concentrated as Quebec's, although Toronto did account for twenty-two (24 per cent) in addition to its General Sympathetic Strike, which I will deal with later. Ottawa had eleven strikes, London seven, Hamilton six, St. Catharines and Windsor, five each. Major mining strikes took place in Cobalt and Kirkland Lake, where 2,200 and 525 miners, respectively, struck for eight and twenty-one weeks. In both cases the miners were defeated by intransigent mining companies, although not before there had been discussions of a northern Ontario-wide general strike.[21]

In Toronto, newly organized workers in the meat-packing industry, organized on an industrial basis, took on the giants of the industry, including Swift Canada, as over 3,000 workers struck in the stockyards area after the companies refused to negotiate with the union. After just over a week on the picket line in early May, an IDIA board was agreed to by both sides and reported unanimously on May 29, mainly in favour of the workers, granting a forty-eight-hour week, a weekly guarantee of forty hours, overtime pay, a formal grievance procedure, and seniority provisions. This settlement became the model for the industry and workers in Montreal, Ottawa, Hamilton, and Peterborough fought for it in the summer of 1919 and the spring of 1920.[22] Beginning in July almost 2,000 Toronto garment workers, led by the International Ladies Garment Workers Union (ILGWU), struck over forty shops for twelve weeks before winning wage and hour concessions. Both of these industries involved high proportions of ethnic workers and their successful strikes suggest the expansion of both trade union organization and class struggle to new and difficult terrain.

Ontario's shipyard workers, who in 1918 had organized a Marine Trades and Labour Federation of Canada, engaged in a series of seven strikes covering almost all the province's shipbuilding centres. Bridgeburg, Collingwood, Fort William-Port Arthur, Midland, Welland, and Toronto each witnessed strikes involving work forces ranging from 100 to 1,300. In the metal trades, which included many of the same trades as shipbuilding, 1919 saw the machinists attempt to gain Ontario-wide uniformity of wages and conditions. Their major aim was to gain the eight-hour day and forty-four-hour week and in the spring of 1919 metal trades meetings were organized province-wide to prepare for that struggle. Moving beyond IAM exclusivism, its vice-president, John McClelland, worked for "complete affiliation of the metal trades," and "in the meantime" organized metal trades councils as the basis for a strike that would "completely close down the industry until a settlement is reached." The Toronto campaign became the central battle for the war for recognition of the metal trades councils as bargaining agents and for the eight-hour day. The demands were sent to the employers on April 1 and tools were dropped on May 1 by some 5,000 Toronto metal trades workers. In Peterborough, Brampton, Hamilton, Kingston, Ottawa, Brantford, and St. Catharines other workers followed suit.[23] The results of these strikes varied but by and large they were defeated.

In the West, Manitoba's strikes revolved totally around the epic struggle in Winnipeg and the General Sympathy Strike in Brandon, which we will turn to later. In Saskatchewan the pattern was similar, primarily involving sympathetic strikes. In Alberta, however, a successful Calgary metal trades strike in April and May won shorter hours and higher wages for machinists, moulders, and other metal workers. In addition, UMWA District 18's over 6,200 coal miners left the pits at the end of May and stayed out until September 1, when they returned on the advice of One Big Union leaders. This General Strike was exceptional, because as a "100 per cent" strike involving the maintenance people it transgressed UMWA custom, and in the fact that some of the firebosses, the foremen in the mines, also took part. By July what had started partially as a sympathy strike with Winnipeg had been transformed into a major struggle for recognition of the OBU, which would play itself out over the next few years.[24] In British Columbia the District 18 strike spread into the southeastern coal field and a series of small logging strikes, under the leadership of the new (later, OBU) B.C. Loggers Union, took place. The major activity in B.C., however, also revolved around the June sympathy strikes.

The three General Sympathetic Strikes generated by local industrial struggles were in Amherst, N.S., Toronto, and Winnipeg. The sensitive work of Nolan Reilly has provided us with a model study of the community background to the Amherst General Strike, an event that had gone almost unnoticed in historical study. In Amherst, the local Federation of Labour, under the rubric of One Big Union, led a general strike that spread out from the Canadian Car and Foundry workers' demands that they receive pay equal to that of their 4,000 Montreal co-workers, who had won in a three-day strike in early May. The company's intransigence led to a city-wide walkout involving all of Amherst's major employers. While proceeding from local causes and representing the culmination of a decade of industrial conflict in Amherst, the strikers identified themselves with the national struggle, as their enthusiastic correspondence with the OBU suggests.[25]

Events in Toronto in 1919, while less dramatic than those in Amherst, nevertheless caused Prime Minister Borden and his government considerable consternation.[26] As elsewhere, the metal trades were central in the crisis. Toronto's extensive foundries, machine shops, and metal factories had been at the core of war production. The city's metal trades workers, who had organized a joint council in 1901 and who had endorsed a call for industrial unionism in 1913, led the battle to enforce collective bargaining and a "fair-wage schedule" on the Imperial Munitions Board.[27] This struggle first came to a head in the spring of 1916 when Toronto machinists tried to extend gains they had made in some shops in December, 1915, to the entire city. In addition, Hamilton machinists demanded parity with their Toronto comrades. The joint threat of a general metal trades strike in Toronto issued by IAM District 46 in March, and a machinists' strike in Hamilton, led to the appointment of a three-member government commission to investigate the munitions plants in Toronto and Hamilton and the general extension of the Industrial Disputes Investigation Act (IDIA) to all war industry. This commission, however, which the Trades and Labour Congress (TLC) regarded as a victory, eventually proved meaningless when Hamilton employers refused to abide by its recommendation of the nine-hour day and wage increases. The subsequent Hamilton-wide strike of some 2,000 workers, which included a coalition of machinists (IAM), engineers

(ASE), and unorganized, unskilled workers, ended in a major defeat for Hamilton workers at the hands of Canadian Westinghouse, National Steel Car, the Steel Company of Canada, Otis Elevators, and Dominion Steel Foundry. Although Toronto IAM members, for the second time in only a few months, threatened a general strike in sympathy with the Hamilton workers, the IAM international leadership managed to prevent it. The Metal Trades Council did help move the Toronto Trades and Labour Council significantly to the left during these developments. The late March extension of the IDIA to cover shipbuilding and munitions led to a furious response from the TTLC, which "emphatically denounced this uncalled for and unwarranted action" and accused the TLC executive "of not fulfilling their obligation to the workers of Canada."[28] Thus Toronto and Hamilton metal trades workers as early as the summer of 1916 found themselves moving in opposition to state labour policy and already identifying their differences both with the TLC leadership and to some degree with their own international officers, such as McClelland and James Somerville, all of whom were continually promoting patience and industrial peace.

By the time of the next major metal trades struggle, which came in May, 1919, the metal workers exercised considerable control over the TTLC. In a May Day meeting, the TTLC voted to contact all Canadian Trades and Labour Councils to get support for the metal trades fight for the eight-hour day. Moreover, they "requested sympathetic action to bring about the result desired." A May 13 meeting demanded that metal trades employers negotiate and then issued a call for a general strike convention for one week hence. While this motion noted western strikes in Winnipeg and Calgary and other Ontario strikes, its major interest was in the Toronto Strike.[29] The vote in favour of a general strike by forty-four unions representing 12,000 workers led to hurried correspondence between Toronto politicians and Ottawa.[30]

Ottawa's intervention led only to an offer of arbitration, which the workers scornfully declined, but again the employers scored a minor publicity coup by offering a compromise forty-eight-hour week, although not agreeing to Metal Trades Council recognition.[31] The sympathetic strike commenced on May 30 with 5,000 to 15,000 workers leaving their jobs. The strike's strength predictably lay in the metal trades, in shipbuilding, among some groups of building trades workers, especially carpenters, and among garment workers. Its major failing was the decision by

Table 6
General Strikes in Sympathy with Winnipeg, May-July, 1919

Location	Dates	Number of Workers Involved	Duration in Strike Days
A. Brandon	May 20-July 2	450	10,200
Calgary	May 26-June 25	1,500	31,700
Edmonton	May 26-June 25	2,000	24,000
Saskatoon	May 27-June 26	1,200	24,000
Prince Albert	May 28-June 23	300	5,000
Regina	May 29-June 26	350	1,500
Vancouver	June 3-July 4	8,000	160,000
New Westminster	June 13-23	537	3,400
Victoria	June 23-July 7	5,000	28,000

B. Atikokan, Ont.	Neepawa, Man.	Melville, Sask.
Fort Frances, Ont.	Souris, Man.	Moose Jaw, Sask.
Rainy River, Ont.	Battleford, Sask.	Radville, Sask.
Redditt, Ont.	Biggar, Sask.	Yorkton, Sask.
Sioux Lookout, Ont.	Hudson Bay Jct., Sask.	Prince Rupert, B.C.
Dauphin, Man.	Humboldt, Sask.	McBride, B.C.
Minnedosa, Man.	Kamsack, Sask.	Fernie, B.C.

civic employees and especially the street railway workers to stay on the job until their contract expired on June 16. The strike lasted until June 4, when it was called off by the Central Strike Committee at the request of the Metal Trades Council. The committee of fifteen that ran the strike included nine metal trades workers, four building trades workers, and two garment trades workers.[32]

The Winnipeg General Strike we will simply pass over in order to discuss the rather less well-known wave of general sympathy strikes. Compilation of these is somewhat risky since the Department of Labour's official version and even its manuscript materials do not necessarily conform to all strikes mentioned in the labour press or even in the various security reports that crop up in the Borden Papers and elsewhere. Table 6 lists those identified in Department of Labour data (A) and then adds a list compiled from other sources (B).[33]

In Manitoba many small railroad junction towns such as Dauphin supported Winnipeg, as did workers in Brandon. The strike in Brandon, the longest of all the sympathy strikes, was extremely solid and orderly. It eventually involved civic workers who had fought and won their own strike in April but who still came out in solidarity as repression mounted in Winnipeg. Controlled throughout by the Brandon Trades and Labour Council, the strike extended to unorganized workers who were guaranteed "full protection" by the labour council.[34]

The list of small Saskatchewan railway junction towns makes clear the support of railroad shop workers and of some running trades workers, although the brotherhoods exerted all the pressure they were capable of to prevent this. Prince Albert's sympathy strike mainly involved Canadian Northern workers. In Saskatchewan's larger urban centres a similar pattern prevailed. Regina workers initially supported a general strike but only a minority eventually struck, mainly from the railroad shops. In Moose Jaw, shopcraft workers, street railway workers, civic employees, and some building trades workers provided the strike's backbone. Saskatoon's sympathy strike was the most successful in the province and included the Sutherland CPR shop workers, street railway workers, freight handlers, postal workers, teamsters, and at least eleven other local unions.[35]

In Alberta, as elsewhere in the West, both Edmonton and Calgary workers had flirted with general strikes earlier. In Edmonton, the Trades and Labour Council had endorsed a general sympathy strike in October, 1918, to aid the Canadian Brotherhood of Railway Employees. Events in 1919 led to a vigorous left-right struggle for control of the Edmonton TLC that culminated in late April in the expulsion of the carpenters, led by SPC militant Joe Knight, Federated Labour Union, No. 49, which included Carl Berg and Sarah Johnson Knight, and the UMWA, Local 4070. As a result of the expulsions, the machinists and street railway workers also left the council. Despite this serious split, a successful sympathy strike was organized. The Federated Railway Trades (shop workers) introduced a motion in the ETLC calling for a meeting of all Edmonton trade unionists to plan for a strike. At that meeting the machinists successfully moved for a strike vote of all unions to report to a Central Strike Committee composed of representatives from both sides of the previous split. This vote resulted in a 1,676-506 vote for a strike with thirty-four of thirty-eight unions casting pro-strike ballots; eleven locals, however, failed to vote. Major strike support came from railway carmen, machinists, railroad shop workers, street railway workers, coal miners, building trades workers, and civic employees. The strike held until the committee called it off and was marked by a minimum of disorder of any kind. This partially resulted from the tacit support the strike received from pro-labour Edmonton Mayor Joe Clarke, whom RCMP security regarded as less than trustworthy.[36]

In Calgary the huge CPR shops were central both to the city's economy and to its trade union movement. Carmen, machinists, and all the other Railroad Shops Federated Trades exercised a considerable thrust for and experience of amalgamation. During the war years, the machinists came to dominate the CTLC and, as Taraska has argued, forged "a new working-class solidarity which led to class conscious action." Militance and political lobbying on the part of munitions workers led to a Provincial Munitions Commission ruling that war contracts should go only to union shops. Thus, by the end of 1915 the war shops were fully unionized. Skilled machinists' leaders such as Socialist and Labour alderman A. Broach, R.J. Tallon, and H.H. Sharples came to dominate the local council and to push it successfully into local politics. Tallon became president of Division 4 of the Railway Employees Department of the American Federation of Labor in 1917, which represented over 50,000 shopcraft workers on the Canadian railways. The division, created to negotiate directly with the Railway War Board, entered negotiations with the CPR in April, 1918. After heated negotiations the board offered parity with the United States McAdoo Award, which was rejected by an overwhelming Division 4 vote. Armed with this rejection, Division 4 leaders threatened a nationwide rail strike. A series of walkouts led to dire threats from the government and the active intervention of the AFL, which ordered Division 4 to accept the board's offer. In September reluctant railway shop workers did so but in Calgary trouble flared up quickly when the CPR victimized some freight handlers who had not been formally allowed to enter Division 4. The freight handlers struck, demanding the McAdoo Award. Calgary Labour Council unions voted in favour of a general strike in support of the freight handlers and a shopcraft workers' strike began on October 11, 1918. Street railway workers and civic employees also struck in sympathy. The threat to prosecute under Privy Council Order 2525 banning all strikes proved futile when Alberta courts refused to uphold it. A compromise, arranged by Senator Gideon Robertson, ended the affair in late October but general strike tactics had definitely been sustained. This set the scene for the following year's city-wide metal trades strike in April and the subsequent sympathy strike in May and June. Predictably, the major support during the general strike came from the CPR Ogden shops and the Metal Trades Council. One outstanding feature of this strike was the creation of an extremely active Women's Labor Council.[37]

In British Columbia, the SPC-controlled Vancouver Trades and Labour Council (VTLC) responded more slowly and deliberately to events in Winnipeg. In mid-May VTLC president Harold Winch of the longshoremen and secretary Victor Midgley wired Winnipeg congratulating the workers for their "cohesion," which "augured well for the future."[38] The following week they warned the Borden government that any military interference in Winnipeg would force them to call a general strike and simultaneously requested that all Vancouver trade unions take a vote on the question.[39] One week later they issued the following demands:

Realizing that while there are many problems that face the workers that cannot be solved under capitalism, and that the end of the system is not yet; also realizing that the present situation is a political one, due to the action of the Dominion Government in the Winnipeg strike, and that as taking care of the soldiers . . . are working class problems, the majority of the soldiers being members of the working class, therefore be it resolved that the following be the policy of the workers in Canada now on strike, or about to come on strike in support of the Winnipeg workers:
1. The reinstatement of the postal workers . . . .
2. The immediate settlement of the postal workers' grievances.
3. The right of collective bargaining through any organization that the workers deem most suited to their needs.
4. Pensions for soldiers and their dependents.
5. A $2,000 gratuity for all those who served overseas.
6. Nationalization of all cold storage plants, abattoirs, elevators . . . .
7. A six-hour day.

They closed by calling for the strike to continue until either the demands were granted or the government resigned and called new elections.[40]

The strike, which commenced on June 3, initially saw thirty-seven unions out but this actually increased in the first few days of the strike. As elsewhere, it found its major support among the metal trades, in the shipyards, and on the street railway. Unique to Vancouver as a major port, however, was the militant support of longshoremen, sailors, and other marine workers. As in Calgary, a series of women's meetings met with enthusiastic support. While the SPC provided leadership and intellectual sustenance, their reluctance and fears were manifest. Even at the final preparation meeting on June 2, William Pritchard posed the question less than enthusiastically: "Their comrades were in the fight, and it was now a question of standing by them, and, if necessary, going down with them – or, later, going down by themselves. His advice was: 'If you are going to drown – drown splashing!'"[41]

The strike ended in confusion a week after Winnipeg's return to work. A recommendation from the strike committee to go back earlier had been voted down by rank-and-file militants. The strike committee's final report to the VTLC indicated that forty-five unions had struck over the course of the strike, but admitted the initial vote had been a narrow 3,305-2,499 victory. Although 57 per cent of those voting favoured the strike, the under 6,000 votes represented only 40 per cent of VTLC members.[42]

In Prince Rupert a sympathy strike had commenced earlier, on May 29, when railroad workers left their jobs; in Victoria the sympathy strike developed slowly with considerable reluctance being shown by Victoria TLC leaders. Nevertheless, almost 5,000 workers left their jobs on June 23, following the lead of the Metal Trades Council, and remained out until early July. A smaller sympathy strike also took place in New Westminster.[43]

These Canadian events captured the attention of European militants. On June 14, 1919, in Turin, Italy, Antonio Gramsci described "The Revolutionary Tide" that had brought "the struggle on a world scale." "The revolution can no longer be exorcized by democratic swindlers, nor crushed by mercenaries without a conscience," the Italian revolutionary argued. His youthful optimism stemmed partially from his view of current world struggles, but he argued that the particular struggles of Canadian labour indicated "industrial strikes have taken on the overt character of a bid to install a soviet regime." Meanwhile, in Glasgow, John MacLean enthused about "the great Canadian strike," which, he argued, had stimulated American labour's "general rank-and-file strike which terrorized the union leaders." While these claims appear exaggerated in retrospect, the important point here is that

1919 was an international event, or as MacLean termed it: "class war on an international scale."[44] It was no more limited to Canada than it was to Winnipeg within Canada.

One little-known example of the international nature of the uprising can be drawn from Newfoundland, then a self-governing British colony in the North Atlantic. The story of Newfoundland's working class largely remains to be written, but in the years 1917 to 1920 it resembled closely the Canadian and international pattern of revolt. In the immediate pre-war years Newfoundland fishermen and loggers had commenced to organize. The meteoric rise of the Fishermen's Protective Union, representing both groups of workers, led not only to industrial gains but to great political success and legislative reforms. In 1917, St. John's workers created the Newfoundland Industrial Workers' Association (NIWA), an avowedly industrial unionist organization that immediately proceeded to organize workers across the island. Thus, Newfoundland workers conformed to the international wave of industrial unionist unrest. The NIWA found its leadership in the railway shops of the Reid Newfoundland Company and among local socialists and drew its membership from St. John's metal shops and the foundry. Its major industrial battle against Reid Newfoundland was a three-week strike of 500 railway workers in the spring of 1918 that involved threats of an island-wide walkout and extensive sympathetic activities in St. John's.[45]

The international literature on the post-war upsurge has blossomed of late and the comparative insights offered by international labour and working-class history open some interesting avenues for investigation.[46] First, however, let us eliminate a few dead ends of previous Canadian interpretation.

In the aftermath of the strike, the *B.C. Federationist* concluded: "The first lesson that workers must learn is that only by organization and cohesion, not only in each centre, but throughout the country, can they resist the encroachments of capital."[47] Similar statements have often been used to buttress a "western revolt" notion of 1919, arguing that only workers west of the Lakehead behaved "radically." The lesson, however, surely lay not in a regional understanding of the revolt but rather in the reverse – namely, the necessity of perfecting nationwide organization.

To be sure, there is no doubt that the AFL and TLC leadership, not to speak of the railroad running trades leadership, played reprehensible roles, blocking such nationwide organization along the lines of One Big Union. They undoubtedly exploited their image as respectable labour leaders who believed in the sanctity of contracts. But this was not a simple East/West fight. At the 1917 TLC convention in Ottawa the debate on the executive's collapse on the issue of conscription and their decision not to resist the law once enacted revealed no simple regional vote. In a lengthy debate twenty-eight delegates spoke with only nine fully supporting the executive of which only two actually supported conscription. The nineteen speakers who opposed the executive included eleven eastern delegates and eight westerners.[48] Eastern opponents included moderate Toronto socialists John Bruce and Jimmy Simpson and Montreal radical machinists Tom Cassidy and Dick Kerrigan. Cassidy engaged in the debate's major rhetorical flight, albeit prescient in light of events in 1919:

> When the machine guns are placed on the streets of Winnipeg to shoot down strikers, also in Montreal, Vancouver Island, and other places, it shows that these organized soldiers are willing to shoot their fellow workingmen. I am not afraid to die. . . . The masters of the world must be whipped. . . . We have only one enemy and that is the international capitalist class.

When the vote finally came the major amendment, introduced by Alberta leaders Farmilo and Ross, failed narrowly 101 to 111. Since there were only forty-four western delegates present, it should be clear that there was considerable eastern opposition to conscription as well. Indeed, when a conciliatory division on conscription itself was taken only ten delegates voted in favour of the calling-up of manpower.

At the 1918 TLC convention in Quebec, where seething western discontent eventually led to plans for the Calgary Conference of March, 1919, similar non-regional divisions were evident. Westerners represented only forty-five of 440 delegates. While radical motions were consistently lost and elections to executive positions saw moderates emerge victorious, nevertheless there were far more votes for radical positions than simply those of the West. For example, the one roll call vote on a Winnipeg motion to release all conscientious objectors from prison was narrowly defeated 99 to 90. The minority radical vote was composed of fifty-eight eastern delegates and thirty-two western, while the conservative vote included two westerners and ninety-seven easterners. The clear lesson to be learned was that the West should send more delegates.[49]

When the TLC met in Hamilton in the fall of 1919 the battle

between craft unionism and the OBU for control of the labour movement was raging. In that context, and with OBU members and sympathizers either departed or expelled, it should not surprise us that the convention witnessed much Red-bashing. Yet there was also an undercurrent of support for industrial unionism and disgust for the TLC's failure to support Winnipeg workers. There was vociferous eastern criticism of the TLC leadership. Toronto delegate Birks denounced "organized officialdom within the trade union movement as something opposed to the spirit and mind of the rank and file." District 26 leader J.B. McLachlan introduced a motion for a general strike demanding the restoration of freedom of speech and of the press and the repeal of the Criminal Code amendments passed during the Winnipeg General Strike. Toronto carpenter McCallum, St. Catharines' delegate Grant, and Ottawa stonecutters took similar stands. As one delegate argued, "the boss beat us because we were divided into small locals." Winnipeg's George Armstrong availed himself of this opportunity to condemn "the machinery of the AFL which made massed action impossible." Battles went on within the international unions as well. The 1920 convention of the IAM saw bitter debate about the expulsion of OBU supporters, and Montreal and Toronto machinists led a losing but fiery effort to defend their comrades.[50]

The fight in the Canadian labour movement thus rested on different views of labour's future organization, rather than on regional peculiarities. Nor was syndicalism central to the debate. The western SPC leaders looked to the OBU as the way forward, but the OBU was certainly not syndicalist. An organization led by the SPC could never have been anti-political and thus analyses stressing the supposed "turn" to politics after Winnipeg are spurious. The political aims of the SPC never varied.[51]

The strike wave, of course, gained SPC leadership only begrudgingly for that very reason. The SPC doubted the wisdom of the industrial actions but had no choice but to lend its leadership skills to the working-class militancy that engulfed the nation. They never, however, viewed 1919 as a nascent revolution. They were politically too experienced for that. While Joe Knight and Carl Berg in Edmonton allowed their rhetoric to exceed the SPC line in the heady days of June, 1919, the leading Vancouver comrades never lost sight of the limitations of the situation. Thus, *The Soviet* could argue, displaying the syndicalist tendencies of Knight and Berg:

In Winnipeg and Toronto today the same condition is observable.

The General Strike by paralyzing industry, paralyzes government. The Strike Committees are forced to rule the cities, to "exempt" certain industries and services in order to provide for elementary human needs; they must police the cities themselves. Willy-nilly "this production for use and not for profit" is undertaken for the benefit of the workers. It displaces the capitalist government which operated for the benefit of the bourgeoisie. . . .[52]

Vancouver's *Red Flag*, on the other hand, was consistent and cautious. The OBU, it noted, simply represented:

... a decided urge towards industrial unionism which has lately become very insistent. We have referred to this movement several times and have criticized it and analyzed it. That is our function. We don't initiate movements, we seek to understand them. We realize that beyond a very transitory influence, great movements are not caused by individuals, they are the result of conditions.[53]

Simultaneously, the *B.C. Federationist* editorialized: "Neither the Seattle nor the Winnipeg strikes were revolutionary upheavals. They were strikes in the one instance for higher wages, and in the later case, for the recognition of the right to collective bargaining. Is that a revolutionary strike?" The same editorial cautioned against violence and promoted discipline "because the ruling class have the guns, and if blood is shed, it will be the blood of the working class." In a revolution, it continued, it was necessary to "control the means of coercion," and there was no such opportunity in Canada. A week later the *B.C. Federationist* again emphasized, "The strike is not a revolutionary strike," and argued instead: "The issue is political. The workers must take the matter up on those lines, and wring political concessions from the master class, and beat them at their own game."[54] All of this fits well with William Pritchard's now famous aphorism: "Only fools try to make revolutions, wise men conform to them."[55]

Ironically, Aaron Mosher, the president of the Canadian Brotherhood of Railroad Employees, shared the SPC perspective to the degree that he recognized that radical leaders could not be held responsible for the labour revolt. In a letter volunteering his services to Prime Minister Borden, he noted:

Numerous telegrams we are receiving from our local branches throughout the entire west asking authority to strike and the fact that some of our members have gone on strike after authorization was denied them, leads me to believe that it is not just a few labour agitators at Winnipeg who are causing the unrest. In most cases, I am sure the rank and file in the labour movement are forcing the leaders to take the stand they have taken, and it would be well to look into this phase of the situation.

Commissioner Perry of the Royal North West Mounted Police argued similarly in his "Memorandum on Revolutionary Tendencies in Western Canada":

At the foundation of all this agitation is the general restlessness and dissatisfaction. The greater number of labour men, and probably of the community as a whole, are in an uncertain, apprehensive, nervous and irritable temper. Perhaps these agitators are but the foam on the wave.

Let us take Mosher's advice and Perry's metaphor and close this paper with a consideration of the causes of the "wave" of unrest.[56]

Eric Hobsbawm, some twenty years ago, suggested that "The habit of industrial solidarity must be learned . . . so must the common sense of demanding concessions when conditions are favourable, not when hunger suggests it. There is thus a natural time lag, before workers become an 'effective labour movement.'" Writing ten years later, Michelle Perrot argued: "The strike is a weapon of conquest, the major instrument of a working class more and more desirous and capable of improving its lot, more and more fascinated by the possibilities of the strike."[57] By 1919, Canadian workers had certainly become an "effective labour movement" and they also had developed in wartime conditions a considerable fascination with "the possibilities of the strike." Indeed, as this paper argued earlier, the 1919 revolt represents a return, albeit at a higher level of intensity, to the pre-war pattern of conflict. This intensification was fuelled by the addition of new groups of workers to the struggle. These new groups included public-service workers, West Coast loggers, and previously unorganized or at best partially organized groups of industrial workers such as those in Toronto's and Montreal's packing houses and garment shops. Among these last groups of workers, as also in Winnipeg and certainly as in the coal mines of District 18, another crucial new ingredient was present – ethnic solidarity. In 1919, momentarily at least, the divisiveness of ethnicity was surpassed in the struggle. A Canadian working-class movement that had been swamped with new immigrants from eastern and southern Europe in the pre-war years had matured, coalesced, and to some degree at least, commenced the process of incorporating the new workers into the movement. These "new" Canadian workers, as we are only now coming to realize, often were not "new" to the working class. Indeed, Finns, Jews, and Ukrainians often arrived with a more extensive socialist background than their much celebrated English and Scot immigrant comrades.[58]

In addition to the new ethnic component of the labour movement, women workers were more noticeably present. The new involvement of public-sector workers brought groups of telephone operators and civic employees, while organization also spread to department store clerks and waitresses, and, of course, into the heavily female garment trades. In Winnipeg, Toronto, Calgary, Vancouver, and elsewhere women workers played important roles in the 1919 strikes, both as strikers and as members of women's labour leagues and councils, which, in some cases, emerged during the general strikes.[59]

The structural transformation of the working class generated by the Second Industrial Revolution and by the ongoing process of the concentration and centralization of capital, which on some levels weakened the working-class movement, simultaneously stimulated an enhanced capacity for collective resistance at the workplace. Thus, scientific management and other managerial innovations, which attacked what Robert Morris has usefully termed the "moral economy of the skilled men," began the process of generating an industrial union response.[60]

The rapid urban expansion generated by monopoly capitalist growth also played its role in the revolt. The working-class neighbourhoods of Toronto's and Montreal's garment districts or those associated with the huge metal plants and railroad shops in those cities and in the West became centres of workers' lives and slowly began to generate working-class community institutions. North-end Winnipeg is perhaps the most celebrated example, but all Canadian cities developed equivalent districts. While sometimes ethnically segregated, these areas often took on instead occupational associations as in Toronto's stockyard area or even Toronto's Junction district. In this period before the automobile's dispersal of the working class, a relationship continued to exist between domicile and workplace. Witness after witness before the Mathers Commission complained of poor and expensive housing in Canadian towns and cities. This near-universal complaint also undoubtedly contributed to the working-class revolt of 1919 and helped to widen it beyond simple workplace issues. Thus the general and sympathetic strikes extended past organized workers to embrace many workers outside the unions.

Also helping to widen the conflict in a similar fashion were the interrelated issues of inflation, the cost of living, and war profiteering. Recent econometric work on real wages in the first three decades of the twentieth century confirms that "real wage rates declined significantly during the First World War."[61] The new national index compiled by Bertram and Percy shows a low of 85.5 in 1917 (1913 equals 100), while Eleanor Bartlett's work on Vancouver shows the low point as either 1917 or 1918, depending on the choice of indices. What is clear in these studies and in earlier studies of Montreal, Toronto, and Winnipeg is that workers suffered a real decline on a national basis during the second half of the war. Moreover, the political dynamite in this situation was the clear dichotomy between a government that refused "fair wages" and conscripted manpower and a government that allowed blatant profiteering and refused to conscript wealth. The transparency of the relationship between capital and the state in the war years allowed socialist propaganda to reach a growing and increasingly sympathetic audience. Demands for nationalization of abbatoirs, cold storage plants, and elevators, which might at first seem surprising, must be viewed in this context. The coincidence of these consumer demands with intense struggles at the point of production helped to deepen class conflict into something approaching conscious class struggle.[62]

The violent repression in Winnipeg, the strike trials and the martyrdom of the leaders, the creation of the Royal Canadian Mounted Police, the conscious victimization of thousands of strikers, the TLC's retreat into craft exclusivism, all suggest a bleak aftermath and a story of defeat.[63] Yet as late as September, 1919, Commissioner A.B. Perry of the new RCMP, an acute observer of labour radicalism, warned of the continuing "general state of unrest," which he found "far from satisfactory."[64]

Indeed, the seeds of industrial unionism would survive the defeat of 1919 to sprout later. Moreover, if the 1920's and early 1930's appear as a period of relative national labour quiescence, the phenomenon is far from unique. The working-class movement in other advanced industrial countries also slipped into what Yves Lequin has recently termed "the great silence," a period stretching from the end of the great revolt until the resurgence of industrial unionism in the mid-to-late depression years.[65] The fascination with industrial councils and various other welfare capitalist schemes, which was so evident in the Mathers Commission and in the National Industrial Conference, also had ambiguous results. The seemingly tame industrial councils often provided the basis for the new thrust to real industrial unions when the time was again propitious for working-class struggle.[66]

Defeats should thus not be confused with failure, and perhaps the SPC leaders should be allowed to write their own epitaph. In Winnipeg, F.W. derived the following "Lessons of the Strike":

> This is only a local momentary defeat on a world-wide battle front. Remember that permanently we cannot lose. Every struggle is a lesson in class solidarity. Every brutal act of suppression brings capitalism nearer to its inevitable doom. . . . Courage, fellow workers. Study your class position and you cannot lose.[67]

Meanwhile in Vancouver, Comrade C.K. addressed "The Burning Question of Trade Unionism," echoing a Daniel DeLeon pamphlet title. Developing a "dialectical" position against the old "philosophy of misery" school, he argued that trade unions must be viewed not simply as they are but rather as they might develop. The events of 1919, he wrote, led inexorably to the workers' recognition of the need for political action. He closed on an optimistic note which, although too reminiscent of Second International evolutionism, nevertheless might be a message for all of us in this period of renewed attacks on labour:

> There is a benevolent appearing old gentleman wearing long white whiskers clad in a nightshirt and carrying a scythe. He is known as "father time." The fact is not generally known but he is a socialist of the most pronounced revolutionary type. He is very busy among the trade unions these days. He is working for us.[68]

5

The Transformation of Women's Work in the Quebec Cotton Industry, 1920-1950

Gail Cuthbert Brandt

Feminists of all theoretical persuasions agree that the horizontal and vertical segregation of women's work constitutes a primary obstacle to the achievement of equality between the sexes. What remains contentious is the appropriate paradigm to explain the existence and persistence of this segregation. Idealists have stressed the importance of gender roles and patriarchal culture; materialists, the role of women as a reserve army of labour and the significance of women's segregated work for industrial capitalism. In more recent analyses of the sexual division of labour, materialist feminists have emphasized the dialectical relationship between class and gender, and one author concludes, "Capitalism, biology, ideology and the actions of men and women all play their part in ensuring not only that they [men and women] participate [in the labour force] in different ways, but also that women are subordinate to men."[1]

The cotton cloth industry in Quebec provides a particularly interesting context in which to analyse this persistent sexual division of labour. A product of the tariff protection embodied in the National Policy, it was a large-scale industry characterized by a high level of corporate concentration and a heavy reliance on female labour. With its pricing agreements and interlocking directorships, the industry constitutes an excellent example of the development of monopoly capitalism at the end of the nineteenth century. By 1919, the manufacture of cotton cloth was dominated by three companies – Dominion Textile Company Limited, Montreal Cottons Limited, and Canadian Cottons Limited. Twelve cotton mills with an average of 871 employees per establishment were located in Quebec and employed a total of 10,454 persons. The value of their products reached $57,530,438, a sum exceeded only by forest products.[2] Women represented a significant component of the workers throughout the first half of the twentieth century, although their proportional representation fell from 55 per cent in 1891 to 32 per cent in 1951.[3]

Due to its reliance on an agricultural commodity, the manufacture of cotton cloth was a volatile enterprise; but while sharp increases in the price of raw cotton could create serious problems, labour remained the major cost of production.[4] Manufacturers were therefore constantly seeking new methods of transforming the labour process to maximize profits. Any technological or administrative innovation that would reduce the amount and cost of labour was bound to be accorded serious consideration. Moreover, unlike many other Canadian industrialists, the cotton goods manufacturers did not enjoy a period of high and sustained profits during the decade following World War I.[5] It is thus not surprising, given these constraints, to discover an increased emphasis on efficiency, cost reduction, and more effective control of the labour process by management in the 1920's. This thrust for efficiency resulted in a host of managerial and technological innovations that would directly affect the organization of production by gender.

I

Prior to the establishment of the factory system, when textile production was located in the home, spinning was considered women's work. But a series of early innovations,[6] culminating in the self-acting mule spinning machine, "masculinized" the trade. The overwhelming majority of mule spinners were male due to the enormous size and complexity of the machine and to the danger of women's skirts getting caught in the moving carriage. Mule spinners were successful in unionizing since they were difficult to replace, and they "soon gained a reputation as troublesome."[7]

Technological change, in the form of the ring spinning frame (see Figure 1b), however, resulted in a dilution of the skill required for spinning and, ultimately, in the destruction of the strategic place of the mule spinner in the industry. Although the ring spindle was invented in the United States in 1828, it only came into

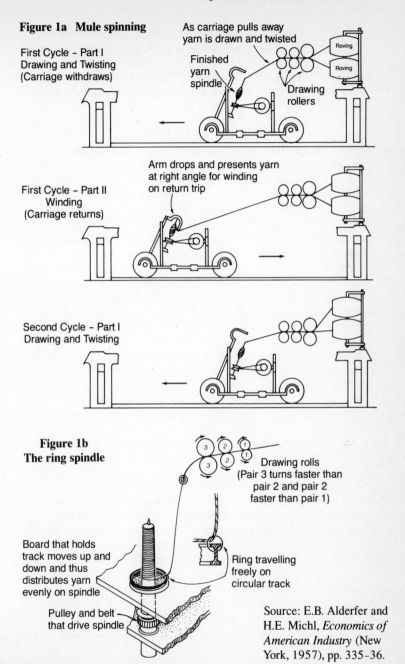

Figure 1a   Mule spinning

First Cycle – Part I
Drawing and Twisting
(Carriage withdraws)

As carriage pulls away
yarn is drawn and twisted

Roving

Roving

Finished
yarn
spindle

Drawing
rollers

First Cycle – Part II
Winding
(Carriage returns)

Arm drops and presents yarn
at right angle for winding
on return trip

Second Cycle – Part I
Drawing and Twisting

**Figure 1b
The ring spindle**

3 2 1

3 2 1

Drawing rolls
(Pair 3 turns faster than
pair 2 and pair 2
faster than pair 1)

Board that holds
track moves up and
down and thus
distributes yarn
evenly on spindle

Ring travelling
freely on
circular track

Pulley and belt
that drive spindle

Source: E.B. Alderfer and
H.E. Michl, *Economics of
American Industry* (New
York, 1957), pp. 335–36.

wide usage after the Civil War. By 1870, however, the number of ring spindles already surpassed the number of mule spindles, and by 1905 there were 17.9 million of the former compared to only 5.2 million of the latter in American mills.[8] For management, the ring spinning frame possessed several important advantages over the mule: it took up less floor space; had no movable carriage; required no great physical exertion to operate; and could turn out about one-third more yarn per operator. The skill component of spinning was significantly reduced for the main task now consisted of piecing together broken ends, replenishing the stock, and doffing. According to one analysis of the work involved in mending broken ends, thirty-two separate hand movements were required; therefore, manual dexterity was identified as the main qualification for the successful ring spinner.[9] Not surprisingly, this type of spinning was assigned to women. One female operative was expected to attend to 1,000-1,500 ring spindles.

In Canada, the replacement of mule spindles by ring spindles proceeded more slowly than in the United States.[10] Like their British counterparts, Canadian mill owners appear to have preferred the "feel" of cloth produced by the mule spinning process. Initially the yarn produced by the ring spindle tended to be coarser and have more twist, so that it was better suited for producing warp thread than weft or filling yarn. As a result of constant improvements, it was possible by the 1920's to produce the finer counts of cotton thread by ring spinning. Mule spinning and the skilled workers it employed were subsequently condemned to obsolescence.

Once it was spun, the cotton yarn used for weft thread required no additional treatment prior to weaving. Warp thread, which ran the entire length of the piece of cloth, did have to be specially treated so that it could withstand the friction of the shuttle being constantly passed back and forth during the weaving process. The necessary preparations consisted of spooling, warping, and slashing. Spooling involved joining together the yarn from several bobbins to form a single continuous thread. This work entailed considerable concentration and speed on the part of the operative, enhanced by the invention of the Barber knotter in 1900. The spooler was described in the following manner: ". . . she – the operator is usually a girl or woman – must be alert and active, and especially nimble fingered."[11]

The yarn from several spools was then placed on a large wooden roller called a warper's beam. Warper-tenders were also usually female. The next phase in the preparation of warp thread was slashing, or the addition of sizing to the yarn to give it greater strength. Running the slashers was men's work because of the lifting involved in installing a set of warper's beams in the slashing machine and because of the skill required in determining the proper quantity of sizing to be administered. In the early nineteenth century, the working conditions associated with the slashing process were atrocious: extremely high temperatures (over 100° F) and the unpleasant smell of sour starch resulting from poor ventilation made this work particularly obnoxious. After the warp threads had been sized, each thread then had to be drawn through the loom harness to produce a sheath through which the shuttle bearing the filling yarn could travel. This delicate and tedious work was performed by the "Drawing-In girls." When the drawing-in was completed, the warp was ready to be installed on the loom.

Within the domestic production (putting-out) system, weaving was primarily a male activity, but with the introduction of the power loom and the transfer of weaving to the factory, women also found employment in the weave sheds. The introduction of the automatic loom and the electric stop in the latter part of the nineteenth century facilitated the transfer of this work to women. The Northrup loom, which came on the American market in 1894, combined the following features:

> a bobbin changing device, a filling hopper from which bobbins are automatically transferred to the loom shuttle, a particular shuttle which can be threaded automatically by the motion of the loom, devices that act to stop the loom if the shuttle is not in position, and a warp stop-motion to prevent the making of poor cloth.

It was no longer necessary to stop the loom nearly every eight minutes to replace the shuttle when the bobbin became empty. Automatic threading also eliminated one of the major occupational hazards for weavers, the "kiss of death," which consisted of sucking the thread through the shuttle an average of 500-1,000 times per day. With each threading, the operative inhaled cotton fibres, dust, sizing, and dye stuffs and consequently often fell victim to serious respiratory diseases.[12]

The automatic loom resulted in significant labour savings: whereas a weaver in the past was assigned six to eight power looms, now she was expected to attend fourteen to thirty automatic looms. Many of the essential traits of the accomplished weaver were those normally associated with women: nimble fingers; long, slender hands; and a careful attention to detail.[13] By contrast, not even the most experienced and intelligent female weavers were considered potential candidates for the position of loom fixer, since it required the "masculine" characteristic of mechanical ability. Since weavers were paid by the piece, the loom fixer could directly affect the earnings of the individual weavers, depending on his willingness and ability to repair the weaver's looms. Thus he exercised a significant degree of control over the labour process and the semi-skilled operatives within the weave room.

The introduction of the automatic loom also resulted in the division of the weaver's work into a number of separate tasks that could be carried out by less skilled and less expensive help, much of it female. Battery hands loaded the full bobbins into the bobbin-changing device; doffers removed the finished cloth; and cleaners kept the loom free of dirt and dust. In this way, it was possible to increase the number of looms attended by one weaver.

The final stage in the manufacture of cotton cloth was inspection. Yard after yard of material was carefully examined for flaws and graded according to its quality. This work was also performed primarily by women since it was clean, light, and monotonous work. Excellent eyesight and unlimited patience were definitely required for this work.

As the preceding account demonstrates, although women and men worked side by side in some departments, occupational segregation by sex was intrinsic to the cotton industry. This segregation assumed both horizontal and vertical forms. In general, men were assigned to tasks requiring either a considerable amount of physical strength or a recognized degree of experience and skill, often defined in terms of the conventional wisdoms of the age. Between 1890 and 1910, various improvements in textile machinery resulted in the transformation of what formerly had been skilled male work into semi-skilled female work. Techno-logical change in this period thus worked to create new employ-ment opportunities for women.

Occupational segregation was replicated and reinforced by the demographic divisions of the work force and by wage differentials. The vast majority of female operatives were single young women; in 1911, 77 per cent of the women in the Quebec cotton industry were under twenty-five years of age. The comparable figure for males was only 45 per cent.[14] Few women continued to work after marriage, a trend that reinforced the popular conception of women as temporary workers and mitigated against male employees and employers viewing them as candidates for positions requiring more than a few months of training.

Nearly all work associated with production in the mill was paid according to the piece rate system. At first glance, this situation would appear to obviate any monetary advantages in employing women in men's places, since they were paid at the same rate. However, the sex hierarchy of jobs resulted in a sex hierarchy of pay: skilled male workers were paid on an hourly basis while women and adolescents were paid by the piece. When markets were sluggish and production had to be cut back, foremen often put women on short time rather than reduce the working hours of men. Whatever the reasons, the evidence is incontrovertible that female operatives earned less than their male counterparts: in 1926, male frame spinners in Quebec earned the equivalent of 30.7 cents an hour while female spinners made only 24.3 cents; male weavers pocketed 33.5 cents per hour while female weavers took home 27.7 cents per hour.[15]

The employment of women was also facilitated by the labour shortages experienced during World War I. As "Florida," a Magog worker, recalled, "Dans ce temps-là c'etait facile de se placer car le monde était parti pour la guerre."[16] In an attempt to secure sufficient experienced workers, the Magog branch of Dominion Textile published a bilingual recruiting pamphlet in 1917. Among other incentives for female workers, it listed the existence of a crèche, operated by Catholic nuns, that could accommodate up to 200 children of working mothers.[17] Before 1914 there was also a general acceptance of French-Canadian working-class women being employed outside the home, at least under certain economic circumstances. Mindful of the exodus of their parishioners to the United States during the latter part of the nineteenth century, members of the French-Canadian clergy welcomed the construction of textile mills that could offer steady employment to many family members. Just as the political elite in the United States had favoured the entry of young Yankee women who could not be absorbed by agricultural production into the textile industry, so, too, many curés and some bishops regarded the utilization of surplus female labour by Quebec's textile manufacturers as a positive development.[18] Since the family was considered the cornerstone of French-Canadian society, the mill managers' practice of recruiting entire families and permitting relatives to work together undoubtedly helped mould this positive valuation. At least one curé felt justified in falsifying a baptismal certificate in order that a young girl could get a job in a cotton mill and thus contribute to the support of her large, needy family.[19]

By 1920, then, Quebec's powerful cotton companies had experienced significant technological change, much of it destined to attract women to the mills. They had also recruited the requisite female work force. Capital's concerns now turned to rationalizing the labour process; the results would be devastating for women workers.

II

If one single word summarized the major concern of cotton manufacturers in the decade following World War I, it was "efficiency." Scientific management, time and motion studies, the acquisition of improved machinery, systems designs, and bonus schemes to increase worker productivity were some of the methods proposed to ensure greater efficiency and profitability. Additional evidence of increased mechanization and the endorsement of Taylorism by the Quebec cotton industry during this period were presented before the Royal Commission of Enquiry into the Textile Industry (Turgeon Commission). In his testimony, Blair Gordon, the president of Dominion Textile and of Montreal Cottons, stated:

> Over the period 1920-1930, the Dominion Textile Company Limited gave a great deal of attention to progressive moves in the field of application of labour to machinery. The aim of such work was two-fold:
> 1) To reduce the labour cost per unit of production.
> 2) To increase the earnings of the skilled individual worker.
> A cardinal principle was that the skilled worker's time should be devoted as far as possible to skilled work, and that the unskilled portion of the work should be given to unskilled workers. . . . Extensive studies were made in all Dominion Textile Company mills of machine performance etc., and basic data serves as the foundation for job assignments and resultant piece-work rate setting.[20]

Gordon spoke as if the cotton work force were sexless. But the corporate aims he articulated would, given the gender-based organization of production, have a different impact on men and women.

Although Gordon identified as "skilled" jobs that were performed in many cases by women (tenders, spinners, and weavers), women continued to be excluded from positions that conferred control over the work process and over other workers. While it is a relatively easy task to distinguish unskilled work from skilled, it is much more difficult to establish criteria that will satisfactorily distinguish between semi-skilled and skilled work.[21] Research conducted into the cotton industry in Britain demonstrates that the intensification of capitalism resulted in some workers successfully establishing their claim to skilled status, although their jobs required no extensive training. Skill is thus in part a social construct, whose very existence tends to benefit certain interest groups. The presence of a sex hierarchy within the cotton industry ended up circumscribing the experience of a mass of female operatives who could never achieve skilled status and over whom male supervision was always required. Skill distinctions served both the managers of the mill and the male operatives, albeit unequally: the former were able to classify much of the work as unskilled or semi-skilled and to reap substantial savings by employing a cheaper class of labour; status distinctions among workers produced gains for some at a cost to others, rendering worker solidarity problematic. Male operatives could achieve a certain degree of occupational mobility by mounting the skill hierarchy; once they reached the level of "skilled" worker they were able to use this position to defend their own interests.[22]

An analysis of the short biographies of long-time employees of Dominion Textile, published in *Les Moulins des Cantons de l'Est*, confirms much of the above, illustrating the marked difference in the work experience of female and male production workers.[23] After an initial period as unskilled workers or learners, the women moved into semi-skilled positions where they would remain until retirement. In some cases this meant working at the same job for fifty years. Male workers were much more likely to be promoted, which enabled them to move from unskilled to skilled positions, such as card grinder or loom fixer, and on eventually to supervisory posts. Such mobility, of course, was enjoyed by a minority of male workers; for French-Canadian male workers also, there were very real obstacles to securing the best jobs in the industry.[24]

Nonetheless, the ambitious and capable French-Canadian male worker, who remained in the employ of a company for several years, could improve his situation in a way that a female operative could not. He could, for example, take advantage of the evening training courses offered by the individual companies.[25] A survey of the articles dealing with vocational training for workers in the textile industry, which appeared in the *Canadian Textile Journal* from 1895 to 1951, turned up few references to women. It was mentioned that female students could study design at the textile college in Ste.-Hyacinthe, established by the province of Quebec in 1945.[26] It is all too clear that conventional attitudes pertaining to women workers – that they were temporary and secondary wage-earners, uninterested in or unsuitable for upgrading of skills – prevented women from breaking out of established occupational patterns: the structure of male authority in the family was reproduced in the factory.

Although the increased division of labour and the resulting creation of low-skill positions had the potential to augment the female component of the work force in the cotton industry during the 1920's, technological changes during this decade in general led to a reduction in female employment. Several changes in textile machinery had a direct impact on the quantity and quality of women's work. Long-draft spinning, automatic spooling and winding devices, automatic warp-tyers and drawing-in machines, and improved automatic looms all reduced the amount of semi-skilled labour in the production process. Long-draft spinning resulted in less treatment being required to produce quality yarn, thereby reducing the number of spinners. After one mill introduced automatic spoolers and warpers, only half as many operatives were required as previously. The Barber Warp-Tying machine, which made its appearance in the early 1900's, accomplished the work of twenty female operatives; and the drawing-in machine could "draw in about six times as many warps per day as a girl can draw in by hand on the same grade of goods."[27] Refinement in looms resulted in fewer interruptions in weaving, the assignment of more looms per weaver, and higher levels of production by fewer weavers.

These tensions associated with the sexual division of labour were bound to have important repercussions on the interaction of female and male workers. A clear indication of the uneasiness between them is to be found in the strike at the St. Anne's branch of Dominion Textile on May 15, 1923. Nine loom fixers initiated the work stoppage to protest an increased workload with no increase in wages. They were also protesting work performed by women and girls during the noon hour and the resultant violation of the fifty-five-hour law. Six and a half days later they returned to work when the company promised to rehire a dismissed loom fixer and to replace the women by men, who could be free to run their looms during the lunch hour if they so desired. The loom fixers were so satisfied with this resolution of the dispute that they were willing to resume work, even though their own hours of work and compensation remained unchanged.[28]

Other industrial disputes and interviews with female workers[29] underline how important it was to female workers which particular man exercised authority over them. The foreman had a tremendous amount of power over his workers – to allocate workloads, to assign the most productive machines to certain workers, and ultimately, to dismiss. Not surprisingly, female operatives were willing to incur wage losses by striking to retain foremen they liked. In November, 1911, for example, 300 "girls" at the Hochelaga mill in Montreal struck to secure the reinstatement of a foreman. Similarly, sixty-three women and eight men employed in the card room in the Magog mill stopped work on May 3, 1920, in an attempt to have a discharged overseer rehired. These workers were able to keep 500 other employees from working. Both of these incidents also demonstrate that semi-skilled female workers were in a position to engage in militant activities. Their work formed a crucial part of the productive process, so that when they withdrew their services they could affect all operations within the mill.[30]

III

The negative consequences for female operatives of technological innovations, deskilling, and the routinization of work in the 1920's were but a portent of the difficulties they would encounter during the Great Depression. As employment opportunities decreased and competition among workers increased, there was a concerted attempt to reorient women to the domestic sphere and to reinforce the patriarchal system in order to reduce competition between men and women in the workplace. From 52 per cent of the work force in 1911, female workers fell to 39 per cent in 1931 and to 33 per cent by 1941. It is most likely that the proportion of women in the industry was even lower during the worst years of the depression.[31]

There are several reasons for the sharp decline in the female component of the work force during the depression. According to the Turgeon Commission report, many employers "gave preference to male employees and particularly those with dependents." Married women, in particular, experienced difficulty in retaining employment. Female workers in the Valleyfield and Magog mills reported that the companies frequently dismissed female employees once they married:

On renvoyait des femmes mariées.

Il fallait donner notre place aux autres. Ils nous renvoyaient, les femmes mariées au lieu d'en 'slacker' d'autres.

On renvoyait les femmes mariées pour donner la chance aux hommes mariés. C'est à ce moment que les hommes commencent à filer.

These discriminatory policies reflected public opinion in the province. In Quebec, as throughout the rest of Canada during these years, there was a widespread opposition to married women working outside the home. Priests, politicians, and publishers cajoled the French-Canadian woman to resume her proper place in society, as *la reine du foyer*. The belief that wives belonged at home was also shared by many men in the working class. Half of the husbands of female cotton workers I interviewed, who married during the 1930's, insisted that their wives stop working after the wedding.[32] Nor were the unions immune to such views. According to "Alphonsine," "Le syndicat passait par les maisons faire signer les gens pour qu'on renvoie les femmes mariées." When she voiced concern about her own possible loss of employment, she was assured by union leaders that she would not be adversely affected since they knew her husband was ill.[33]

This opposition to women's gainful employment was not restricted to married women. Throughout the depression, the Canadian and Catholic Confederation of Labour, with which the National Catholic Textile Federation was affiliated, recommended not only the dismissal of married women, but also a restriction on the use of all female labour. A 1939 resolution provides an excellent summary of the menace of the single young woman:

Ce régime facilite une trop grande émancipation de la jeune

fille de telle sorte qu'un bon nombre se degagent de la tutelle de leurs parents pour aller vivre en toute liberté d'action et souvent de conduite, ce qui entraine une foule de conséquences graves relativement à la morale.

Le Travail Feminin contribue à retarder les mariages, ce qui occuperait ces jeunes filles dans leur foyer respectif, milieu naturel de l'exercice de leur activités.

Ces jeunes filles et femmes remplacent les jeunes gens et les hommes et entretiennent l'ère des bas salaires obligeant les patrons consciencieux à engager une main d'oeuvre féminine pour concurrencer avec les compétiteurs.[34]

A more moderate assessment of the male workers' attitudes toward women in the industry is provided in a brief presented to the Turgeon Commission:

L'ouvrier n'a pris partie ni pour no contre le mouvement féministe. Il a cependant tendance à restreindre le travail féminin. Il reconnaît que dans bien des cas le travail de la femme est une nécessité de la subsistance. Il regrette la concurrence que la jeune fille fait à l'homme de quarante ans et plus. Il considère que normalement le travail de la femme à l'usine devrait n'être que temporaire, la fonction de la femme vis-à-vis la famille et la race réclamant la conservation de ses forces et sa présence à la maison.[35]

Provincial minimum wage legislation, introduced in 1925 and which applied only to women, added an economic rationale to the ideological bias against women's paid employment. At mills in Sherbrooke and Trois-Rivières, jobs were redistributed in favour of young men and married men so that the employers could avoid paying minimum wages to the female workers.[36] Women were prevented by law from working nights. Female spinners in Magog were thus discharged as a new all-male night shift was created, even though many of the men had to commute from Sherbrooke.[37] In August, 1935, the provincial government revised the minimum wage legislation to make it applicable to men who replaced women on the job; nevertheless, the textile companies continued to replace female operatives with men who were paid lower wages. Women who earned the required amount ($12 in the metropolitan Montreal region and $10.08 in the rest of the province for a forty-eight-hour week) were said by the industry to constitute a "high wage bracket."[38]

Women who were successful in keeping jobs during the depression were more likely than previously to be in unskilled positions. Whereas most women who began work in the 1920's were rapidly able to obtain work as spinners or weavers, ten years later it was much more difficult to move beyond unskilled positions such as cleaners and battery hands. At Dominion Textile's Montmorency branch, the female battery hands were obliged to sign a document renouncing a promotion to avoid being replaced by lower-paid learners. Another woman who was interviewed worked as a shuttle filler from 1932 to 1939 and was only provided an opportunity to learn to weave after war was declared and many of the male workers left.[39]

Technological transformations continued apace and even quickened during the depression. Annual reports issued by the Quebec cotton companies throughout the 1930's outlined major expenditures for plant modernizations and the installation of new machinery. While workers found themselves without jobs, and sometimes investors without dividends, company officials continued to make expansion of productive capacity by means of increased mechanization a top priority. In his 1935 study of employment trends in the province, Leonard Marsh concluded that "the complicated processes formerly performed by skilled workers are continually broken down and simplified until the task approaches the routine. The skilled operative is replaced by the 'machine minder.' Mechanization, immensely increased output and large-scale operation have all proceeded together."[40]

The result was that there were fewer opportunities for women to find employment of a semi-skilled nature in the mills. Increasingly they found themselves working as doffers, battery hands, packers, and labellers. Testimony presented to the 1936 textile enquiry suggests that not only was the work women were asked to perform in the 1930's less skilled but it was also of a heavier nature. Paulette Cabana, age nineteen, and Isabelle Vachon, age twenty-four, worked as doffers; the first for five years and the second for the better part of nine years. Both reported that they were required to push a truck loaded with hundreds of bobbins of roving to the elevator, or to the other end of the department when the elevator malfunctioned, an average of ten times each day. In return for their physical exertion, they received $1.45 to $1.90 per day.[41]

That women were more vulnerable than men to deskilling in times of economic distress is indicated by the census data. In

1931, 37 per cent of female production workers laboured at unskilled occupations, compared to 43 per cent of men. Ten years later, the comparable figures were 57 per cent of women and 47 per cent of men. A more specific example of this trend is provided by the occupation of weaver. In 1931, nearly one-quarter of female workers and 18 per cent of male workers were weavers; in 1941, only one-fifth of the former and 21 per cent of the latter were so designated.[42]

As in most other industries during the depression, women workers' militancy was held in check by the insecurity that confronted them on a daily basis. They did not possess the leverage necessary to negotiate successfully for improvements in their working conditions. Of nine work stoppages in the cotton industry recorded by the federal Department of Labour, in only one did women appear to play a significant role. Even during the industry-wide strike in 1937, they were not highly visible. While male workers walked the picket line, female strikers were cast in a supporting role, making mountains of sandwiches in union halls and church basements. Solidarity was not necessarily utterly destroyed, but it may well have assumed less visible forms, such as in sharing workloads and in providing mutual moral support.

IV

The eruption of hostilities in Europe and Canada's entry into the war resulted in a dramatic increase in business for the domestic cotton manufacturers. The demand for cotton was virtually insatiable since it was used in over 10,000 articles required by the armed forces. Production and profits soared, but managers in the textile industry found it increasingly difficult to maintain a full complement of experienced workers. A submission to the War Labour Relations Board by the United Textile Workers of America claimed that "manpower is leaving the textile industry as fast as it can." Given that the laws of supply and demand were now clearly in the workers' favour, the industry urgently sought state intervention to ensure the existence of an adequate and affordable work force. This intervention ultimately assumed various forms: the designation of the cotton industry as an essential war industry; tightly controlled limits on wage increases; the abrogation of workers' rights to leave jobs considered essential to the war effort; and a full-fledged publicity campaign to draw women into the workplace.[43]

The shortage of experienced and skilled workers in the textile industry was a major concern for industry officials from 1941 onward. Initially, however, the director of National Selective Service, Elliott M. Little, did not believe it was necessary or desirable to recruit women into the labour force *en masse*:

I would like to feel that there was a reservoir of trained or partially trained women workers on which we could draw when the day arrives: but until we see the whole picture and have a better understanding of our needs I would not feel justified in urging a mass movement of women to the training schools and factories. The reason we have not yet included women in the program is plain enough. As you know we still have some unemployed employables in this country . . . .

By 1943 the federal government did have "the whole picture"; there was a shortage of 13,179 textile workers. In some departments in mills operated by Dominion Textile, it was reported that up to 50 per cent of the men had left to join the armed forces. Women, as a reserve army of labour, were now very much in demand.[44]

The efforts of National Selective Service to recruit women to textile work were met head on by countervailing forces that tended to impose limits on the size and scope of women's participation in the labour force. The employment of women on night shifts continued to be prohibited by provincial regulation. Led by members of the clergy, who now had less fear of francophone migration to the United States, Catholic French-Canadian leaders denounced the entry of married women into the work force. Work in the war industries was deemed to imperil women's morality and family solidarity. Despite the unprecedented scarcity of workers, some cotton cloth manufacturers felt constrained to respect prevailing sentiment about women's proper role in society. In their annual report for 1943, the directors of Dominion Textile observed:

The number of female employees in our mills has increased by about 1400 and we now employ approximately 1000 more men than we did in 1939. A partial displacement of men by women on the day shifts has been offset by the large number of men employed on night shifts compared to peace time when the mills were not operated at night to any great extent. The net result is that women make up a little under 40 per cent of our working force and this condition is not subject to much change without offending very influential opinion.[45]

The aspirations of female workers themselves also contributed to the ongoing labour crisis in the textile industry. Once again they demonstrated that they were not nearly as malleable as National Selective Service officers and manufacturers might have wished. Comments from both government and union sources indicate that women were just as likely as men to leave low-paid employment for the high-wage defence industries. According to a government report, three-quarters of the entire labour shortage in the Canadian textile industry in September, 1944, was accounted for by female workers. This trend was accentuated by the lack of concerted effort on the part of industry officials to train female workers to assume the most skilled jobs in the mills. The editor of the *Canadian Textile Journal* noted that prior to 1943 the industry had done little to avail itself of the War Emergency Training Program. Moreover, in numerous articles dealing with the pressing need for more specialized training for textile workers, there was no discussion of how women might be included. The latter were well aware that their services were wanted on a short-term basis to meet the existing emergency. One directive emanating from NSS headquarters instructed regional officers that "Employment in textile mills should be brought to the attention of applicants as continuing work which offers a measure of permanency and which also provides an opportunity for the applicant to learn a trade. This will be of interest to women who are apprehensive that, with the cessation of hostilities, employment will not be readily available." But mill executives clearly did not intend to provide women with long-term employment. A survey of their post-war plans, published in 1944, revealed that "Employment is expected to be available for returned men without previous experience in the textile trade. The view was expressed that sooner or later married women whose husbands are working will be given a low priority, either by concerted government action or by government ruling, the vacancies being filled by ex-service personnel."[46]

An analysis of labour disputes occurring within the cotton textile industry during the war illuminates women workers' discontents. In ten of fifteen walkouts, women formed over 40 per cent of the personnel in the departments in which the disputes originated. In two cases they appear to have initiated the protest. In February, 1940, 150 female and twenty-five male cone winder tenders at the St. Gregoire de Montmorency mill walked off the job to protest a reduction in the piece rate. The work stoppage lasted six days and eventually affected 600 other workers. Three years later, at the same factory, the entire spinning department, composed of 275 female and seventy-five male operatives, refused to resume work unless thirty-seven other employees who had been fired for not reporting to work on Epiphany (January 6) were rehired. These incidents suggest that with their re-entry into the mills, women were once again playing a more central role in the manufacturing process and had regained some leverage to voice their protests.[47]

The employment of women during the war did not, however, effect any long-term alteration in the sexual division of labour. When war ended, those women who had held jobs previously performed by men found they were transferred to "female" jobs. The introduction of night shifts on a widespread basis during the war resulted in a higher proportion of spinners and weavers who were male, so that women were in direct competition with them for post-war employment.

The reconversion of the cotton industry to peacetime conditions also signalled the beginning of another massive modernization campaign. Textile machinery, worn by the frenetic pace of wartime production, needed to be replaced and still greater efficiency achieved if the cotton goods manufacturers were to be successful in protecting their markets from foreign competition and new synthetic fibres. More efficient machinery requiring less inter- vention on the part of the worker was installed, buttressed by more time and motion studies and the extension of the bonus system of payment to more production workers. The increased complexity of the machinery and the reduction of work requiring manual dexterity meant that this phase of automation continued past trends in eliminating women from waged work.

In the post-war period, the most important strike in the cotton industry occurred in 1946, when the United Textile Workers of America, led by Kent Rowley and Madeleine Parent, left their jobs in Montreal and Valleyfield. Newspaper accounts and inter- views with former workers indicate that female workers were more visible on the picket lines than they had been during the 1937 strike. Given the depression-induced hostility to women working in the mills, this is not surprising. The Valleyfield and Montreal conflicts, major battles in the Canadian post-war strike wave, demand further and deeper scrutiny, especially in terms of the role of women workers. But there can be no question that after decades of confinement and marginalization, women workers were no longer strategically placed to participate actively in militant protests. Forced out of work, or shunted into the peripheral jobs of inspection, folding, sewing, and packaging, Quebec's women textile workers had seen their productive lives transformed between 1920 and 1950. Once central to the labour process, they existed, by the late 1940's, only on its edges. Small wonder that union lists for the Valleyfield local of the UTWA indicated a definite under-representation of female adherents, 26 per cent of signed members in November, 1944, and a bare 8 per cent in August, 1945.[48]

V

The preceding account demonstrates that no single factor can adequately explain the persistence of the sexual division of labour within the Quebec cotton industry. As materialist feminists have argued, the interrelationship between ideas about gender and economic organization is crucial for understanding this division. More specifically, the various stages of development within the industry and attendant technological transformations, ideological formulations, and the actions of male and female workers themselves all contributed to a workplace ordered by gender. Two countervailing trends can be discerned – immutability and flexibility. On the one hand, a gender hierarchy persisted throughout the entire period under consideration. The highest-ranking production positions in terms of status, authority, and monetary rewards remained a male preserve. On the other hand, the gender identification of specific jobs could vary; for example, during the initial phase of factory production, spinners were predominantly male; later, predominantly female; and subsequently, both male and female.

The degree and manner in which women were integrated into the work force were influenced by several interrelated factors. Before 1920, women in Quebec found unprecedented employment opportunities in primary textile production. By 1911, they accounted for over half of the industry's workers; technological developments had enabled them to assume many of the semi-skilled jobs and even to replace skilled male labour. Short-term fluctuations notwithstanding, it was a period of expansion for the Quebec textile industry and of a sustained demand for workers. The employment of women throughout this period seems to have raised few objections. It was assumed that women worked out of necessity and that their contributions to the family wage economy were crucial. Through their attitudes and actions, mill managers, bishops and priests, and heads of families helped create a significant role for French-Canadian women in the early industrialization of their province.

After 1920, technological innovation worked against female employment in the industry, and the continued introduction of labour-saving machinery throughout the depression years aggravated the situation. There was no longer sufficient work to keep all employed, and increasingly women and men were in direct competition for certain jobs. By denouncing paid employment for women, the clergy, intellectuals, and union leaders sought to eliminate this problem. Companies introduced machinery that not only decreased the number of jobs available but also increased the likelihood that the workers who operated it would be male.

With the labour shortage engendered by World War II, one might have expected a reversal of the female employment trends encountered in the 1930's. There was an outpouring from government agencies of propaganda addressed to all groups of women to assume gainful employment to help the war effort. But in the province of Quebec there were conflicting messages. Again, the clerical, intellectual, and working-class elites joined forces to denounce women's work in war industry, particularly when it was performed by wives and mothers. Even textile managers felt compelled to exhaust all methods of recruiting additional men to resolve the labour crisis rather than call on women to take up the slack. Although the proportion of women engaged in the industry, and the range of jobs performed by them, did increase during the war, these gains were short-lived. When companies encountered the next set of adverse conditions, they manipulated the female work force to help resolve them.

Throughout all of this, women were not passive pawns in the service of corporate capitalism. Individually and collectively, they sought to defend their interests whenever they were in a position to do so. However, by 1951, their removal from a central role in the manufacturing process left them few opportunities or resources with which to remonstrate.

Part III

Advanced Capitalism and Accommodating the Class Struggle

Years of class struggle etched into the very substance of labour-capital relations certain basic antagonisms. These often erupted in large-scale generalized conflict, especially during wartime, when inflationary pressures, increased need for production, and labour scarcities all stimulated workers to raise specific demands and, moreover, increased the likelihood that such demands could be realized.

World War II was a context of this sort. During the 1940-44 years, the Liberal state, guided by the experience of more than three decades of explicit intervention in the class struggle, passed a great deal of legislation aimed at stabilizing class relations and accommodating class struggles. This is the subject of Jeremy Webber's analysis of wartime compulsory conciliation. When, during the immediate post-war years, class struggle surfaced with renewed vigour, the state followed suit with a series of legislative enactments that granted the workers' movement certain legal rights in collective bargaining. This overt involvement of the state was one indication that the raw class relations of earlier forms of capitalism were now being mediated by a relatively autonomous agent. Whereas nineteenth- and early twentieth-century capitalism had often sought to crush class struggle, advanced capitalism in the post-World War II years moved more effectively to accommodate it, holding brute force in a more restrained reserve. The legitimation that the state would confer on trade unions and collective bargaining would be accompanied by important curbs

135

on the class struggle: union agreements not to strike during the life of a contract, to abide by procedures established by state dictates, and to honour the increasingly common management rights clauses of collective agreements. Legitimacy thus bore a specific cost, with unions expected to accommodate their memberships to particular contractual relations.

Out of World War II, then, developed a complex industrial relations system in which federal and provincial legislation and labour codes increasingly governed significant parts of the class struggle. Unions living within this industrial legality, and there was little likelihood of any union dropping out of it, consequently cultivated professional, bureaucratized leaderships to fight on the legal terrain of the new order. This process was accentuated in the Cold War years of the late 1940's and early 1950's, when many labour bodies drove Communist organizers and other dissidents into retreat. Having achieved legitimization through state recognition and its own purges of much-maligned "subversives," the Canadian trade unions enjoyed some two decades of relative tranquility, consolidation, and, in terms of the rising public sector, expansion. The latter development, admittedly not a consequence of militancy but of the state's granting of bargaining rights to its employees, many of whom were women, forced the state to assume the role of employer at precisely the time that a vocal women's movement began to be heard within trade union circles.

The forces accommodating workers thus appeared to be breaking down as a wave of unauthorized "wildcat" strikes focused attention on the militancy of younger workers in 1965-66, as Quebec labour struck out in new directions as the Quiet Revolution unleashed new aspirations within the French-Canadian working class, and as women workers grew increasingly restive.

By 1975, moreover, a fundamental shift in the direction of worldwide capitalist developments hit hard at advanced Western capitalist economies, and even harder at those countries, like Canada, dependent on resource exports. The tide appeared to be turning against the Western capitalist economies and, as well, against the working class. Between 1975-85 Canadian federal and provincial governments launched a number of direct attacks on the trade union rights established in the late 1940's: worker organizations were being delegitimized. As the Maroney and Palmer essays indicate, women and public-sector workers would feel the negative consequences of this new context most forcefully, necessitating new forms of class struggle. Within this period of class struggle, however, many workers would find that they faced forces of accommodation entrenched within the upper echelons of the labour movement itself, where a bureaucratized stratum had lived for decades with the "benefits" of the post-war settlement.

6

The Malaise of Compulsory Conciliation: Strike Prevention in Canada during World War II

Jeremy Webber

Canadian governments have always wished to avoid the economic disruption caused by strikes; during World War II, this desire was particularly compelling. Ottawa's chief tool for accomplishing this aim was compulsory conciliation, the regime of government-sponsored mediation enshrined in The Industrial Disputes Investigation Act, 1907 (IDIA).[1] Before the war, this regime constituted the dominant thrust of the federal government's intervention in disputes between labour and capital. As the war progressed, however, the government came to recognize that conciliation alone would not achieve an acceptable level of industrial peace. It therefore began to intervene more directly in the class struggle, attempting to reduce conflict first through wage controls, and then, with the passage of order-in-council PC 1003 (February 17, 1944),[2] through the adoption of the principles embodied in the American Wagner Act:[3] compulsory recognition of workers' representatives, compulsory collective bargaining, the surveillance of labour relations by permanent administrative boards, and the forbidding of certain "unfair labour practices." But throughout this process of increasing governmental intervention, compulsory conciliation remained a key element of Canadian policy, serving, even under PC 1003 and post-war legislation, as the federal government's last line of defence against strikes and lockouts.[4]

I

What was "compulsory conciliation"? Essentially it was a legal

138

regime designed to ensure that before a work stoppage occurred a third party would intervene in the dispute and attempt to achieve a settlement. Strikes, lockouts, and changes in working conditions were therefore prohibited until a board had met with the parties and, if no settlement was reached, delivered a report containing non-binding recommendations "for the settlement of the dispute according to the merits and substantial justice of the case."[5] These *ad hoc* "Boards of Conciliation and Investigation" were composed of three members, one being nominated by the employees involved, one by the employer, with the influential chair being chosen by the first two (or, if these two could not agree, by the Minister of Labour). From the activities of boards, as well as from the structure and wording of the statute, there appear to have been two main functions a board could serve: (1) conciliation, in which it would encourage the parties to settle the matter amicably through discussion and compromise, and (2) adjudication, in which it would set itself apart from the parties, listen to their presentations, determine in its own wisdom the "right" or "just" solution, and then communicate its decision to the public at large, which would presumably exert pressure on the parties to respect the board's recommendation. These two basic approaches were by no means mutually exclusive: often they would both be used in one investigation.

The turbulent labour climate of World War II posed a severe challenge to this regime. Developments in union organization and the new economic circumstances of the war generated widespread labour unrest. In the late 1930's, the aggressive organizing drive of the CIO had come to Canada.[6] In most provinces there was no legal obligation for employers to bargain with their workers, nor any efficacious unfair labour practices legislation.[7] As labour relations deteriorated, Ottawa's determination to prevent strikes stiffened. To support the allied war effort, it embarked on a large-scale reorganization of the economy designed to boost the production of war material. The economy became, in large measure, a public enterprise devoted to achieving maximum industrial output. In such an environment, strikes were seen as more than mere nuisances: they were direct challenges to a great national endeavour.

While the state yearned for industrial peace, it had little desire to make substantive changes in the worker/management relationship. Intervening with legislation to favour one side or the other would, the government surmised, endanger the fragile consensus that was the cornerstone of Liberal politics: let the parties determine their own relations; the government should simply find a way of encouraging this process without having the parties resort to a strike or lockout. The government's commitment to the purely negative goal of strike prevention meant that when it did finally intervene it did so in particular ways with specific consequences. First, legislation generally did not purport to deal with the causes of dissatisfaction but rather erected a number of hurdles that unions had to leap before legal strikes could be declared (on the assumption that the intermediate steps would result either in a settlement, or at least in a narrowing of the issues to the point where a strike was no longer worthwhile). Second, the Department of Labour treated the reports of the resulting conciliation boards as stages in a long process of conciliation rather than as authoritative pronouncements of equity and justice that it should encourage the parties to accept. Third, delays, the failure of employers to comply with conciliation board reports, and the promotion of inadequate compromises on matters of crucial importance to the labour movement seemed all too often the outcome of intervention by officials or boards. While the government publicly argued that compulsory conciliation was an *expeditious* means of airing the issues, obtaining a decision on the merits, and achieving compromise, then, it often appeared simply to wish to delay industrial strife.

The malaise resulting from the tension between the government's preoccupation with strike prevention, on the one hand, and reluctance to grapple with the substantive content of labour relations, on the other, afflicted the boards themselves. A department that saw the conciliation process primarily as a device for postponing strikes gave little guidance regarding either the means by which a board should proceed or the normative basis on which issues should be decided. J.L. Cohen, labour lawyer and employee nominee on several boards, voiced a common complaint when he wrote:

> [Ottawa prefers to] appear to be filling the role of umpire between competing social forces and behind that role . . . to conceal the fact that as a government it has failed to discharge its primary duty of prescribing the rules. Umpiring without rules is a makeshift process and that in great measure marks the whole attitude of government today on the question of labour relations and collective bargaining.[8]

Gradually, however, Ottawa did move to prescribe more rules, reluctantly defining its policy preferences and reducing the autonomy of the parties. The government's first piece of wartime labour legislation was order-in-council PC 3495 (November 7, 1939), which simply extended the scope of the IDIA (formerly confined to disputes in "public utilities") to cover all defence-related industries.[9] For these sectors of the economy, there were now two official stages of third-party intervention: conciliation boards under the IDIA, and the pre-existing system of informal conciliation pursued by "industrial relations officers" under the Conciliation and Labour Act.[10] While the latter system was purely voluntary, no legal strike could occur until the requirements of the IDIA had been satisfied. This led to a massive increase in the number of cases dealt with: in 1939, thirty-three applications for boards were received; in 1940, sixty-seven; and in 1941, 143.[11]

The expansion of the IDIA's jurisdiction was supported by at least one major segment of organized labour, the well-established and relatively conservative (in comparison to the CIO activists) craft unionists. On October 5, 1939, a delegation from the Trades and Labor Congress of Canada, which had just expelled the CIO-affiliated unions, met with Prime Minister King to express its agreement with the government's aim of wartime strike prevention and to suggeest the extension of the IDIA as a means of resolving disputes without either work stoppages or compulsory arbitration. At that meeting, it also urged the government to declare itself in favour of collective bargaining and union recognition.[12] This latter demand led to the passage, almost nine months later, of order-in-council PC 2685 (June 19, 1940).

PC 2685 was significant for two reasons: (1) it constituted the government's clearest statement to date in support of union recognition, collective bargaining, freedom of employees to organize into independent unions, and grievance arbitration (in short, the essential elements of American labour law); and (2) it enunciated loose standards of industrial conduct by which government and private action could be judged, both by workers and by conciliation boards. This breakthrough was not without precedent: PC 2685 was modelled closely on a World War I order-in-council that had, after a very brief existence, been superseded by a regime of compulsory arbitration.[13] Nor was it the type of imperative intervention that many people were looking for: the principles were merely advisory and liable to be interpreted even by representatives of the government in ways inimical to labour.[14] But it did provide union organizers with a basis in government policy on which to found their arguments. It was followed by other orders-in-council establishing the first voluntary and then mandatory wage controls.[15]

Still unsatisfied with the degree of labour peace achieved by the IDIA, the intervention of industrial relations officers, PC 2685, and voluntary wage controls, the government in June, 1941, established other mechanisms of conciliation. PC 4020 (June 6, 1941) provided for the appointment, at the Minister of Labour's discretion and without the participation of the parties, of *ad hoc* "Industrial Disputes Inquiry Commissions," which would make preliminary investigations into disputes, attempt to secure settlements, and report back to the minister concerning the issues involved and whether or not the appointment of a more formal IDIA board was justified.

On September 16, 1941, the government passed yet another order-in-council, this time requiring that before a strike could occur in an industry subject to the IDIA, a government-supervised strike vote must take place if the minister so wished. PC 7307 was especially unpopular with organized labour because it gave the minister broad discretion to define who could vote: "all employees who in his opinion are affected by the dispute or whose employment might be affected by the proposed strike. . . ." Thus, the minister could, and sometimes did, include employees who were not even members of what would later be called the bargaining unit (e.g., foremen or clerical staff). In addition, the strike had to be approved by a majority of those *entitled* to vote, not merely of those actually voting. Writing in *Canadian Forum*, George Grube criticized PC 7307 in terms equally applicable to much of Canada's wartime labour law: "Its aim is purely negative. It puts further delays and obstacles in the way of possible strikes, without doing anything whatsoever to deal with the causes of strikes." On November 13, 1941, PC 7307 was amended to make it less objectionable, but on September 1, 1944, six months after the passage of PC 1003, it was repealed.[16]

The entry into force of PC 1003 (February 17, 1944) on March 20, 1944, brought new stability to Canada's labour laws. Following the American model, the federal government enacted a comprehensive labour code designed to promote collective bargaining, a code essentially the same as that governing Canadian workers today. These measures had teeth: a union that had the support of the majority of a plant's work force would be recognized by the government as the bargaining agent for that plant and the employer was obliged to enter into negotiations with it; a regime of compulsory arbitration was substituted for the freedom of strike during the term of a collective agreement; more effective means were provided for punishing such unfair labour practices as discrimination by employers against pro-union employees. The new regime thus did away with recognition strikes, which had been common under the old dispensation,[17] and which the public, familiar with the American experience under the Wagner Act, had increasingly come to consider as unnecessary. Indeed, Ottawa, under pressure from all segments of organized labour, had already ordered Wagner Act principles be applied to employees of Crown corporations; and in April, 1943, the Ontario government, in a vain attempt to save its electoral life, had enacted The Collective Bargaining Act, establishing compulsory recognition in that province, providing for the certification of bargaining agents, and placing the scheme under the supervision of a "Labour Court."[18] To deal with those issues insusceptible of agreement, however, compulsory conciliation was retained. Thus, strikes and lockouts were still prohibited until the parties had submitted their differences to a two-step process: (1) intervention by an individual "conciliation officer," and (2) investigation by an IDIA-style conciliation board. Much the same procedure therefore existed as under the IDIA at the beginning of the war, but the field of inquiry had shrunk from questions of recognition, wages, working conditions, and breaches of the collective agreement to the consideration of a single overriding issue: union security. Within this narrower compass, Ottawa remained unwilling to establish precise norms, although it still earnestly wished to prevent strikes. The cause of the malaise of compulsory conciliation – the contrast between the government's desire to intervene and its reluctance to make a formal decision favouring one side or the other – persisted.

This, then, was the background to the wartime emergence of government labour legislation and policy. But how did the malaise of compulsory conciliation "work" in the concrete context of class struggle?

II

Events preceding the 1941-42 strike at Kirkland Lake portray clearly a number of characteristics of compulsory conciliation in the early wartime environment.[19] The strike is also significant in that it contributed to public support for compulsory recognition and thus helped to edge the federal government toward the reforms of PC 1003.

The Kirkland Lake dispute was fought squarely on the issue of recognition: Local 240 of the International Union of Mine, Mill and Smelter Workers (Mine-Mill) sought to enter into a collective agreement with the management of several gold mines in the area; the latter refused to meet with union representatives, even though the union apparently had the support of a substantial majority of the miners. The first attempt at conciliation occurred on June 21, 1941, when the department's chief conciliation officer, M.S. Campbell, was dispatched to Kirkland Lake to prevent the impending clash. He was unable to persuade the companies to speak with the union and, on July 18, 1941, Local 240 applied for an IDIA board. This request was not immediately granted, although the union specifically asked that no further delay occur. Instead, on August 2 the parties were informed that an IDI Commission would investigate the dispute. It had no more success than the conciliation officer in persuading the employers to meet with the union. The commissioners did, however, get the companies to agree to a compromise: management would negotiate signed agreements, but only with committees elected by the workers in the various mines. The union rejected the proposal, and was supported by the membership in a vote held on the IDI Commission's request.

Indeed, the members of Local 240 saw employee committees not as a reasonable compromise, but as capitulation, resulting in a form of company unionism. The IDI Commission, however, reiterated in its report to the minister its support for the committee plan and went on to declare that had Conciliation Officer Campbell not assured the union that a board would be appointed, it would have recommended against establishing a board at all.[20] In effect, this suggestion came close to compulsory arbitration of the issue, for if the department had accepted it, the union would have been forced to choose between declaring an illegal strike and acquiescing in the committee plan. As it was, the commission did propose that the union leaders be summoned to Ottawa for a consultation with the minister. This meeting occurred on August 19, and once again the men, backed by an overwhelming strike mandate received four days earlier, expressed their opposition to the committee plan. Even this did not spell the end of the proposal;

to the government, employee committees remained the most likely solution to the difficulty.

Local 240's attempt to gain recognition provides a perfect example of an all-or-nothing demand – one based on principle. If, on a matter of consequence, all the concessions necessary to get agreement must come from one party, there are no longer any inducements, short of the threat of economic force, that can be used to pry them loose; either the issue must be fought out on the picket line or the government must use its influence, through legislation or otherwise, to secure a solution. During World War II, the government was reluctant to adopt either alternative, and it therefore attempted to delay the inevitable conflict, while proposing saw-offs that often served merely to annoy the parties. While such an approach did indeed prevent strikes, it tended to undermine conciliation as a method for promoting consensual agreements, making it into one long endurance test. Dissatisfaction with this state of affairs was not limited to union ranks. In a series of dissenting opinions delivered in conciliation board decisions dealing with disputes over union security (under PC 1003), a company nominee, J.S.D. Tory, criticized from the employer's perspective the practice of recommending compromises when principles were involved:

> The issue here demonstrates that there is an honest difference of opinion between the parties with respect to the ultimate status of trade unions in industry. At the moment this difference appears to be irreconcilable and any suggestion that the parties merely forget about the main issue and in the meantime compromise the claim seems to me to be a wholly unwarranted procedure. If there were any practical value in the arrangements for maintenance of membership and check-off in a particular case I should be prepared to give them earnest consideration; but in a case where it has been demonstrated that neither of these arrangements will assist the Union, and where the suggestion is made that these arrangements are put into affect [sic] merely as compromise, I am inclined to the view that this would serve only to emphasize the real issue between the parties and that instead of lessening the friction between union and non-union employees, it would only tend to increase it. . . . In my opinion, it by no means follows that the refusal of an employer to agree to provisions for a union shop, maintenance of membership and check-off amounts to a nega-

tion of collective bargaining. Genuine collective bargaining can and does exist without any necessity for agreement on these particular items, which are merely the subject of collective bargaining.

In Tory's view, compromises in such circumstances could only be justified as interim steps toward the complete adoption of the alternative policy; if the end was indeed worthwhile, he reasoned, the conciliation board or the government should have the courage to advocate it openly.[21]

On August 22, Local 240's long-awaited conciliation board was appointed. Normally, the board would have met with the parties, accepted briefs and oral presentations, and then tried to conciliate the dispute. When at last the board convened in early October, however, the hearings took a most unusual turn: immediately after the parties' initial presentations, the employers withdrew from the proceedings, declaring that because they were "*unalterably* opposed" to recognizing the union, there was no reason to participate. This was undoubtedly a tactical mistake. (The employers later apologized, claiming that their counsel had acted without authority.) The board, relying on the language of PC 2685 and the invocation of that order in PC 7440, delivered a unanimous report in favour of recognition, asserting that on the basis of the orders-in-council, "it is difficult to . . . find any authority for the proposition that an employer is to have any voice in selecting the employees' union, or other bargaining agency, or to impose any conditions of his own as to just what union or what type of union or bargaining agent he is prepared to bargain with. . . ." It had no illusion "that the recommendation is likely to be more than a mere formality," however:

> The employment of such a technique [the companies' withdrawal from the proceedings] together with the doubt as to jurisdiction under the Act [to deal with recognition problems] would seem to leave the broad question of collective bargaining to be dealt with by Parliament or Cabinet Council rather than by the old process of conciliation boards under the Industrial Disputes Investigation Act.[22]

The companies, predictably, did not accept the board's report. The union therefore applied for the supervised strike vote required by PC 7307. After another vain attempt by department officials to get the parties to agree, rules were drawn up for the conduct of the vote and approved by the union. The companies demanded some modifications, and two days before the vote was to be held the union was informed of the revised rules. These were completely unacceptable to the union. Among other things, *everyone* on the payroll except the president, management, and directors of each company were to be eligible to vote. Intense lobbying by union leaders and sympathizers from across Canada followed, and the day before the vote the provisions were modified to limit the constituency. On November 8, three and a half months after the first government conciliator had intervened in the dispute, the calling of a strike was approved by 63 per cent of those eligible (67 per cent of those voting).[23] Further formal and informal attempts at conciliation failed.

The strike began on the evening of November 18. After a bitter three-month fight, during which the government intervened yet again unsuccessfully to have the matter referred to binding arbitration (the workers turned down the proposal, fearing a revival of the employee committee plan), the union admitted complete failure on February 12, 1942, and those men that the company would accept returned to work. In the end, the lack of financial support and the knowledge that Ottawa would not use its leverage in support of recognition made it impossible for Local 240 to carry on. Delays resulting from the conciliation process meant that the strike had occurred during the harsh winter months, after the employers had much time to prepare, and this obviously contributed to the failure.

III

As was apparent in the Kirkland Lake dispute, informal attempts at conciliation often continued long after the conciliation board had brought down its report. Union leaders frequently encouraged this practice, either because they hoped that increased pressure by government would lead to more concessions, or because they realized that the area of disagreement had, through the negotiating process, become so narrow that the membership would be unwilling to bear the cost of a strike for the meagre potential gain. This post-conciliation-board intervention was usually sufficiently restrained that no resolution was achieved, the ultimate confrontation merely being delayed. Occasionally, however, when a strike appeared imminent in an industry of great importance to the war effort, the government did act more directly to influence the content of the negotiations in order to achieve a sure settlement.

Disputes between the Electro-Metallurgical Co. in Welland, Ontario, and Local 523 of the United Electrical, Radio and Machine Workers of America and the confrontation at three Montreal aircraft factories in 1944-45, provide good examples of the government's reliance on repeated attempts at conciliation to narrow the parties' differences while postponing a work stoppage. They also demonstrate some of the techniques Ottawa used to procure concessions.[24]

The Electro-Metallurgical dispute was officially brought to the department's attention in July, 1944, by the Ontario Labour Relations Board, which recommended the appointment of a conciliation officer. In accordance with the provisions of PC 1003, the union had referred the matter to the Labour Relations Board after negotiations had continued for more than thirty days without success. Industrial relations officer Harold Perkins was immediately dispatched to Welland to settle the dispute. He met with the parties, but no agreement was concluded, the matters at issue being the union's desire for a union shop (where membership in the union would be a condition of employment) and the check-off of union dues. A conciliation board was established, consisting of Alexander Brady as chair, a United Church minister as employee nominee, and lawyer J.S.D. Tory as employer representative. After investigating the dispute and attempting to achieve a settlement, the board was unable to come to a unanimous decision. The majority recommended that the union should drop its demand for a union shop, obtaining instead a maintenance-of-membership clause (so that once a worker became a union member, he would have to retain his membership until the end of the collective agreement) and a voluntary check-off provision, in which a member's choice of check-off would be irrevocable during the term of the collective agreement. The minority report, by the company nominee, opposed any form of union security, arguing that the union shop and compulsory check-off violated individual rights, and that the compromise proposals were not of any value in themselves, merely constituting the first steps in a movement toward complete union security.[25] The majority's recommendations were accepted by the union, but not by the company.

The board's reports were delivered in mid-November, 1944. By January, 1945, the union was demanding that the government force Electro-Metallurgical to comply with the award, threatening to strike if no settlement could be reached. The department concluded that more vigorous encouragement of the company was needed. On January 24, 1945, the following memo was sent by Assistant Director of Industrial Relations J.S. McCullagh to Deputy Minister of Labour Arthur MacNamara:

> Yesterday I endeavoured to reach Mr. Harry Taylor of Toronto, whose company controls Electro-Metallurgical. I had in mind suggesting to Mr. Taylor that if he would authorize the Company to institute a check-off, we might get the Union to drop, for the time being at least, the maintenance of membership demand, but if the Company refuses to make any concession, there is every indication of a strike which would undoubtedly be embarrassing to the Minister, being in his Constituency.

Taylor, however, refused to have the company change its policy without an express government directive on the point.

At this time, increased pressure was put on the union not to call a strike. MacNamara took the position that because the parties had signed a provisional agreement covering matters other than union security, a strike would be illegal under PC 1003. Representatives of the department attempted to persuade the union that maintenance-of-membership and the voluntary check-off were not worth striking over. The company sent a letter to the union claiming that "any action interfering with the vital war production of this plant in relation to this issue, would not only be illegal, but would also be grossly unpatriotic during the present war emergency."[26] Union members responded by asking their MP, the Minister of Labour, to intervene personally to settle the dispute. This led to another attempt at conciliation, this time by J.S. McCullagh. Early in February he met with the parties, proposing that instead of the check-off the company provide the union with facilities for collecting its own dues. He also won a further postponement of the strike to allow consideration of this proposal. A week later he was back in Welland attempting to get more concessions from the company, specifically a clear commitment from Electro-Metallurgical that it would pay the person responsible for collecting dues. Calling each party in turn, he tried to get them to modify their positions, advising the union in particular that it would be most unwise to strike over such a small issue. Finally, on February 13, 1945, fully seven months after the initial reference to the Ontario Labour Relations Board, a settlement was reached. Electro-Metallurgical's war production continued uninterrupted; the confrontation over union security was delayed until the summer of 1946, when a strike did occur.

In the Montreal dispute, the government did not rely so heavily on repeated instances of conciliation, but rather sought to manipulate the constitution and proceedings of the conciliation board itself in order to achieve a favourable result. This more intense involvement reflected the high priority the government gave to the production of aircraft during the war.

The dispute arose out of negotiations for a new collective agreement between three Montreal aircraft factories (Fairchild Aircraft Ltd., Noorduyn Aviation Ltd., and Canadian Vickers Ltd.) and Lodge 712 of the International Association of Machinists. A number of issues were in question, but the most contentious was the lodge's demand for a union shop and check-off. Negotiations between the parties failed to lead to a settlement, and in June, 1944, the union applied to the National Wartime Labour Relations Board for a conciliation officer. According to the agreement between Ottawa and Quebec regarding the administration of PC 1003, however, the union should have referred the matter to the Quebec Wartime Labour Relations Board, since the provincial boards had responsibility for ensuring that the requirements of PC 1003 were satisfied and for recommending that a conciliation officer be appointed. Mr. Justice G.B. O'Connor, chairman of the national board, therefore contacted M.M. Maclean to discuss whether the national board should insist that the normal procedure be followed. This, of course, would result in delay. After stating his desire not to offend the Quebec authorities and mentioning that the union would probably accept a postponement, O'Connor remarked: "Personally, I can see the advantage of delay because the War is drawing to a close and every day gained brings us nearer to the time when the demand for aircraft will be less vital." In the end, the Quebec board quickly gave its permission and a conciliation officer was appointed. Nevertheless, delay was to play an unusually large role in the proceedings before the board.[27]

The conciliation officer's intervention did not produce a settlement, and he recommended that a board be appointed. When the nominees of the parties failed to agree on a chair, Maclean, following normal practice, asked Mr. Justice Oscar Boulanger if he would be willing to participate and submitted the necessary documents to the minister for signature. The minister and his deputy, however, did not like the choice, apparently fearing that Boulanger would submit a report recommending too strong a union security clause. They therefore suggested that another chair be found, but this proved impracticable since Boulanger had already been informed that he would be appointed. The deputy minister then suggested that some way be found to restrict the board's consideration of union security, perhaps having it present an interim report on the other matters, deferring the union security discussions until after the decision had been rendered in a separate case involving Montreal Tramways (where the chairman was more to the minister's liking). This expedient was adopted (with the reluctant agreement of the union) and the board adjourned indefinitely.

The Montreal Tramways case, however, took longer than expected, and in November the Fairchild board asked if it could resume its own investigation. MacNamara wrote Maclean, "I should think Mr. Justice Belanger [sic] might proceed if we could find some way to tell him not to go farther than the agreement arranged with the packinghouse employees. I refer to the Union security clause resulting from Mr. Justice Richard's recent activity in Toronto." Boulanger was summoned to Ottawa for discussions with Maclean, but he refused to be bound by the Richards award and the board's adjournment was extended until January. By this time, the union was becoming most impatient with the delay (the board had not met since August), and it protested to the department. Finally, on January 24, 1945, Maclean authorized the board to go ahead. Majority and minority reports resulted, Boulanger agreeing with the employees' nominee that a particularly strong maintenance-of-membership clause be included in the agreement. The last item in the department's file dealing with the dispute is a memorandum from MacNamara to Maclean dated March 31, 1945, suggesting that if the recommendations were reasonable, the department should get Minister of Munitions and Supply C.D. Howe to put pressure on the aircraft companies to make the concessions necessary to secure an agreement.[28]

IV

Boards were often unsure whether they should attempt to adjudicate disputes or simply find some workable settlement between the parties. From the department's propensity to continue to seek compromise after a board had reported, it might appear that the government looked on the appointment of a board as essentially another step in a long process of conciliation. Certainly the government did not feel bound by any authoritative force in the board's decision. Indeed, its manipulation of the board in the

Fairchild dispute would indicate that the whole process was perceived to be merely a useful tool for levering the parties closer together. Conciliation probably was the dominant role of the officers and boards: of the 124 applications for conciliation under PC 1003 that had been completely dealt with by July 1, 1945, fifty had been settled by conciliation officers and twelve by boards. Adjudication did not appear to be terribly effective at resolving disputes: of the sixty-two cases in which a settlement had not been reached prior to the board's report, forty-eight remained unsettled on July 1. Yet to dismiss out of hand the adjudicative role would be to ignore a major facet of the boards' activity. They were a schizophrenic institution, pulled between mediation and judgement, and often the latter approach predominated, especially in the minds of the board members themselves.[29]

Ore can see the influence of the adjudicative conception of the board's role in the emphasis on the need for the parties' nominees to behave with some impartiality,[30] in the increasing use of board decisions as precedents,[31] in the unions' frequent demands that awards be enforced, in the legalistic arguments occasionally dealt with by boards,[32] and in the department's readiness to take down a written record of the proceedings if the circumstances warranted.[33] Maclean's response to MacNamara when the latter succumbed to the malaise of compulsory conciliation and labelled the appointment of a board "a waste - of time - money and effort" also indicated an appreciation for the board's judicial function. Maclean said:

> Even though at the moment it might appear in some of these cases where we are now establishing Boards of Conciliation that there is a waste of time, effort and money, I think that in the long-run it will be helpful and even necessary in order that there may be a body of opinion built up as a result of decisions of Boards which will set the pattern for both employers and unions on the union security issue.[34]

These two notions of the boards' role sometimes came into direct conflict. One case that clearly illustrated the tension between the boards' adjudicative and conciliatory roles was the 1944 dispute concerning Okanagan Valley packinghouse workers.[35]

This dispute, between Locals 1, 3, 4, 5, 6, 7, and 8 of the Fruit and Vegetable Workers Union and sixteen of twenty-eight packinghouses in the Okanagan Valley of British Columbia, arose out of negotiations for a second collective agreement between the parties. The chief issue was the union's demand for a union shop and check-off. It differed from many wartime disputes in that it occurred in a conservative, agricultural region of the country among workers whose numbers were subject to great seasonal fluctuations (there were 111 permanent and 2,195 seasonal employees in the plants directly affected). A great deal of attention was focused on the conciliation board's proceedings because of the fruit growers' fear of the impact of union power on their volatile industry, and because of the union's desire to achieve a victory in this new organizational terrain.

A conciliation board was appointed in mid-October, 1944, consisting of W.E. Haskins as the employers' nominee, B.G. Webber as the employees' nominee, and Dean F.M. Clement of the UBC faculty of agriculture as chairman. Because of the "wide ramifications" of the dispute, the regional director of the Canadian Congress of Labour, Danny O'Brien, asked that a written record be kept of the hearings. The employees' nominee and the chairman concurred in this request and, upon the department's approval, a stenographer was hired. From the beginning, then, the hearings took on a judicial appearance, the parties looking on the process as a means of creating new industrial norms.

The board in the Okanagan case sat for an unusually long time – sixteen days – but was unable either to achieve a settlement or to agree among themselves on a suitable solution. Haskins and Clement recommended that the existing agreement simply continue in effect, with no union security clause at all; Webber, on the other hand, suggested that permanent and seasonal employees who worked more than thirty days per year be subject to a union shop and check-off and that the parties agree not to strike or lock out during the term of the collective agreement. But the board's conclusions were not as straightforward as they appeared. During the course of the hearings, Clement had written to Maclean asking that the latter send him a copy of the Richards award in the Toronto meatpacking case (the same report that was recommended to Boulanger in the Fairchild Aircraft dispute). Then, when the Okanagan board's reports were delivered to the department, Clement, without informing the parties' nominees, sent along what amounted to a third report (marked "not for publication") suggesting a compromise along the lines of the Richards award (voluntary check-off, maintenance-of-member-ship, and a "no strike/no lock-out" clause). He prefaced his suggestions with the remarks:

The majority report [which Clement signed] is, in my opinion, a fair one. It is based on the evidence submitted. I think the Board has carefully weighed the various practical considerations.

There is, however [,] a question of principle that cannot be overlooked. Having in mind the question of principle and a consequent desire to arrive at some compromise solution about midway between the two extremes, the following suggestions were offered: . . .

The schizophrenic nature of the board had resulted in a schizophrenic report: the adjudicative function was completely separated from that of conciliation, Clement proposing one set of recommendations for public consumption and precedential value, but suggesting another set for resolving the actual case at hand.[36]

The dispute in the packinghouses remained unsettled. Consequently, in February, 1945, O'Brien approached the B.C. Minister of Labour to say that a strike vote was being contemplated and to request more conciliation. At the same meeting, he criticized the parties' nominees on the board for being too reluctant to compromise (although there is evidence that, on the contrary, the employee nominee had attempted to secure a settlement and that at that time O'Brien had rebuked him for departing from the union's position). Apparently, the union had decided it did not want a strike in the Okanagan and preferred a compromise along the lines of Clement's suggestions rather than no union security at all. The B.C. minister therefore requested that the board be reconvened for "amplification" of the report; on March 2, 1945, Maclean complied with this request. The board only met once, however. Clement believed that an agreement might be reached more quickly if he conciliated the dispute on his own. Intensive negotiations with the parties did indeed lead to a settlement. The agreement was very similar to the Richards award, containing a voluntary check-off, irrevocable by the member for the duration of the collective agreement, and a maintenance-of-membership clause.[37]

V

Boards frequently were required to pass judgement on the merits of disputes, but on what principles did they base their decisions? Governments were reluctant to establish authoritative standards by which labour disputes could be resolved. The union/management relationship itself did not produce many commonly accepted principles of industrial conduct. And despite the sanguine hopes of many, the long history of conciliation in Canada had contributed very slowly, if at all, to the formulation of such norms. Only rarely was an adjudicator able to break out of these confinements to find a solution that met the chief concerns of both parties. A stunning example of such an award was that of Mr. Justice Rand in the 1945-46 Ford arbitration. In a dispute over the union's demand for a union shop and check-off, Rand ordered that all workers in the plant pay union dues (to be deducted by the employer and remitted to the union), but that membership in the union be optional. This new form of union security, known as the "Rand formula," was extraordinarily successful, serving as a durable precedent in subsequent disputes. Its genius lay in its ability to satisfy the most forceful arguments of both parties: individual liberty was protected, the problem of free riders averted.[38]

But the Rand award was the exception that proved the rule. By and large, boards were unable to find principles satisfactory to both parties, and they therefore looked to outside sources for direction. The most obvious and authoritative source was the series of orders-in-council passed by the federal cabinet, especially PC 2685 and PC 1003. Several boards began to probe the nature of collective bargaining in order to derive solutions to particular disputes. In the 1944-45 conciliation concerning the Upper Canada Mines in Kirkland Lake, one of the government's favourite chairmen, Cecil A. Wright, stated the problem and his preferred solution as follows:

> With the legislative policy of leaving disputes over such issues as "union security" to Conciliation Boards whose recommendations have no effective sanction and for whose guidance on such matters no governmental policy has been laid down, we are not concerned. Much the same situation prevailed at the time when Boards were left to settle disputes by recommending the recognition of unions as bargaining agencies, even though, after June, 1940, PC 2685 may be said to have furnished some guide in this connection. In such circumstances a Board can only act on what it believes to be reasonable on the particular facts taking into account what it believes to be the broad – if vague – implications of compulsory collective bargaining legislation which was designed to prevent disputes ripening into more active industrial warfare.[39]

The implications were indeed vague, judging from the variety of principles deduced by boards. For example, in the John Inglis dispute of 1944, the majority report came up with clearly defined principles. First, it reasoned that the acquisition of different types of union security "can much increase the power for doing good by the right kind of Union, while it correspondingly increases the power for evil of the wrong kind of Union." It was obvious that the former should be encouraged and the latter discouraged, so the board proceeded to define the ideal union: "A Union vigilant in protecting its members from injustice, sincerely concerned in advancing the interests of the industry which affords employment to its members, and at least not unmindful of the welfare of the consuming public on whom the industry depends." The performance of the actual union was then compared to this ideal type, and the amount of union security gauged accordingly.[40] In another dispute, the employee nominee explained in a "supplementary report" his agreement with the board's decision to deny the union's demand for a voluntary, revocable check-off as follows:

> While I regard the check-off as an aid to union stability, which is important to good collective bargaining, I do not think that it should be made the means of initiating that stability, saving perhaps cases where it appears that an employer's unfair labour practices have prevented a union from establishing itself on a solid footing.[41]

Apparently, in this board member's view, compulsory collective bargaining legislation merely established unions' right to recognition and freedom from unfair labour practices; any other form of union security had to be won by the union in the economic contest with the employer. As if to emphasize the indistinct nature of collective bargaining's implications, the majority of the board in the Electro-Metallurgical dispute fastened on the bare necessity of compromise to justify its award. It declared:

> ... as is often the case where collective bargaining is of relatively short duration, the element of fear is the cause of the present disagreement. . . . There is plainly no remedy for this condition of mutual fear except a frank readiness of both parties to place more trust in each other. Such trust may be expressed in and promoted by a moderation of the demands made, and a readiness on the other side to accept the moderated demands.

Genuine collective bargaining, in consonance with the essential principles of a democratic state, must reflect a spirit of give and take. It is obvious that it can grow sturdy and effective only where compromise is present. It must seek agreement with the minimum of mutual irritation. To this type of collective bargaining there is little alternative except harsh industrial struggle or a highly rigid prescription of industrial relationships by the state, under which both employers and employees would lose much of their present free decision.[42]

All these expressions of principle did little to provide unambiguous standards for future decision-making. Without a clear expression of governmental policy or a social consensus to support them, any concrete recommendations appeared to be merely the personal opinions of individual board members. It is not surprising, however, that universal norms were slow to emerge. The fundamental assumption of conciliation and collective bargaining was that the parties themselves were best able, through negotiation, to determine their own relationship. The terms and conditions of work were *ex hypothesi* not a matter of moral judgement, but of contract.

VI

Compulsory conciliation was, above all, a flexible institution. It could serve many different roles, depending on the objective of the government and the initiative of the board members (especially the chair). Most often, it promoted the mediation of disputes, the boards and officers striving, as Alexander Brady or Cecil A. Wright did, to find some workable compromise between the parties. When no such compromise emerged, however, or when from the first a board perceived itself to be essentially a judicial tribunal, conciliation boards did adjudicate the dispute, ruling on the justice of the parties' demands. Although these decisions seldom led directly to a settlement, they could serve to legitimize governmental pressure on the parties to make concessions, or serve as precedents in subsequent decisions. In addition, boards occasionally acted as administrative bodies, implementing, sometimes in a surreptitious manner, governmental policy (as in Ottawa's attempted manipulation of the Fairchild Aircraft board, or the promotion of wage guidelines through PC 7440). Finally, compulsory conciliation could be used as a mechanism of delay, merely postponing work stoppages.

From its inception, compulsory conciliation's chief purpose was the prevention of strikes. The most certain method of doing this was to get the parties to come to an agreement. Mediation, with its informal, confidential, probing method, was useful for finding the elusive compromise. Direct governmental pressure was sometimes applied as an aid to this tool, extracting concessions from reluctant parties. Adjudication could also promote agreements in several ways: the mere threat of a public report on the causes of the dispute could induce compromise; the report itself might have sufficient authority to be accepted; the award might serve as the justification for more forceful governmental intervention; or the adjudicators' solution could serve to reinforce one party's position in subsequent negotiations. In the absence of strong governmental action, however, the attainment of an agreement without a strike always depended on the possibility of compromise. If the parties were so committed to their particular positions that neither was prepared to budge, conciliation would be unavailing; the threat or use of economic force alone would solve the difficulty. The statutory form of compulsory conciliation reflected these considerations. The regime postponed strikes in order to allow third-party intervention a chance to succeed. There was ample provision for conciliation by both officers and boards. Only if a negotiated settlement could not be reached would a board make a formal recommendation. Adjudication served as the method of last resort to induce a settlement; if it failed, the resolution of the difficulty was left to the threat or application of economic coercion.

During World War II, however, the government departed from this formula. It wished to prevent all strikes, even those after the normal conciliation procedures, yet at the same time it was reluctant to compel concessions from unwilling parties or legislate standards of industrial conduct. It therefore attempted to prevent or at least delay strikes by extending the conciliation process beyond the adjudicative stage. This had several consequences: (1) with no finality to the conciliation process, the pressure to make concessions was reduced and, as a result, negotiations tended to stretch out over long periods; (2) the authority of board decisions was undermined, the reports coming to be treated merely as additional opinions on what might be suitable settlements; (3) disputes lacking the necessary prerequisite of conciliation – the possibility of compromise – remained subject to a conciliatory process long after it became clear that the disagreements would only be resolved by job action; (4) Ottawa's attempts to postpone strikes through conciliation prompted demands that it intervene more forcefully to remove the cause of disputes, and although the government was thus seen as the body responsible for attaining industrial peace, it refused to take the steps necessary to prevent strikes; (5) the promotion of delay when there was no reasonable hope of attaining a compromise prejudiced the interests of employees, for the employer had more time to prepare for the strike, and during the negotiations the employees remained subject to the old working conditions.

From these drawbacks resulted the malaise of compulsory conciliation: the sense of acute frustration caused by prolonged involvement in a process that aimed at achieving settlements but that so often failed to secure forceful resolutions. It is true that frustration is, to a certain extent, endemic to any labour dispute that approaches the stage of a work stoppage: no one wants to strike or lock out, yet it is often hard to make the compromises necessary to secure an agreement. Indeed, in collective bargaining generally there exists a tension between the sometimes violently opposing attitudes of the parties and the need to achieve a *modus vivendi* for mutual benefit. Ordinarily, this tension, when it becomes too great, is relieved by the catharsis of a strike. During World War II, Ottawa's strong opposition to work stoppages restricted this method of release, generating more frustration, focusing dissatisfaction on the government itself, and structuring the character of class struggle in new directions.

7

Feminism at Work

Heather Jon Maroney

In Canada, as elsewhere in the advanced capitalist world, fifteen years of ideological and cultural struggle have resulted in the diffusion of the vital sense that women have rights and will not be bound by convention, prejudice, or male privilege.[1] In any contemporary evaluation, however, it must be recognized that the present women's movement differs markedly from that of the sixties. In Canada, two developments are particularly significant. A recent successful campaign to include equal rights for women in the Canadian constitution has strengthened liberal feminism and its orientation to the state. But since the mid-seventies, a radicalization of working women – most immediately visible in several important public- and private-sector strikes – has profoundly altered the organizational and ideological balance of forces within the women's movement as a whole. It is this latter development that forms the substance of this essay.

By the end of the seventies, working-class feminism in Canada had become a distinct current in the women's movement. In contrast to the university-based feminism of the sixties, it was rooted in the workplace and oriented, first of all, to the practical achievement of more concrete and, hence, more limited goals. It had its own outlook on what feminism should be:

Of course jobs are a feminist issue: and equal pay and training. Getting women into non-traditional jobs is important right now, because of what will happen with tech change. Of course, in my union when they think they're getting down to the nitty-gritty real feminist issues, the men always ask "How's the day care in your town?" – the whole motherhood thing. They don't want to talk about sexual harassment or anything to do with sex. After all, it's not just cross-class, it's workers harassing workers. But unions give you power, and they educate you. It's the only way to unite the working class, through unions and working together.[2]

Underlying the development of working-class feminism are dramatic increases in labour-force participation during the 1950's and 1960's for women over twenty-five with children. Women have risen from 17 per cent of membership in trade unions in 1966 to 27 per cent in 1976.[3] Although the most important single contribution to this increase in unionization was a top-down legislative conversion of provincial and federal staff associations into unions in a rapidly expanding public sector, women workers' readiness to unionize and their militancy in strikes testify to a consciousness that wage work is no longer an episode before marriage and child-raising but a permanent feature of their lives, a recognition that is a crucial component of proletarian consciousness. In these recently formed Canadian public-sector unions of clerical and service workers, the combination of a relatively weak bureaucracy and a majority female membership has facilitated the entry and expression of feminist consciousness. As governments have sought to resolve their fiscal crisis through rationalization, semi-professionals like teachers and nurses have met increasingly proletarianized working conditions, pay restraints, and job insecurity, have moved away from corporatist associations or professional aspirations, and have affiliated to trade unions in great numbers. Despite their conservative and sometimes confessional origins, public-sector unions, particularly those in the Quebec Common Front, have proved to be both militant and relatively open to women's demands. In some cases, women teachers and nurses, traditionally ruled by an ethic of service and self-sacrifice, have raised explicitly feminist demands in contract negotiations.[4]

Two other developments have begun to bring more women into the trade union orbit and, this time, into the male-dominated heavy industrial unions. First, the entry of women into non-traditional jobs in steel, mining, rail, manufacturing, and forest products has been the focus of widespread propaganda by both government and labour, making a greater political impact than the restricted numbers of women would seem to warrant. For government, affirmative action promised a trendy, low-cost alternative to the enactment and enforcement of rigorous equal value legislation; selective promotion of a few both promotes individualism and serves the interests of formally qualified professional and managerial women.[5] Government publicity and human rights provisions notwithstanding, campaigns by coalitions of unions, socialist feminists, and job-seekers have been necessary to overcome actual employer barriers against female applicants.[6]

If, in this first instance, women have come into unions, in the second, the large industrial unions (especially United Steel Workers of America and United Auto Workers) have turned to women. With recession-induced instability and shrinking employment in the manufacturing sector, unions, forced to find new ways to secure a membership base, have supported organizing drives in small plants or have moved to sign up clerical and service workers (at Blue Cross, Fotomat, in legal aid, and so on). Taken together, these developments imply the numerical feminization of the centres of male working-class power and of the labour movement as a whole. These inroads are fragile, however, as layoffs reduce or eliminate the numbers of women machinists, miners, and smelter workers.

In established unions, trade union feminists, often on staff, have set up or given new political life to official union committees on the status of women, have worked for women's caucuses, and have animated unofficial cross-union formations - such as Organized Working Women (Ontario) - as a base to agitate against sexism. Highly developed caucuses leading to committees first appeared in Quebec, where they had led several campaigns: for equal pay legislation; for maternity and parental leave; against sexism in the schools; for women's liberation reports and resolutions that, in line with the "ideological" character of the Centrale des Syndicats Nationaux and the Centrale des Enseignants du Québec, go far beyond work-force equality to call for abortion rights and the socialization of housework; and to criticize marriage as an oppressive institution.[7] Across Canada, their success has been marked by the establishment of equal rights committees in all the provincial labour federations, the establishment of the Canadian Labour Congress (CLC) women's conferences, and rapid and dramatic changes in policy. Although the Quebec federation's concern with the global aspects of "la condition féminine" is exceptional, many unions now have the essential elements of a program for workplace equality through economic and social measures; equal value demands; across-the-board rather than percentage wage increases; affirmative action; day care; and parental leave for childbirth, adoption, or abortion.

Despite the advance represented by the institutionalization of these committees, the intersecting structures of sexism and bureaucratic power in the labour movement replicate and thus serve to reproduce prevailing gender structures. Even where the membership is predominantly female, women are consistently underrepresented in governing bodies and feminist forces are weak in relation to an entrenched male leadership. Although their paucity can be partially explained by the difficulties for women of adding a third set of union responsibilities to their double day of paid and domestic labour,[8] the independent effect of sexism must be taken into account. While the commentators in "Women and Trade Unions"[9] recognize that many men in unions are supportive of, if sometimes confused by, women's attempts to redefine gender boundaries, they nevertheless point with remarkable consistency to sexism on the part of male workers, women's internalization of stereotyped behaviour, "business unionism," and bureaucratic control as blocks to female participation.[10] Since the current leadership was politically and ideologically formed during the post-war defeat of feminism (and, incidentally, of the left), it owes its position at least in part to male privilege.[11] To put the question sharply, immediately equalizing women's representation in union power structures would require either that some male power brokers lose their positions of financial and sexual privilege or, an unlikely alternative, that the number of such positions be almost doubled to accommodate women. Thus the question of representativeness in general is raised by women's demands for equality. In the rank and file as well, a pro-woman economic program has sometimes generated conflict between male and female workers.[12] Even if political education tends to homogenize the ideology of trade union *activists*, convention resolutions do not necessarily represent the views of the membership. As recently as 1971, many Quebec unionists still thought that men had a prior right to jobs and that women should, in any case, stay at home, union policy to the contrary.[13] Even allowing for economically irrational employer resistance, so-called "women's issues" such as day care, rights and benefits for part-time workers, and maternity leave seem sometimes to have been included in contract demands merely as bargaining points to be traded off.[14]

The resources of unions, never elastic, are particularly stretched by basic defensive tasks in the current recession, whether because of loss of membership from layoffs or intense strike activity. In this situation, continuing pressure from rank-and-file and more particularly women's caucuses is necessary to ensure that social concerns are taken up by the union.[15] In this regard, trade union feminism has passed through two stages of development. Having taken the first consciousness-raising and mobilizing step, it has gone on to formulate claims *from the point of view of women* as a special group: the right to work, equal pay, and so on. In agitating for the acceptance of these demands, women have sometimes breached gendered ghetto walls and created a class demand supported equally by, and understood to be in the interests of, women and men – again, equal pay is the classic case in point.

But at no point has feminism reformed the institutionalized forms of politics – bureaucratic by some accounts, patriarchal by others – that cyclically alienate women and impede their participation.[16] Formal norms of political procedure, for example, can be manipulated to define *what can be heard*, to block rank-and-file initiatives, or to reinforce existing ideology. That bureaucratic responses are not limited to male power brokers but ingrained in union functions was shown at the 1980 CLC Women's Conference, where a proposal from the floor for plenary discussions and time to evaluate the conference was blocked by the chair, a president of a national public-sector union and a noted feminist; militancy was not stressed, and the discussion of how to acquire power was limited to lobbying.[17] Thus, only a certain range of feminist complaint and militancy can be taken account of and women who have not yet learned the ropes (or those who go too far) are ruled out of court. Lest this process be thought of as simply one of self-censorship or internalized submissiveness on the part of women, it should be emphasized that "ruling out" not only takes place from the chair of conventions but is often backed up in private life. On balance, trade unions provide organizational continuity, material resources, and an established constituency in contrast with the more ephemeral, poorer, yet creative, self-directed, and consciously holistic structures of the autonomous women's movement. Nevertheless, formal democratic norms have provided a means for trade union feminists to take advantage of the political and ideological space created by general feminist agitation, whether that be as a result of real sensitivity to women's needs or merely to their explosiveness.

Trade union feminists are caught in a contradictory situation.

Their position inside the labour movement is vulnerable and their room to manoeuvre depends on the extent of feminist radicalization and trade union miltancy of women in the rank and file – which, in turn, exists in a complex relation with general feminist and class mobilization. In isolation, trade union feminists, especially union staff, are not only subject to the usual pressures of bureaucratic and reformist integration of normalized union practice, but must also bear the brunt of sexism inside the unions. On their other side, feminist peers outside the labour movement often expect that a maximal program for women's liberation can and should be propagated without modification in the trade union arena and that any failure to do so amounts to a sell-out of women's interests. The task has been complicated by the existence of real resistance among rank-and-file women (let alone men) to sexual and cultural issues "expressed in feminist jargon" – particularly to abortion and lesbian rights. The resources that have been available to staff women have been far from adequate to carry out general consciousness-raising programs on these questions (or even on basic trade unionism) among the workers whose interests they are supposed to represent. And, although their position allows them to speak with the political weight of the trade unions in the broader women's movement, what they say is restricted by the ideological horizon of the constituency that they represent. Overall, they must mediate between the feminist movement, including its working-class component, and working-class sexism and sexual oppression.

A second grouping of trade union organizers located mainly in British Columbia has adopted a feminist-syndicalist approach by attempting to construct exemplary independent unions in female-dominated industries – for example, the Service, Office and Retail Workers Union of Canada (SORWUC) among restaurant, office, and bank workers, and the Association of University and College Employees (AUCE), both formed in 1972. The initial success of their organizing drives demonstrated how lessons derived from sixties women's organizing – small group consciousness-raising, a stress on democratic, anti-hierarchical principles, and feminist policies of day care, equal pay, and promotion – could be applied to the class ends of union solidarity. In the process, they disproved the contention of male-dominated trade unions that service and clerical workers were too difficult to organize.[18] Relying on support from women's groups, the New Democratic Party, and CLC and Congress of Canadian Unions (CCU) locals and members for long-term leaflet campaigns and essential financial support during strikes, feminist-syndicalist organizers urged women workers to unionize (along with men) not just for economic defence but to combat their special exploitation in the labour market as women.

Since 1978, however, the limitations of feminist syndicalism have become clear. First, employer resistance in the banking sector successfully used both threats and co-optation to limit the union drive.[19] In the face of what turns out to have been a tactical error in deciding to organize on a branch-by-branch basis, coupled with a financial inability to gain first contracts in certified locals and to carry cases through the Canadian Labour Relations Board, most of the bank locals were decertified, the United Bank Workers dissolved, and several hundred women left without union protection. Second, SORWUC, unable to mobilize adequate support from outside the CLC and unwilling to "compromise" its democratic constitution as the price of entry for CLC power, eventually split on the question of integration into the central, with those opposed to the move bitter about what they saw as raiding by rival (and johnny-come-lately) CLC affiliates. Faced with similar financial and political weaknesses, the AUCE has voted to lobby the CLC for admission as an independent union in order to protect the democratic and feminist aspects of its constitution. In evaluating their tactics in British Columbia, we have to weigh organizing skills, willingness to organize small work units, and a capacity to create union organizers out of women workers against a purist reaction against "big" unionism. Some of SORWUC's financial weaknesses may be offset by its adhesion to the CCU, which is largely based in British Columbia, but it still remains in opposition to the CLC and, thus, isolated from the largest female-dominated public-sector unions.

In addition to feminists working within union structures or struggling to set up feminist unions, working-class feminism has also arisen in the course of strikes. Two strikes in Ontario – at the Fleck plant near Exeter in 1978 and at the International Nickel Company at Sudbury in 1979 – illustrated spectacularly how feminism among working-class women strengthens economic struggles and how their mobilization can have an important political impact on the women's movement.

At Fleck, an automobile parts plant, a newly certified UAW local composed overwhelmingly of women struck for a first contract and over wages, union security, and working conditions.

As the strike dragged on for months it took on an increasingly class-political tone as a battle about the right to unionize. The UAW, the parent union, rallied to its support with plant-gate collections and busloads of mostly male workers for mass picketing. At the same time, it became a test case for feminism, and socialist feminists in particular saw it in these terms. The general potential for radicalization in the interplay of class and feminist forces was manifested in this strike. By its very nature, a strike situation is an intensive consciousness-raising process. With work rhythms disrupted, the opportunity and the necessity to think collectively and strategically break through the fatigue, political passivity, and mystification of normal production. Militant strike action by women is also an objective challenge to their economic exploitation, their individuation into the illusory privacy of the family, and the ideological construction of women as passive dependants protected by men, which is at the core of women's place in the contemporary capitalist sexual division of labour. At Fleck, the strikers explicitly articulated this challenge. They attributed management and police harassment to a complacent assumption that they would be easily intimidated because they were women; instead, maintaining that men would not have been able to hold out so long, they saw their own capacity to resist arising from their *solidarity as women*. By mobilizing union women's committees and groups from the autonomous women's movement for picket-line and financial support, trade union feminists brought a feminist perspective to the strike and, more importantly, legitimated "the women's movement" in the eyes of the strikers (and other unionists), at the same time as non-union feminists were given a deeper understanding of class conflict. Finally, the Fleck strike shows the importance in such radicalization of the interplay between "spontaneous" struggle and conscious intervention "from the outside." As well as the crucial role played by trade union and other feminists in this regard, some journalists also brought a feminist concern to their investigation and reporting of the strike, eliciting the strikers' responses to their situation as women and playing back through the media an ideologically more sophisticated version of the strikers' own feminism.

Historically, the Fleck strike helped to popularize a militant feminist ideology. The intensity of the struggle, and the determination and sharpness with which sex and class lines were drawn, gave it the kind of drama that makes news. The strikers' individual and collective courage, conviction, and humour caught the imagination of people well beyond the organized labour and women's movements. They became popular working-class heroines with a message that captured the essence of working-class feminist ideology: women have the right to work; wages are a woman's concern; unionization is a basic weapon; women can find strength from one another in struggle. For feminist strategy, the lesson that they confirmed was that, given the right political conditions, self-organization in struggle will radicalize, mobilize, and broaden feminist consciousness and action.

If the Fleck strike showed the radicalization of women at the point of production, then the strike in Sudbury against INCO demonstrated a different possibility: the role of class-conscious feminism in promoting solidarity between the union and the community. During a previous strike in 1958, a mass meeting of "wives" had been manipulated to make it appear that they were in favour of immediate and unfavourable settlement. In 1979, however, partly at the initiative of members of a local women's centre, a women's committee, "Wives supporting the strike," was formed to counter the reputation and repetition of 1958. Mobilizing the power of women in the community and including aspects of normally private "domestic" work (children's clothing, Christmas parties, layettes, community suppers) in an overall program of strike defence partially overcame the structural split in the working-class community between wage-work and housework, which is expressed as conflict between women and men. But the resolution was not complete. With the mobilization of women, new conflicts were generated. From the power base of the wives' committee, some women pressed, against union opposition, for a greater voice in the direction of the whole strike. An important political issue was thus posed: what should the relation of wives' committees be to strike steering committees when both women and men are dependent on wages and men's working conditions indirectly affect women's household work? Family and marriage relations were affected by the partial sublimation of gender conflict. A preliminary study[20] indicates that, despite the added tensions of economic hardship, family relations were considered to be more satisfactory when men spent more time in the household. Some of the readjustments were precarious, with men pressuring their wives back into the kitchen after the strike. After some initial compliance, however, many women have sought part-time work and become reactivated in local women's committees.[21]

The Sudbury strike thus raised the link between class and

feminist demands, connected via socialist commitments. At present, working-class and socialist feminists together form a strategically located, mutually dependent, but functionally differentiated nucleus for a class-conscious current in the autonomous women's movement. Although trade union feminists are the critical links for this nucleus, they have not been an independent leadership for the women's movement as a whole. Socialist feminists have effectively supported working women's struggles, single-issue and national campaigns (most notably the promotion of International Women's Day as a unitary day of protest and celebration),[22] have contributed to the development of theory, strategy, and ideology, and have consistently sought to play a leadership role for both class-conscious and other feminist forces. But they have little permanent organization, no co-ordination at the level of the Canadian state, and no publication. There are also tensions in the current's whole development, and its homogeneity should not be overestimated. Only in British Columbia and Saskatchewan have there been province-wide organizations that included both unionized and non-unionized women. In other centres in Ontario, city-wide socialist-feminist organizations exist. Even on IWD, the day of symbolic unity, political differences have developed over the relative weight to give demands for abortion rights and maternity leave or how to present demands for lesbian rights. As well as contradictory evaluations of the political impact of these issues by organizers, these disagreements reflect the unevenness of political development of the constituencies involved. For, if trade union feminists are caught between the differing expectations of the bureaucracy and the rank and file, socialist feminists, lesbian and straight, are similarly placed in a conflicting relation with labour and other feminist and socialist currents. Through such activities, trade unionists have come to a greater awareness of non-economic aspects of feminism and have, in turn, become leaders able and willing to defend these issues to other women. At a recent IWD, two women from Fleck were talking about the Lesbian Organization of Toronto whose presence was signalled by banners, picket signs, and buttons. While one was uneasy about the presence of "all those lesbians," her friend responded, "Well, that's the women's movement, and you'll just have to get used to it."

The popularization of feminist analyses of sexuality, rape, and violence has set the stage for the class transformation of earlier concerns with sexual objectification. Sexual harassment on the job has come to be considered a major women's issue in the labour movement. Unlike other women's issues (such as day care, maternity leave, equal pay), sexual harassment focuses directly on sexuality and on the antagonism that pits women, individually and collectively, *against men as agents of their oppression*. Since women are harassed not just across class lines by men in supervisory positions but also by fellow workers, this issue is potentially explosive inside the working class.

Although, strictly speaking, sexual harassment is a feminist issue of sexual politics, it has a class dimension as well. "Quid pro quo" harassment by a supervisor tells women that they hold their jobs only at their bosses' pleasure, reinforcing both class and gender subordination. Although supervisors are also implicated, the more prevalent form, "harassment as a condition of work," is in large part carried out by co-workers through unremitting comment on a woman's appearance, sexual activities, and desires – real or fantasied – often in a joking manner that men aver as "harmless" and even flattering to women.[23] Such statements assert that a woman's sexuality is not hers alone but an aspect of her public personality that belongs by right to any man who wishes to appropriate it through comment.

The direct result of sexual harassment is to keep women in line (in culturally specified places and ways) or to keep them out of where they are not supposed to be. In the labour force, sexual harassment strengthens both vertical hierarchy and horizontal divisions to maintain women in their traditionally inferior position. It is the intimate way in which working-class men police their privileged position in the labour force and let women know they are transgressors on male territory, particularly when they enter non-traditional jobs. Culturally sexist attitudes and behaviour also prevent women's full participation in unions: feminist activists in particular are attacked as "lesbians" and their clothing is scrutinized. Even if all men do not harass or support harassment by silence, its pervasiveness cautions women against trusting men. Structurally, sexual harassment pits all men against all women at the same time as it makes working-class women the target of cross-class sexism. The net result is to reinforce male solidarity across class lines, to blur class divisions through working-class sexism, to fragment the solidarity of a working class that has two sexes, and to reinforce class domination.

More than just equalizing the division of mundane tasks, the generalization of feminist consciousness in the working class requires breaking through the psychological barriers of prevailing gender types and adopting liberated norms. All aspects of femininity and masculinity, including sexuality, must be reformed if women, men, and the relations between them are to change. To fear feminism is also to neglect the countervailing forces of class solidarity – whether from shared experience of economic struggle or the ties of kinship and community – that bind women and men alike into class.

As a result of the radicalization of women workers that I have described here, the women's movement in Canada has reached a turning point. The possibility has opened up for a decisive expansion of "second-wave" feminism's social base, and at the same time the opportunity has been uniquely created for a fusion between the two modes of social opposition, cultural on the one hand, class-based on the other, which normally traverse the contradictory universe of advanced capitalism in mutual isolation. The turn, however, to a class-conscious feminism has not been made by the movement as a whole; nor, correlatively, has working-class feminism articulated the full range of programmatic concerns that sixties feminism itself placed on the historical agenda.

The price of not completing the turn is the continued dominance of liberal feminism and the exclusion of socialist feminism from mainstream political debate. Actually, the most anodyne forms of state-sponsored feminism, or radical feminist ideology wedded to reformist tactics, have succeeded in presenting themselves as feminism *tout court*. Socialist feminists were uninterested or in disarray at the time of the discussion on the constitution in 1982, while better-organized liberal feminists successfully lobbied for the inclusion of an equal rights plank in the Bill of Rights. This achievement should not be discounted; it succeeded where the more protracted efforts of the U.S. pro-ERA (Equal Rights Amendment) lobby failed. However, despite its popular resonance, it made only a limited appeal for equality within the juridical-political framework of the capitalist economy and state. An opportunity was missed to campaign for constitutional guarantees for reproductive freedom, the rights to equal work, pay, unionization, self-determination for national minorities, freedom of sexual orientation, and basic economic security for children as important prerequisites for women's equality, particularly for oppressed minorities, and to point out the role of the state in reproducing gender-stratified class hierarchies. Even more recently, liberal and radical feminists and politicians at all levels of government have

joined together with Christian fundamentalists in an anti-
pornography campaign that, because it offers state censorship
as a solution, has a practical appeal for many people partially
radicalized by feminist critiques of sexual exploitation and harassment. These developments have helped to legitimate the Canadian
state as amenable to women's issues and to align the politics
of sexuality on the right.

A starting point for the necessary work of correction is to realize
that the women's movement of the sixties was ideologically limited
by its restricted social base – specifically the absence of significant
numbers of working-class and unionized women. If its analysis
of culture and sexuality was strong, its understanding of the state
and class politics was not. Formulated as a call to "smash the
family," feminist analysis could not explain why working-class
women as well as men have fought to defend the possibility of
family life. Thus, sixties theory, produced by a particular contradictory dynamic of class and sex struggle, was often age- or
class-biased and too abstract to serve as a basis for policy
formation. All the same, it *did* contain crucial insights not easily
available to working-class activists.

Workplace struggles do not generate an insistence on the
positively liberating aspects of eroticism or on the need to challenge
the family as an institution. On the contrary, as contemporary
capitalist developments undermine family stability, and as the
fallout from the "disco-*Goodbar*" commodification of sexuality
and from rising rates of social violence produces a climate of
fear and uncertainty, one reaction is to defend it. But defensive
responses to maintain the illusory privacy of individual family
life against impersonal economic rationality are not the only reason
for protectiveness about families. As Humphries and Luxton have
pointed out, kinship networks have also traditionally provided a
support base for working-class struggles.[24] Their steady disin-
tegration in late capitalism thus has a mixed import for class-
based politics.

Although there has been a tension between feminist and class
politics throughout the history of the women's movement, its form
of expression has varied radically according to the circumstances.
Much of the sixties emphasis on sexuality and the family as a
site of conflict between women and men reflected not just the
characteristics of feminists as individuals or the specific character
of the cultural conjuncture, but the student/youth social composition of the new left where female-male relations revolved

intensely in a movement-defined space that was simultaneously political, erotic, and emotional. In contrast, feminists in the labour force are placed in another powerful relation with men as fellow workers and union and class members. This surely makes their gender situation even more complex – both richer and more confusing. Ehrenreich has put the dilemma well: "We are all pulled in at least two directions. On the one hand, as feminists, we are drawn to the community of women and to its political idealization as a sisterhood of free women. It is this sisterhood, this collectivity of women, that we believe to be the agent of revolutionary change. On the other hand, we are pulled by . . . 'fleshy, familial ties' to a community of men and women – fathers, lovers, brothers, sons, neighbours, co-workers – out of which comes our sense of class solidarity."[25]

By now, however, an accumulation of common experience has created the conditions to overcome differences between the two generations of feminists that arose out of their different work and sexual histories. While middle-class feminists have entered the work force for a variety of biographical and financial reasons, feminist critique has been diffused through the mass media, co-optative educational reforms, trade union projects, and so on to other working women. In addition, the issue of sexual harassment has been a vehicle for women workers to confront the ways in which their (economic *and* sexual) oppression is reproduced through maintaining and exploiting female sexual vulnerability.

Today the economic conjuncture in Canada is changing in ways that may help to advance these theoretical and strategic issues by moving the questions of work and family to centre stage in the labour movement. Like most of the advanced capitalist world, the Canadian economy is undergoing a process of structural transformation that seems likely permanently to reduce labour requirements, creating rising unemployment and producing enormous social dislocation and suffering. Whether as a result of technological change or deindustrialization resulting from a shift in the global division of labour, high levels of unemployment have already hit workers of all ages, sectors, skills, and educational levels. In particular, an "alarmingly high rate of unemployment among female clerical workers – as high as 26 per cent in 1985 and 46 per cent in 1990 – has been projected for the main area where women found work in the expansionist 1960's.[26] If these labour reductions are introduced simply in the interests of capital, the consequences for women workers and their movements could be disastrous: sharpening gender inequalities in work, wages, and social power that erode the membership base of unions and undermine the capacity to resist.

Coming to grips with this problem presents an important opportunity for feminists and unionists because it poses the questions of work, gender, and family in one integrated movement. First, simply to carry out defensive struggles it is necessary for the labour movement to combat primitive sexism generated by competition over the remaining jobs, a consequence of unregulated but systematic disemployment. Although women experience disproportionately high rates of unemployment that are often disguised by under-employment in part-time, seasonal, or under-qualified work or by being swallowed up in family membership,[27] their continuing visibility as workers provokes attacks that they are "responsible" for the loss of male jobs. To deal with job loss in general, Canadian trade unions have already initiated a call for the reduction of the working week in order to redistribute employment more equitably in order simply to work less. To be effective, such a campaign must take on the question of women's and men's relationships to work and family. In the short run, demands for the redistribution of work must also find ways to integrate affirmative action and equal pay policies that have only recently become part of the labour movement's *active* policy. To be effective in the long run, however, what is required is a reconsideration of the nature of work in late capitalist society. Gorz has suggested that in conditions of job scarcity the possession of a job becomes a social privilege that serves to fragment sections of the working class – to confer privilege on the traditional organized proletariat, which is politically fragmented from the unemployed and the new mass workers.[28] Indeed, possession of a job/salary or "breadwinner power" has long been a material basis of male privilege within the family.

Whatever the success of efforts to redistribute work, the social effects of economic transformation may also affect relationships within families and marriages. For men, a loss of work puts not only economic survival but also personal identity at issue. Deprived of breadwinner power, men will be willy-nilly "freed" from a hitherto forced reliance on a masculine ethic of work, stripped of a material base of male power, and faced with the prospect of rebuilding individual character structure and relationships with women on something other than these patriarchal bases. Simple resistance is, of course, possible, but so are other outcomes. As part of a complex process, some men will, through an interest in their wives' wages, move to support equal pay while others who find themselves dependent or unemployed over the long term may, like the Sudbury miners, become more responsible for domestic and child-care activities, with positive results for family relations. Given the real need and widespread acceptance of women's right to work, women are likely to resist measures reminiscent of the 1930's that scapegoat them or solve the crisis on their backs. Class struggle, in the 1980's, is necessarily a battle involving both sexes.

8

The Rise and Fall of British Columbia's Solidarity

Bryan D. Palmer

British Columbia, like most Canadian provinces, has a history of class struggle. It is a record that peaks at episodic moments of confrontation.[1] For 130 days, throughout the summer and fall of 1983, the province's working class found itself in the midst of just such an epic battle. Hundreds of thousands of people marched in protest rallies; new converts to labour's ranks were introduced to picket lines and an ethos of collective resistance; the media offered people a constant barrage of sensationalist comment on general strikes in the past and the meaning of one for the present. In bars, recreation centres, living rooms, and parks, not to mention workplaces, little else was discussed except the raging battle between the province's Social Credit government and the labour-led opposition. To have lived through these 130 days is to have been a witness to the reality of class struggle, and of how, in certain circumstances, it can restructure the politics of everyday life. No one who was there would understate what was happening in the summer and fall of 1983. Mike Kramer, secretary-treasurer of the British Columbia Federation of Labour (BCFL), commented, "I'm convinced there were people who thought there were going to be troops in the street . . . it was talked about. Would they call the army in? . . . In Ottawa we had the NDP critic for defence getting an assurance from the minister that they weren't going to be using people from Chilliwack [an army base] and bring them in here." Five months later the *Globe and Mail* correspondent, Ian Mulgrew, would write: "Class warfare used to be a joke in this province. In the spring of 1984 no one is laughing."[2]

What happened during these turbulent 130 days when, in the words of a Vancouver *Sun* editorial, "Just how close the province came to spilling over the brink we need not speculate"?[3] An easy answer would be Solidarity, a word that summons up an entire history of working-class struggle and internationalism, and the name that the 1983 opposition took up as its own. But Solidarity itself was created within a particular historical context, a product of a specific economic and political conjuncture.

In examining the rise and fall of British Columbia's Solidarity this essay explores the character of contemporary class struggle within that conjuncture. It highlights the role of the state in the making of class relations in the post-World War II years and focuses on the ossification of labour's leadership.[4] For the experience of Solidarity is nothing if it is not a stark reminder that a particular layer of labour leadership, which grew to power and maturity in the context of a post-war settlement among capital, labour, and the state, is now unable to challenge those forces that are, in effect, restructuring class relations and reconstituting the post-war pact on terms entirely unfavourable to the workers' movement. In the words of Solidarity activist and postal worker leader Evert Hoogers, those who led British Columbia's workers in the opposition of 1983 "had no sense of the importance of real working-class struggle, because for years they had based their successful union strategies on legalisms, the social contract, and being able to extract deals from employers and the state in exchange for a very pliant and non-confrontational labour movement."[5]

I

Solidarity was born not because a labour leader or a neo-conservative politician took particular steps. Rather, as a mass movement its origins lie in a series of developments in the post-war history of class relations in advanced capitalist countries. Those developments conditioned specific responses on the part of those personalities who then came to occupy positions of prominence in the Solidarity summer and fall. But one must never lose sight of those structural factors that set the limits within which individuals operated. "Men make their own history, but they do not make it just as they please; they do not make it

under circumstances chosen by themselves, but under circumstances directly encountered, given and transmitted from the past,"
wrote Marx, adding that this "tradition of all the dead generations
weighs like a nightmare on the brain of the living."[6]

Traditions that would indeed prove oppressively limiting in 1983
were rooted in what were commonly perceived as the labour and
progressive victories of the 1940's. In that decade the first planks
of a welfare state were laid, and a system of industrial pluralism,
premised on workers' rights to join unions of their choice and
bargain collectively with employers, was institutionalized. To be
sure, the conception of a welfare state freely and benevolently
developed to provide for the "lowly" is more an ideological than
historical creation, just as recognition of unions, the automatic
employer check-off of union dues, and the establishment of
collective bargaining grew out of more than the state's liberal
sense of workplace democracy and justice. The benefits of the
1940's were as much attempts to control and rationalize the labour
market as they were humanitarian innovations, as much a response
to escalating class struggle as they were the voice of concerned
authority. Thus the Family Allowances Act, Canada's first universal welfare program, was something besides the rhetorical state
interest in the well-being of all Canadian children. It was designed
to maintain purchasing power and the family, both forces of
stability, and, more significantly, it also aimed to undercut the
more radical CIO unions' demand for a minimum industrial wage.
The 1940's thus saw labour struggles and demands linked to the
arrival of the welfare state, and before the decade had ended
old age pensions, unemployment assistance, and expansion of
health care had also been introduced. In conjunction with the
1948 Industrial Relations and Disputes Act, which finally secured
workers freedom of association and established procedures for
collective bargaining, these developments sealed a post-war pact
among labour, capital, and the state. Struck at just the moment
that Communist influence in the unions was being vigorously
opposed (and, shortly, to be driven out or silenced),[7] this post-
war settlement was rooted in the perceived need for orderly
industrial relations. They were to be governed by legally constituted
codes and procedures that specified how and when unions were
to be certified and where, when, and under what conditions class
struggles might be allowed to erupt. The pact also grew out of
an awareness of the need for a social safety net that would catch
those displaced by capital, albeit a net that set assistance rates

so low as to effectively coerce labour into the marketplace of waged work rather than allow too many the option of welfare.[8]

The post-war settlement and its legalistic structuring of trade unionism in the direction of certification procedures, the impact of the Cold War rout of the Communists in the unions, and the very complacency and contentment of a rank and file that lived with the securities of prosperity and recognized rights rather than the constant combat of earlier generations gave rise to a particular contingent of labour leaders who lived by the rules of the pact of the 1940's.[9] In order to deal with the day-to-day experiences of a class struggle increasingly channelled into elaborate modes of arbitration, the theatre of collective bargaining, and precise grievance procedures, labour's leaders inevitably drifted away from the mobilization drives of the 1940's.[10] Once organizers, trade union officials often became complacent bureaucrats, enamoured of what the post-war settlement secured for their members, dedicated to the victories of small reforms and modest economic gains at the bargaining table. Former British Columbia worker activist Bill White captures something of this when he writes:

> When you had to go out and sell your union to every member you worked harder to prove it was worth it. . . . Now the leaderships can lay back in the head office and pay themselves big salaries because they know the dues are going to come rolling in anyway. . . . When I see the face of a labour leader on the T.V. now it's always fat. All jowls like hogs ready for the knife, it's hard to imagine the sight of any of them striking fear in the capitalists' hearts.[11]

The post-war pact was thus continued and deepened in the thirty years stretching from 1945-1975, willingly embraced by labour's mainstream leaders. In British Columbia, moreover, the pot was sweetened by a Labour Code reputed to be among the most progressive in the country.[12] And if the New Democratic Party was not always labour's erstwhile advocate, it could win power in B.C. and it promised labour a better deal than any other political party on the electoral scene.[13]

Won through struggle, developments such as these were also granted, legitimized, and bankrolled by the state. Equally significant, they were paid for out of the generalized post-war prosperity of North America. By the mid-1970's that prosperity was winding down in a distressing Canadian spiral of deindustrialization, persistent structural unemployment, and debilitating inflation. As the latter erosion of the dollar chipped away at the competitiveness of Canadian products throughout the 1970's, unit labour expenses, measured against similar costs of the country's major trading partners (many of which were now rebuilt economically after the devastation of World War II), soared between 1965-1975. Canada's competitiveness dipped to new lows. The deficit on the current account of the balance of payments accordingly climbed to an unprecedented $4.757 billion. Resource economies like that of British Columbia, dependent on marketing forest products to the advanced capitalist economies of the West, were particularly hard hit.[14] Having geared its policies toward export,[15] the Canadian state sought answers to the dilemmas of a new international division of labour, in which Third World countries underpriced their products to secure much needed American dollars.[16] Canada's high-wage marketplace pushed the state to attack the earning power of Canadian labour. The federal guidelines of the Trudeau Liberals' Anti-Inflation Board[17] limited worker wages in 1975 and, to buttress this policy and ease public spending, the government jettisoned its post-war policy of Keynesian expenditure and replaced it with a gradualist strategy of monetary restraint.[18] The gloves were off; the post-war settlement was ended covertly.

Signs of this appeared in two parallel developments. First, legislation aimed to curb workers' power grew more threatening as the 1970's gave way to the 1980's. The state's discretionary coercion replaced an era of industrial pluralism, securing wage controls, exempting public-sector workers from collective bargaining, and ordering private-sector workers back to their jobs if they struck in defiance of tightening restrictions.[19] Second, the persistence and mushrooming character of the deficit provided the ideological and economic legitimation for the rise of the political right. This political tendency had ready answers for the plight of Canadians in the 1980's, advocating "privatization" and "restraint." In contracting out services once paid for by the government and cutting back on social programs, the new right promised liberation from rising taxes and a return to the individualistic self-reliance that it claimed made for greatness in the economic realm.[20]

What the state had given, then, it could reappropriate. When, in the face of a global restructuring of the economic order, North American successes soured and prosperity passed, trade union rights and human entitlements were often mistakenly felt to be deeply entrenched. As Panitch and Swartz have noted, "The reforms achieved in the 1940's were thought to be irreversible and cumulative."[21] They were not. In the cynical anti-worker words of 1960's counter-culture hero Bob Dylan:

> You know this shirt I wear comes from the Philippines
> And the car I drive is a Chevrolet
> It was put together down in Argentina
> By a girl makin' thirty cents a day
> Well, it's sundown on the union . . .
>
> All the furniture it says made in Brazil
> By a woman who slaves for sure
> Bringing home thirty cents a day to a family of twelve
> You know that's a lotta money to her
> Well, it's sundown on the union . . .
>
> You know capitalism is above the law
> It say it don't count unless it sells
> When it costs too much to build it at home
> You just build it cheaper some place else
> Well, it's sundown on the union . . .[22]

Less lyrical, but more direct, are the words of a former Communist and president of the once-powerful British Columbia-based Boilermakers and Iron Shipbuilders Union of Canada: "When you add it up there's not one gain the labour movement has won since the depression that isn't under attack in some quarter. . . . It's a mistake to think things can't go backwards."[23] Solidarity would emerge out of this post-war context, a response to those of the new right who would fire the opening shots in a war that would rage across the summer and fall of 1983.

II

In British Columbia, 1983 was an election year. Contested in May, the electoral battle involved the social democratic New Democratic Party and the populist neo-conservative Social Credit, a coalition of forces dedicated to keeping the province out of the clutches of the threatening socialists. Leader of the right was Bill Bennett, son of former B.C. political boss W.A.C. Bennett and a Kelowna hardware merchant.[24] Pushing a vaguely stated program of moderate "restraint," Bennett emerged victorious. Social Credit won thirty-five of the fifty-seven provincial seats.

Regarded as a stunning victory, the popular vote was in fact indecisive, with barely 50 per cent of the participating electorate casting their lot with the Reaganite colours (red, white, and blue) of the Social Credit machine. Bennett had in fact been sold to the voters by a slick Tory pollster from Ontario, Patrick Kinsella.[25]

"Restraint" had never been anything more than a subdued theme of the campaign. But the Socreds were obviously concerned with the state of the local economy and the impact of the new international division of labour, which by 1983 was being felt in mass shutdowns and staggering unemployment as the large forestry product multinationals wound down their Pacific Northwest operations to exploit the more lucrative potential of the open-shop American South or the low-wage underdeveloped Far East and southern hemisphere. Reported unemployment in British Columbia climbed from 12.1 to 13.8 to 15.6 per cent between 1982-1984. It was a rate surpassed in North America only by Newfoundland and Virginia, and actual unemployment was much higher.[26] Once considered a Canadian paradise, parts of British Columbia were taking on the trappings of a ghost town as people fled the province, housing prices collapsed, and speculative fortunes dissipated. Both capital and the state perceived the need to act. And there were those who were willing to tell them what must be done. Bennett and his cabinet were soon consulting with Michael Walker and his colleagues in the B.C.-based right-wing "think tank," the Fraser Institute, a centre of free-enterprise ideological output known for its antagonism to rent controls, unions, state assistance to the unemployed and disadvantaged, and any and all fetters on entrepreneurial initiative and the free movement of commodities and labour.[27]

Out of these consultations would come the Social Credit budget. Introduced on "Black Thursday," July 7, it contained twenty-six pieces of specific legislation. "Restraint" was no longer subdued. A number of the bills were of peripheral concern, but as a package the legislation was awesome in its direct attack on the areas of labour and social rights and welfare-related services. Broadly defined, the crucial bills fell into three categories: five pieces of legislation aimed their sights directly at the labour movement, especially its public-sector component, undermining trade union practices and virtually destroying collective bargaining; four other bills promised to dismantle established structures, commissions, and offices long established to safeguard essential human rights and protect the powerless; and seven more bills collapsed previously dispersed authority, especially in the fields of education, health, and regional planning, into the offices of cabinet ministers, thereby curtailing local autonomy. Four crucial pieces of legislation were: Bill 2, which removed government employees' rights to negotiate anything but wages (limited anyway under the Compensation Stabilization Act); Bill 3, allowing the state to fire employees at will upon the expiration of a collective agreement (in the case of the British Columbia Government Employees' Union the contract was to lapse on October 31, 1983); Bill 5, abolishing the Rentalsman's office and rent controls; and, finally, Bill 27, which repealed the Human Rights Code, narrowed the definition of discrimination, limited the amount of compensation, and abolished the Human Rights Commission.[28]

In one devastating blow Bennett and the Socreds sought to liberate capital from the fetters of the post-war settlement, striking out at public-sector unionism as the weak link in the chain of trade union defence mechanisms and declaring an abrupt end to the state subsidies and protections for the poor, handicapped, and underprivileged. To be sure, the actual dollars saved in the "restraint" budget were minimal and the continuing crisis of capitalist restructuring coupled with the Social Credit penchant for megaprojects ensured that actual spending in the period of economic cuts rose by more than 12 per cent. The deficit, rather than shrinking, was projected to increase to $1.6 billion. But this did not mean, as some liberal economists have suggested, that the budget was a purely political and ideological act of coercion. The Socreds no doubt inflated the deficit the better to sell their cutbacks, but common sense and a look around the province told many that the government was not fudging the depressing reality of joblessness. The "restraint" legislation was an attempt to restructure in the political arena what was already being reconstituted economically. In order to underwrite the costs of economic transformation to a technologically intensive order in which both the high wage and the social minimum of the welfare state would not prove future impediments to investment and accumulation, the state demanded concessions. The result would be a society in which permanent structural unemployment was accepted and a social stratum of marginalized and abandoned "have nots" created and indeed institutionalized.[29]

"Restraint" was thus not about economics here and ideology there, but about the interpenetration of these realms. "Downsizing" was a case in point. This was the Fraser Institute-Social Credit parlance for firing public-sector workers, eliminating government jobs. One day after the budget was introduced 400 workers, many of them in the targeted Human Resources Ministry, were fired, severely disrupting social services affecting battered wives, abused children, welfare recipients, and the disabled. On October 31, moreover, 1,600 more layoffs were scheduled. The devastating forecasts were that full-time equivalent positions for employees of government ministries would be reduced from 46,806 to 39,965 in 1983-84 and slashed yet again in 1984-85 to 35,410.[30] Done in the name of economy, these job eliminations also had their convenient ideological and political sides. Bennett made much of civil servants' "laziness," lack of productivity, and privileged job "tenure." Michael Walker noted that public-sector workers provided "an ideological consistency and a lag in adjustment to new ideas and political directions." In the age of Bennett's much-vaunted "new reality," "when the government in British Columbia is attempting to make the transition to a new vision of the future, it is appropriate that the continuity of ideas provided by the civil service be broken."[31]

The budget, then, was about class needs where the material and the ideological were inseparable. Not surprisingly, it also ended by being about class struggle.

III

Opposition to the budget was forthcoming almost immediately.[32] The Unemployment Committee of the Vancouver and District Labour Council called an early meeting to create a coalition of community groups and unionists opposed to the threatening legislation. Led by militants in the Communist Party and labour figures active in the radical Action Caucus of the BCFL, this initial organizational effort was soon supplemented by the formation of the feminist Women Against the Budget (WAB). Out of this would emerge the Lower Mainland Budget Coalition. On July 23, two weeks after the introduction of the budget, this body mobilized some 25,000 people in a spirited demonstration that marched through the streets of Vancouver to rally at the Socred megaproject, BC Place. There a contingent of angry speakers denounced the Social Credit project and called for the withdrawal of the entire legislative package.[33] It was a militant and impressive beginning to a movement yet to be formally constituted and named Solidarity, an initial wave of protest that rippled throughout the province in workplace occupations, meetings, and smaller rallies.[34]

On the very day that the Lower Mainland Budget Coalition was created the British Columbia Federation of Labour, headed by Art Kube, finally got into the act. After attempts to dissuade organizers of the BC Place rally from acting "prematurely," Kube and the federation finally threw their support behind the demonstration and launched their own campaign against the budget. On July 15, Kube announced the formation of Operation Solidarity, an attempt to bring all trade unions in the province together, regardless of past differences, jurisdictional disputes, and status (affiliated or non-affiliated) with the BCFL. Meeting in the Operating Engineers' Burnaby Hall, the province's unionists pledged their commitment to Operation Solidarity. Bill Clark of the Telecommunications Workers' Union argued that the budget had to be defeated and claimed that "a general strike, possibly in October, is virtually a certainty." More than 500,000 workers (37 per cent of the entire work force) were now pledged to opposition to the legislation. Within three weeks over $1,500,000 had been raised, all but $200,000 generated within British Columbia.[35]

Operation Solidarity's first major undertaking was a demonstration on the lawns of the provincial legislature in Victoria. Scheduled for mid-week, the July 27 protest brought busloads of unionists, human rights advocates, tenants, feminists, and unemployed workers to the capital. Approximately 25,000 were in attendance, making the rally by far the largest political demonstration in Victoria's history. Speaker after speaker called for the withdrawal of all twenty-six Social Credit bills. Solidarity was the popular theme of the protest, captured in the words of building trades leader Roy Gautier, "An attack on any group must be a fight for us all," and the thundering promise of Hospital Employees' Union (HEU) head Jack Gerow: "When working people unite, social and economic victory is not only possible, it is inevitable." The astounding success of the Victoria rally, coupled with Operation Solidarity-led activities in working-class centres like Nanaimo and Prince George, convinced many of what could be gained by a co-ordinated, comprehensive campaign under the leadership of Kube and the B.C. Federation of Labour. Late July and early August appeared to be the time to build a massive movement of resistance, which only the resources and reach of the BCFL could sustain.[36]

In the words of the federation's Mike Kramer, the Lower

Mainland Budget Coalition's ability to put together "almost 30,000 people overnight" convinced the labour hierarchy of the seething opposition to the legislation outside of the trade union movement. The buses were barely back from Victoria when Operation Solidarity called for a broad province-wide coalition to beat back the offensive bills. Kube had spoken to the Lower Mainland Budget Coalition two days before the Victoria rally, reporting on the progress of Operation Solidarity. At that meeting a motion endorsing a general strike had been tabled. But those present did vote "unanimously to endorse Operation Solidarity and to co-ordinate major actions with it."[37] In the weeks to come, however, the Lower Mainland Budget Coalition would find itself not a partner in protest, but a constituency being led to its liquidation.

On Wednesday, August 3, Operation Solidarity called together representatives from over 200 community-based organizations, convening them in the same Operating Engineers' hall where it had announced its own formation. At this meeting, organized by the HEU's Jean Swanson and Clay Perry of the International Woodworkers of America (IWA), the fate of the Lower Mainland Budget Coalition was sealed. From the chair, Operation Solidarity head Kube moved and secured acceptance of three co-chairs for a new coalition: himself; fired Human Rights Commissioner Renate Shearer; and Father Jim Roberts, a Langara College religious studies instructor and member of the steering committee of the original Budget Coalition. The BCFL would later provide the coalition with three organizers (Swanson and Perry being two of them), two clerical workers, and $90,000. The assembled activists were told to return to their constituencies, nominate delegates, and prepare for a large end-of-the-month gathering. Two days later the Vancouver and New Westminster labour councils called a meeting of the Lower Mainland Operation Solidarity group, where the idea of the new coalition was discussed. Those present regarded the old Lower Mainland Budget Coalition as "not broad enough in its representation" and agreed to launch a new body. Needless to say, many of the original coalition, especially those in Women Against the Budget, thought that "the two groups were being melded without appropriate involvement of the Budget Coalition." But resistance at this point was futile, the result a foregone conclusion.[38]

The very success of Operation Solidarity initiatives and the new province-wide momentum silenced many critics. Over 50,000 people jammed Vancouver's Empire Stadium on August 10 to see the city firefighters and bus drivers join public-sector workers and outraged citizens in a massive and exhilarating show of force, spirit, and solidarity. One day earlier, rallies of 1,000-4,000 had occurred in the small interior communities of Kamloops, Nelson, Williams Lake, and Salmon Arm. Future demonstrations were to take place in Nanaimo, Campbell River, Fort Nelson, Courtenay, and Kelowna, where there was talk of picketing outside the premier's store. Coalitions were springing up across the province. Unity was the cry of the hour, a call with understandable appeal to many, be they trade unionists or unaffiliated with the labour movement.[39]

Such unprecedented protests set the stage for the disbanding of the Lower Mainland Budget Coalition, which by mid-August was collapsed into the new province-wide movement of budget resistance, the Solidarity Coalition. When this body was formally launched in the immediate aftermath of the August 10 rally at a large meeting at the British Columbia Government Employees' Union (BCGEU) hall in Burnaby, there were voices of protest from various quarters. But the meeting, chaired by New Democratic Party (NDP) figure and IWA official Gerry Stoney and by Frank Kennedy, head of the Vancouver and District Labour Council and long associated with the Communist Party (CP), had little time for dissent. "Work was to be done," thundered CP spokesperson George Hewison from the floor, and the liquidation of the original coalition was a *fait accompli*.[40]

By mid-August, then, the structures of a movement of resistance were in place. Solidarity had three massive rallies under its belt and strong indications that it had the support of hundreds of thousands of citizens. Opposition to the budget was clearly widespread and the appeal of the demand to withdraw the legislation was unambiguous. The promise of the movement seemed great indeed.

Yet, in hindsight there was more to Solidarity than a simple expression of opposition. Structurally, the Solidarity Coalition's separation from Operation Solidarity, both of which had their own distinct steering committees and assemblies, institutionalized and legitimized the dichotomization of trade union (economic) and social service (human/political) issues. Given who was paying the bills, this separation inevitably reduced the Coalition to an adjunct of the more powerful Operation Solidarity, which was literally guided by a small contingent at the head of the B.C. Federation of Labour. Politically, the left that had initiated the protest wave in the Budget Coalition was now effectively marginalized, represented on the Solidarity Coalition's steering committee and assembly as the Lower Mainland Solidarity Coalition (LMSC), and swamped by the more than 150 provincial delegates that comprised the new body.[41] Furthermore, the leading figures in the Solidarity Coalition were literally appointed by Kube, among them co-chairs Renate Shearer and Father Roberts. The handpicked provincial organizers included the IWA's Clay Perry, the HEU's Jean Swanson, and Gerry Scott of the NDP and the BCFL. The former duo had been associated with Kube's call to form a coalition well before the official formation of the new Solidarity Coalition. Lest anyone forget where authority lay, Arthur Kube was the only direct link between Operation Solidarity and the Solidarity Coalition, heading the former and appointing himself as one of three chairs of the latter. In their structures the newly created provincial coalition and its labour movement parent, Operation Solidarity, were answers to more than Bill Bennett. They were also answers to who would control the mobilization against the budget.

In the six weeks following the Empire Stadium rally the consequences of this concentration of leadership in the hands of Kube and a few others would become apparent. Kube's approach to the class struggle was one of moderation. As early as 1976 he had stated: "I think I'll have to go to Victoria one day to protest anti-labour legislation. . . . But I'm not going to be getting up each morning crying 'general strike'. . . . Rather than hammering people, I'll talk to them about options." Seven years later he sang the same tune. As some workers and a militant layer of trade union leadership urged work stoppages, Kube resisted even consideration of such tactics, saying, "A general strike is the last thing on my mind," adding that such job action would "scare away a great number of groups."[42]

Tightly controlled by the bureaucratic leadership of the BC Fed, the Solidarity movement would soon be demobilized, structured into moderate channels that de-escalated the pace of opposition. An Operation Solidarity "think tank" in mid-August determined that phase one of the protest, in which mass demonstrations predominated, had run its course. Phase two would involve diversified protests, while phase three, to commence in October, would centre on contract negotiations of the British Columbia Government Employees' Union (BCGEU).[43] Phase two ended up being dominated by an eight-week consciousness-raising drive, in which September and October were given over to local events geared to highlight the harsh impact of the government's program on specific social groups and entrenched rights. Each area was to be targeted during a specific week. Complementing these weekly activities was a petition drive aiming to secure masses of signatures opposing the twenty-six bills of "restraint." A new slogan appeared, plastered on Operation Solidarity billboards throughout Vancouver and its suburbs. Proclaiming that "restraint does not mean repression," it attempted to assure all British Columbians that Solidarity was not opposed to reasonable "restraint," only the excesses of the state's draconian assault on the defenceless.[44]

These initiatives were attempts to co-ordinate activity on terms acceptable to the official Solidarity leadership. Indeed, they had been preceded by press announcements that "Mavericks in Operation Solidarity are about to get reigned [sic] in. A set of guidelines will be laid out by month-end."[45] When militants in the Solidarity Coalition tried to counter this containment of protest by organizing a Women Against the Budget "Stone Soup Luncheon" at the house of Human Resources Minister Grace McCarthy (August 27) and occupying the Vancouver offices of the Social Credit cabinet, proclaiming a "People's Government" (September 16-17), they were either rebuffed or ignored by Kube and others in the Solidarity hierarchy.[46] There was talk in the press of Solidarity's demise. The movement was waning under a leadership that refused to lead.[47]

In fact, the popular will to resist the Social Credit bills had not faded but had been understated by the candlelight vigils and petition signings of September. It remained to be tapped, waiting for an opportunity to express itself. Confined by the Solidarity leadership's defeatist insistence that the mass mobilizations of the summer could not be recreated in the fall, this opposition sentiment lay dormant throughout much of September.

It would explode in the streets of Vancouver on October 15. It was well known that the Social Credit Party's convention was scheduled to take place in mid-October at the Hotel Vancouver. But when the matter was raised in Operation Solidarity circles, with the suggestion that a massive protest be organized to coincide with the event, little resulted. Indeed, there was considerable resistance to the idea within the BC Fed leadership. But people were tired of the inaction of Kube and company and the Lower Mainland Solidarity Coalition virtually insisted that a demonstration be built. It was eventually organized, but within official Solidarity circles there was scepticism about the numbers that could be drawn to the march, and it was decided that there would be no media or billboard advertising for the event. The few speeches to be given were to take place at an obscure downtown enclave, well out of sight of the Socreds and Hotel Vancouver. It was a location "designed to camouflage a small crowd." In the face of Kube's public statement that he hoped "the planned October 15 Solidarity march and rally doesn't get too large," a massive crowd of 60,000-80,000 materialized. For more than two hours it filed past the Hotel Vancouver, fists raised defiantly in the air, its collective voice speaking in chants of anger: "Socreds out! Socreds out!" Few stayed to listen to Renate Shearer read the newly drafted Solidarity Coalition's Declaration of the Rights of the People of British Columbia. Most could not have got close enough to her to hear what she said. Most had already made *their* statement.[48]

The October 15 demonstration was such a striking success because so many people felt the budget legislation's threatening impact had reached the eleventh hour. Introduced in July, the budget's bills simply hung over the province for two months; no attempt was made to pass any of the legislation into law. Then, starting on September 19, the Socreds initiated a series of parliamentary charades that made a mockery of past procedures and democratic traditions. With the NDP having isolated "a dirty dozen" bills that it was prepared to denounce, filibuster, and delay to the best of its parliamentary ability, the Social Credit majority declared war on debate and discussion. Closure, an extreme measure of shutting off parliamentary debate last used in B.C. in 1957, was invoked twenty times. All-night sittings, known as legislation by exhaustion, were common. The leader of the Opposition, Dave Barrett, was ejected from the House twice, necessitating his banishment from the legislature until its next sitting. In three weeks of this legislative siege, seventeen acts received royal assent, including four of the main anti-labour bills. The Socreds now had labour legislation to hold over public-sector unionists' heads in the forthcoming BCGEU contract negotiations, the NDP had been relegated to the sidelines, and the battlelines were clearly drawn between Social Credit and Solidarity. Bennett announced that the legislature would recess on October 21 to provide a much-needed "cooling off" period.[49]

It was in this context that people took to the streets in mid-

October, and it would be this context, as well, that increasingly gave rise to talk of the need for a general strike. When a poll was conducted in the first week of October asking, "If the Solidarity movement were to call a general strike in B.C. in order to bring about new provincial elections, would you personally stay off the job," an amazing 19.7 per cent replied to this loaded wording with an unreserved yes. A further 6.9 per cent said they would consider it, while 23.6 per cent answered with an evasive but telling statement that they had no job to stay away from. Only 45.7 per cent rejected outright the notion of an unlimited general strike to bring the government down. At the first delegated conference of the Provincial Solidarity Coalition, held on October 22-23 at the King Edward campus of the Vancouver Community College, resolutions calling for a general strike came from all quarters. Representative was the Port Alberni resolution, supporting a "General Strike . . . until the entire legislative package has been withdrawn."[50]

This escalating militancy, coupled with the forthcoming contract negotiations of the BCGEU, where the decisive impact of Bills 2 and 3 would be felt acutely within the labour movement for the first time, dealt a death blow to the leadership's phase-two tactics of demobilization. The hour of action was now fast approaching. How did official Solidarity leaders adapt to this situation? In a word, with opportunism.

This opportunism was evident in the labour hierarchy's handling of the demand for the repeal of the entire legislative package as well as in its deflection of the militant leftist call for a general strike. Operation Solidarity heads publicly condemned all of the Socred bills and throughout the summer and fall habitually called for the withdrawal of all the legislation. Indeed, this universal condemnation of the Social Credit program was the cornerstone upon which the movement's solidarity rested, providing common ground where unionists, feminists, human rights advocates, the disabled, minority groups, tenants, and countless others met. But by late October it was clear that labour's leaders were backing away from this original position. They began to retreat into the territory of the post-war settlement, claiming that while labour issues were negotiable the more diffuse human rights area was not. This met with a chilling response from the Solidarity rank and file and in the face of consistent repudiation of this attempt to narrow the issues, Kube and others turned Janus-faced. Stoic in their endorsement of the original demand for the withdrawal of all the legislation, they backed into the actual structures of Operation Solidarity power, where a narrow, legalistic trade unionism was entirely capable of whittling the movement's actual, if not professed, aims down to defeat of Bills 2 and 3.[51]

Just as the official labour leadership backed away from the call to repeal all of the legislation, so, too, would they distance themselves from the unlimited general strike that many unionists and Solidarity activists urged. In its stead a timetable for "escalating public sector job action" was devised. The BCGEU was to be first off the line, leaving work legally for a new contract on Tuesday, November 1. Next would come workers in the education sector (November 8), who had questionable legal status as strikers under the Labour Code, then Crown corporations, the Insurance Company of B.C. and ferry workers (November 10), municipal workers and bus drivers (November 14), and hospital and health employees (November 18). All of this, later events would show, would be avoided if the BCGEU could get a contract and public-sector workers could secure exemption from Bill 3. But this was not clear from the rhetoric of labour's leaders. Kramer, for instance, was claiming that "all of the social services that have been taken away under this restraint program are on the table," promising "a general shutdown in the province" if any legislative repression was employed against Solidarity strikers. With 200,000 workers poised to withdraw their services and private-sector labour leaders like the IWA's Jack Munro talking tough, it looked like a general strike in the making. Certainly the media thought so, as did much of North America, which had the experience in B.C. passed on to it filtered through news reports of the drama of unfolding confrontation. All the while, however, those in the know had a more limited agenda. Operation Solidarity spokesmen (they *were* a gender-specific lot) were instructed to "Avoid use of the term 'general strike'. Let others use it. You are not 'making demands' but 'securing' basic rights as your objective." Teachers' leader Larry Kuehn later agreed that public perception and the leadership's orientation differed. "We didn't respond to these differences," noted Kuehn, "because to announce there was no general strike would have undermined us."[52] Indeed it would have, among *both* their antagonists *and* followers.

In their public statements and escalating strike strategy, then, the labour leadership was rhetorically leading with its left at the same time as its specific intentions harboured a more modest purpose and strategy. Opportunism thus bought the hierarchy a renewed mandate, as Solidarity activists in the unions and the community fell behind their leadership thinking the struggle was moving forward in ways they could support. As October gave way to November it would be clear how many illusions were being cultivated at the top and embraced at the base.

IV

The confrontation commenced at midnight on October 31. Ten days of BCGEU-Social Credit negotiations went nowhere and the Halloween strike was on as 35,000 government workers took to the picket lines. Right from the outset the conflict was depicted as a narrow struggle. An Operation Solidarity press release stated that "The negotiations currently underway can bring a general resolution to the conflict spawned by Bill 3." At a meeting of the Provincial Assembly of the Solidarity Coalition Kube argued: "It's not the case that unions have forgotten human rights and other issues, but we don't know if we will be able to bargain for them."[53]

By mid-week it was apparent that the state was willing to negotiate exemptions for public-sector unions from the already passed Bill 3 and, further, that the Socreds were willing to let Bill 2 die on the legislative table. But more was at issue for the state than a mere settlement. Bennett's chief negotiator, Norman Spector, was convinced that Solidarity was on the run. Many on the right felt that the escalating public-sector job actions would fizzle on November 8, when the teachers were scheduled to join the protest and leave work. Judged to be "the weak link in the solidarity chain," teachers had voted to strike by a narrow 59.5 per cent majority. Looking forward to a failed teacher walkout, the state sabotaged attempts on the part of school boards to exempt their instructors from Bill 3, stalled the BCGEU negotiations, threatened teachers with loss of their certificates if they engaged in "illegal" work stoppages, and used the media to decry the irresponsibility of teachers who would sacrifice children's education on the altar of self-interest and partisan politics. The state thus counted on the teachers' failure and did what it could to coerce and intimidate those in the school system who were considering striking to preserve human, educational, and trade union rights. According to Kube, the government was "gambling on the teachers not going out."[54]

But teachers, who had seen the state lay off more than 1,000 of their colleagues, witnessed the sorry and crude Social Credit efforts to block a resolution of the crisis and feared for the quality of education under an oppressive, centralized ministry assured by the newly passed Bill 6; and they were not to be denied their place in the Solidarity struggle. Eighty-five to 95 per cent of the British Columbia Teachers' Federation membership left work, their strike buttressed by co-workers in the Canadian Union of Public Employees and by college and university faculty, students, and staff. As Victoria and local school boards slapped the striking teachers with injunctions calling for teachers to cease and desist from picketing and return to their classes, Solidarity Coalition supporters from WAB, the LMSC, and the Vancouver Municipal and Regional Employees Union re-established picket lines so that teachers would be able to plead their conscience as grounds for not showing up to work. From across the province enthusiastic strike responses poured into the BCTF offices: "We must not be hectored with the cries of terrorism and anarchy. . . . It has been a great week. . . . We have already achieved change." A projected teachers' collapse, counted on by the state and perhaps even anticipated by a few labour leaders, had turned into an exhilarating success.[55]

At this point, as a general strike appeared both warranted and possible, state mandarins and fearful labour leaders began seriously to search out a compromise. The ferry workers, scheduled to strike November 10, had their job actions postponed until the following Monday. Kube, exhausted and battling pneumonia, appeared at a New Westminster Solidarity meeting visibly shaken by Social Credit intransigence and, in the midst of urging all there to continue to fight for "decency," broke down and wept. The next day he would be bed-ridden. Tough-talking Mike Kramer took over the reins of authority and the IWA's Jack Munro, literally a non-presence for much of the Solidarity summer and fall, eased quietly into the picture. "I guess if they [Social Credit] want a war, we're going to give them a war," he said, his words not exactly ringing with conviction. Kramer promised "massive retaliation" and spoke of "the rumble" that was going to shake all of British Columbia. On Saturday evening, with one day left before the ferry workers and bus drivers were to abandon their posts, it was still possible to think that, in Kramer's words, "an all-out total war" was brewing. In fact it was not. Thirteen days of intense confrontation were all the province would face. And the players were already waiting to take on their roles. As Kramer recalled:

A. We decided that I should be the crazy man and Art was the guy people talked to. It made sense . . . That good guy-

bad guy thing. And we talked about that a couple of times.
Q. And Jack [Munro] would just play naturally the role of labour statesman?
A. That's right. . . . We went around the table and did some soul-searching. . . . We knew the fallout from this would be horrendous.[56]

Fallout or not, Solidarity as a mass movement was now finished, as was any hope of forcing the Socreds to back away from much of their legislative assault on the welfare state. By Thursday of the week of the teachers' walkout all attention centred on the Labour Relations Board (LRB), where a select group of labour figureheads bartered with bureaucrats and government negotiators. Employers' Council head Jim Matkin indicated to Munro and Kramer that terms could be arrived at on the critical labour legislation, Bills 2 and 3, and all that remained was a settlement with the BCGEU. These substantive matters had to be dressed up with some concessions to the Solidarity Coalition, however, which had provided critical support for striking teachers and government workers in November and had mobilized hundreds of thousands in the months leading up to the job actions. On Friday, then, the package that would end the drama of November was in place, and it would be leaked to the press by the next day.[57]

Cleared with the bed-ridden Kube, agreed to by BCTF leader Larry Kuehn and BCGEU spokesman Jack Adams, the peace terms included: the killing of Bill 2; the possibility for all public-sector unions to negotiate exemptions from Bill 3; no reprisals against any strikers; money saved during the teachers' strike to remain in the educational system; and the establishment of advisory committees to hear submissions to the state on human rights legislation, tenants' issues, and proposed changes to the Labour Code that threatened the private sector with some of the state medicine the public sector had recently been swallowing.[58] None of this had been ratified by any of the unionists on strike, nor had anyone breathed a word of such terms to those at the very pinnacle of the Solidarity Coalition.[59] More than that, there is substantial evidence that the Coalition was deliberately misinformed about the state of negotiations at the LRB so that leftist elements could not publicly challenge the settlement before it was signed, sealed, and delivered.[60]

Delivered the settlement would be, but there was no signing and no sealing. The BCGEU finally got its contract on Sunday afternoon. It called for a wage increase of zero per cent the first

year, followed by 3 per cent in November, 1984, and a further
1 per cent the next April; it negotiated the 1,600 offensive layoffs
rather than simply letting the state announce who was to go;
and it sacrificed some union rights on hours and worktime
flexibility. But, and this was critical, it exempted the union from
the provisions of Bill 3. It was supposedly a "no concessions
agreement."[61]

With the BCGEU strike settled, the larger Solidarity protest could
now be wound down. This ceremonial termination would take
place, to the shock of many Solidarity activists, in Bill Bennett's
Kelowna living room. Jack Munro had in fact been ready to fly
to Kelowna to present the settlement terms to Bennett two or
more days before. He left as the BCGEU announced the terms
of its new contract.[62]

Kube, Kramer, and Kuehn insist that it was understood that
Munro was taking a deal to Bennett for symbolic ratification.
In Kube's words: "The deal was Munro was supposed to go to
Kelowna and him and the premier would make a public statement
outlining the agreement made at the LRB." But this expectation
never came to pass. Bennett received a phone call from one of
his cabinet ministers who stressed that he could not announce
the settlement without first clearing it with his caucus. Kube
stressed the necessity of a public statement since only that would
ensure "they couldn't weasel out . . . renege on the total package."
But Bennett refused. A series of phone calls between Munro,
Kramer, and Kube (who was confined to his house on doctor's
orders) finally resolved the issue. Munro insisted on getting a
settlement and won the Operation Solidarity executive to his
position. Kube argued that without a public statement he was
prepared to go ahead with further escalation on Monday, but
he was overruled. ("I was the lonely voice that told Munro to
get the fuck out of Kelowna.") A gentlemen's televised agreement
on the premier's porch, in which nothing was signed, nothing
was sealed, and no concrete settlement terms were stated, thus
ended one of the most dramatic labour and social confrontations
in British Columbia's history.[63]

It would be difficult to convey the feelings of betrayal and
desolation felt in many Solidarity circles that Sunday evening as
people watched their television sets and saw Jack Munro and
Bill Bennett end a part of their lives. At a marathon Provincial
Solidarity Coalition Steering Committee meeting that lasted well
past two a.m., the activist left raked Operation Solidarity figures

Joy Langan, Leif Hansen, and Mike Kramer over the coals. The links forged between community activists and labour unions shattered in a series of ugly recriminations. The next evening the Lower Mainland Solidarity Coalition called a mass meeting. It was an angry wake. For two hours those assembled challenged and chastised Kube, now publicly back on the scene, and pointed accusingly at Kramer, who stood off to the side of the podium. An endless parade of activists marched to the mike to ask how and why the movement had been derailed. An eight-year-old girl "just wanted to know why you sold us out, Art?" He had no answers that satisfied the crowd.[64]

In the weeks to follow it would become clear what had been won and what had been squandered. For the BCGEU, Bill 2 had been dealt a death blow, and all public-sector unions could, if their strength permitted it and if they had something they could afford to give up, negotiate exemptions from Bill 3. The labour movement had won something. The consultations promised around human rights, tenants' legislation, and the Labour Code proved to be as hollow as previous meetings with the Socreds had indicated they would be. The government was able to chastise the movement and argue that the settlement had cost it nothing. Bennett made much of the fact that Munro's IWA had no desire to be a part of any job actions, and he took repeated snipes at the NDP's impotence with reference to "the Solidarity Party."[65]

But the educational sector of the settlement was to be the most controversial plank in the Kelowna accord. The teachers had forced the Social Credit government to negotiate its legislation, something it was loath to do. In the weeks to come Bennett would lead a personal crusade against teacher leader Larry Kuehn and back out of his commitment to keep the money saved during the strike – some $18 million in teacher/staff salaries and wages – in the school system, retaining educational funding at close to 1983 levels. Kuehn realized that the $12 million in teacher salaries would not have saved the educational system from deep cuts, but it would have meant that school boards would have delayed 600 teacher layoffs until December-January. It was Kuehn's intention to "buy time for a fight more favourable to us," since it would have been far more difficult for the government and the school boards to terminate teachers in mid-year than over the course of the summer holidays. Bennett no doubt agreed to the original Solidarity demand, but upon being advised later of its implications he drew back. Munro's acquiescence in Bennett's refusal to publicly proclaim the agreement paved the way for the victimization of the teachers. While $6 million in CUPE wages were funnelled back into the system, the teachers' salaries were not. Teachers were even asked to make up the days lost to the strike, a condition Ministry of Education head Jack Heinrich claimed Munro agreed to. Understandably upset, teachers complained to their federation about "the inconclusiveness of the agreement... and the continuing confusion." From Nanaimo came the demand to exert pressure on the government to "live up to the Kelowna agreement," and the warning that "members would likely participate in a general strike but would not be willing to participate in some kind of phased approach . . . want pretty specific objectives understood."[66]

In the twenty months that followed the settlement Solidarity was transformed beyond recognition. It bears no resemblance today to the vibrant mobilization of less that three years ago. Gone are mass actions. In their stead we have a series of hearings eventually published as *The People's Report*. The movement's newspaper, *Solidarity Times*, folded before the end of 1983. Offices remain, and the highly paid organizers (former BCTF head, Larry Kuehn, instead of going back into the classroom went on the Solidarity payroll) are at work reminding people that Solidarity still exists. Renate Shearer crossed the province twice, explaining to people why the Coalition needed to remain together and aligned with Operation Solidarity. Bureaucratically, Solidarity remains an entity, an adjunct to the labour leadership, channelled into the commitment to defeat the Socreds at the next election. At a December meeting of the Vancouver and District Labour Council, Munro's settlement was defended by IWA officials who insisted on the need to avoid the confrontational tactics of the past: "The way to defeat the Socreds is to struggle for the next three years and get our friends, the NDP, elected." The thundering rhetoric of October – when Kube insisted that "Desperate times require desperate measures. We can, and will, through massive mobilizations, force this government to back off" – gave way to the timidity of 1984, when the BC Fed head murmured that labour would continue "to use all traditional means to fight for fairness in the workplace." Such developments gave the Bennett regime a clear message, and 1984 would witness a series of persistent assaults on labour and human rights. But the will to fight, outside of the building trades, was weak. The humiliating termination of Solidarity as a movement ensured that the struggle in British Columbia would be waged at the level of the lowest common denominator. Rank-and-file militants know the price paid in demoralization and disillusionment for the Kelowna agreement. A movement was bartered for two bills and a contract. When the Action Caucus tried to revive Solidarity II in the summer of 1984, WAB activist Jackie Larkin was reminded of Marx's extension of Hegel's remark that historical developments occur twice, "the first time as tragedy, the second as farce."[67]

V

Solidarity's rise was exhilarating, its fall debilitating. Like so many other moments of Canadian class struggle it was two-sided, containing elements of victory and accomplishment as well as aspects of defeat and failure. But the meanings of Solidarity are not those that come easily to mind in the anti-union context of the 1980's. The failure of Solidarity was not a failure of unions and unionists, many of whom struggled valiantly and sacrificed much for a better society for all British Columbians. Rather, Solidarity's failure was a failure of leadership.

The tragic lesson of November was that while the post-war settlement has been jettisoned by capital and the state, which have consciously opted out on the grounds they can no longer afford to live by the old rules, labour is now led by a powerful if numerically small contingent of trade union officials who are literally trapped in the old guidelines. As bargaining itself is shell-shocked by state directives and anti-worker legislation, pivotal figures in the labour movement remain wedded to an atavistic notion of what is bargainable and what is not. Having assumed the progressive evolution of the welfare state was irreversible, this labour leadership carved up the class struggle into its economic (trade union) and socio-political (electoral) halves. Content with winning their memberships (which, admittedly, grew increasingly apathetic over the course of the post-war years) modest economic gains, these labour leaders cultivated a hierarchical practice of authority within the trade union movement. They depended less and less on combativeness and collectivity and more and more on the institutions and legalistic core of industrial policy in the era of free collective bargaining. But those times are now ended. And as the house of cards that labour's bureaucracy ensconced itself within came tumbling down in the troubles of the 1980's, trade union officials often found themselves trying to deal from the old deck crumbling at their feet. As Solidarity's outcome revealed, there would be no winning hands drawn from such worn cards.

Notes

Introduction

1. Karl Marx and Frederick Engels, "Manifesto of the Communist Party," in *Selected Works* (Moscow, 1968), pp. 35-36.

2. For a defence of Marx and Engels, see G.E.M. de Ste. Croix, *The Class Struggle in the Ancient Greek World* (London, 1981), pp. 42-49.

3. See, for instance, Bettina Bradbury, "The Family Economy and Work in an Industrializing City: Montreal in the 1870s," Canadian Historical Association *Papers* (1979), pp. 71-96; Peter DeLottinville, "Joe Beef of Montreal: Working-Class Culture and the Tavern, 1869-1889," *Labour/ Le Travailleur*, 8/9 (1981-82), pp. 9-40; Michael B. Katz, Michael J. Doucet, and Mark J. Stern, *The Social Organization of Early Industrial Capitalism* (Cambridge, 1982).

4. Note the discussions in David Bercuson, "Through the Looking Glass of Culture: An Essay on the New Labour History and Working-Class Culture in Recent Canadian Historical Writing," *Labour/Le Travailleur*, 7 (1981), pp. 95-112; Gregory S. Kealey, "Labour and Working-Class History in Canada: Prospects for the 1980s," *Labour/Le Travailleur*, 7 (1981), pp. 67-94; Ian McKay, "Capital and Labour in the Halifax Baking and Confectionary Industry during the Last Half of the Nineteenth Century," *Labour/Le Travailleur*, 3 (1978), pp. 63-108.

5. See the attempt at a broad overview in Bryan D. Palmer, *Working-Class Experience: The Rise and Reconstitution of Canadian Labour, 1800-1980* (Toronto, 1983).

6. Note Satu Repo, "Rosvall and Voutilainen: Two Union Men Who Never Died," *Labour/Le Travailleur*, 8/9 (1981-82), pp. 79-102; Wayne Roberts, *'Honest Womanhood': Feminism, Femininity, and Class Consciousness among Toronto Working Women, 1893-1914* (Toronto, 1977); Gregory S. Kealey and Bryan D. Palmer, *Dreaming of What Might Be: The Knights of Labor in Ontario, 1880-1900* (Cambridge, 1982).

7. See, for instance, David M. Gordon, Richard Edwards, and Michael Reich, *Segmented work, divided workers: the historical transformation of labor in the United States* (Cambridge, 1982); also the attempt to read Canadian development in this light in Gregory S. Kealey, "The Structure of Canadian Working-Class History," in W.J.C. Cherwinski and Gregory S. Kealey, eds., *Lectures in Canadian Labour and Working-Class History* (St. John's, 1985), pp. 23-36.

8. Ian McKay, *The Craft Transformed: An Essay on the Carpenters of Halifax, 1885-1985* (Halifax, 1985), esp. pp. 1-26.

9. Note Tom Naylor, *The History of Canadian Business, 1867-1914*, 2 vols. (Toronto, 1975); David Frank, "The Cape Breton Coal Industry and the Rise and Fall of the British Empire Steel Corporation," *Acadiensis*, 7 (1977), pp. 3-34; T.W. Acheson, "Changing Social Origins of the Canadian Industrial Elite," in Glenn Porter and Robert Cuff, eds., *Enterprise and National Development: Essays in Canadian Business and Economic History* (Toronto, 1973), pp. 51-79; Acheson, "The National Policy and the Industrialization of the Maritimes, 1880-1910," *Acadiensis*, 1 (Spring, 1972), pp. 3-28.

10. See the following background studies: Craig Heron and Bryan D. Palmer, "Through the Prism of the Strike: Industrial Conflict in Southern Ontario, 1901-1914," *Canadian Historical Review*, 58 (December, 1977), pp. 423-58; Ian McKay, "Strikes in the Maritimes, 1901-1914," *Acadiensis*, 13 (Autumn, 1983), pp. 3-46.

11. See Greg Kealey, ed., *Canada Investigates Industrialism: The Royal Commission on the Relations of Labor and Capital, 1889* (Toronto, 1973), pp. ix-xxvii; Kealey and Palmer, *Dreaming*, pp. 204-76; Bryan D. Palmer, "They Ride Horses Don't They: Historical Musings on the Canadian State and its Agents," *Our Generation*, 14 (Summer, 1981), pp. 28-41.

12. Paul Craven, *An Impartial Umpire: Industrial Relations and the Canadian State* (Toronto, 1980); Ian McKay, "Review of Craven," *Labour/Le Travailleur*, 8/9 (1981-82), pp. 364-70.

13. See also Laurel Sefton MacDowell, "The Formation of the Canadian Industrial Relations System during World War II," *Labour/Le Travailleur*, 3 (1978), pp. 175-96; Leo Panitch and Donald Swartz, *From Consent to Coercion: The Assault on Trade Union Freedoms* (Toronto, 1985).

14. Mark Thompson and Gene Swimmer, eds., *Conflict or Compromise: The Future of Public Sector Industrial Relations* (Montreal, 1984); Daniel Drache, ed., *Quebec – Only the Beginning: The Manifestoes of the Common Front* (Toronto, 1972); Leo Roback, "Quebec Workers in the Twentieth Century," in Cherwinski and Kealey, eds., *Lectures*, pp. 180-81.

15. Compare the Palmer essay with Des Morton's reading of Solidarity: "A summer-long organizing campaign, borrowing the Polish union's name and logo, created Solidarity, a front of unions, the elderly, and other victims of Bennett's policies. An escalating strike in October and November closed government offices, services and most schools. Only hours away from a near-general strike, B.C.'s government and unions compromised. The concession was modest but real: seniority would be respected in the government's cuts. Unions in the most unionized of provinces were obliged to treat the outcome as a triumph." Desmond Morton with Terry Copp, *Working People: An Illustrated History of the Canadian Labour Movement* (Ottawa, 1984), p. 319.

16. See André Gorz, *Farewell to the Working Class* (London, 1982); and, for rejection of the now popular Gorz position, Michael Burawoy, *The Politics of Production: Factory Regimes under Capitalism and Socialism* (London,

1985); Ralph Miliband, "The New Revisionism in Britain," *New Left Review*, 150 (March-April, 1985), pp. 5-28.

McKay, Class Struggle and Merchant Capital

1.   This essay is a revised and rethought version of "Class Struggle and Mercantile Capitalism: Craftsmen and Labourers on the Halifax Waterfront, 1850-1902," in Gerald Panting and Rosemary Ommer, eds., *Workingmen Who Got Wet* (St. John's, 1980), pp. 289-333, and draws on trade union and other sources that surfaced after the first version was prepared. Throughout I use "Halifax" to refer to both Halifax and its suburb Dartmouth. My thanks to Judith Fingard, who first introduced me to the subject of Halifax working-class history and who has generously shared information and insights with me.

2.   For an analysis of the domination of the Chamber of Commerce by the wholesaler/broker faction of the Halifax bourgeoisie, see David A. Sutherland, "The Personnel and Policies of the Halifax Board of Trade, 1890-1914," in Lewis R. Fischer and Eric W. Sager, eds., *The Enterprising Canadians: Entrepreneurs and Economic Development in Eastern Canada, 1820-1914* (St. John's, 1979), pp. 205-10. See also Larry D. McCann, "Staples and the new industrialism in the growth of Post-Confederation Halifax," *Acadiensis*, VIII, 2 (1979), pp. 29-64.

3.   *Report of the Royal Commission on the Relations of Capital and Labor in Canada,* (hereafter *RCRCL*), *Evidence - Nova Scotia* (Ottawa, 1889), pp. 136, 325.

4.   See E.J. Hobsbawm, *The Age of Capital* (New York, 1979), p. 59; *RCRCL, Evidence - Nova Scotia*, p. 154.

5.   *Acadian Recorder*, 6 May 1884.

6.   *Citizen and Evening Chronicle*, 9 May 1884.

7.   Adopting the useful terminology of Sydney and Beatrice Webb, *Industrial Democracy* (London, 1901), although not, of course, many of their other assumptions.

8.   Gerald S. Graham, "The Ascendancy of the Sailing Ship, 1850-85," *Economic History Review*, 2nd Series, XIX, 1 (1956), p. 7; Rosemary Ommer, "The decline of the eastern Canadian shipping industry, 1880-95," *Journal of Transport History*, 1 (1984), pp. 25-44; Sarah Palmer, "Experience, Experiment and Economics: Factors in the Construction of Early Merchant Steamships," in Keith Matthews and Gerald Panting, eds., *Ships and Shipbuilding in the North Atlantic Region* (St. John's, 1978), pp. 233-49; Public Archives of Nova Scotia (PANS), MG 27, Vols. 42-44, Pickford and Black Registers. The printed records of the Department of Marine and Fisheries, in the *Sessional Papers*, 1890-1910, show the domination of steam vessels in the early 1890's.

9.   See Eric W. Sager, "Sources of Productivity Change in the Halifax Ocean Fleet, 1863-1900," in David Alexander and Rosemary Ommer, eds., *Volumes Not Values: Canadian Sailing Ships and World Trades* (St. John's, 1979), pp. 93-115; L.R. Fischer, "The Great Mudhole Fleet: The Voyages

and Productivity of the Sailing Vessels of Saint John, 1863-1912," *ibid.*, pp. 119-55.

10.   The record of the *N.B. Lewis*, a Yarmouth vessel, suggests that heavy repair costs could wipe out much of the gross revenue from a successful trip to Java: see Clement W. Crowell, ed., *The Novascotiaman* (Halifax, 1979), Chapter VIII.

11.   For mid-nineteenth-century repair facilities, "careening wharves," see the description of Richard Marshall in *Acadian Recorder*, 28 March 1857; and also *Herald*, 24 April 1880, 28 August 1883; *Acadian Recorder*, 21 September 1889; Fielding Papers, PANS, MG 2, Vol. 557, Folder 108; and *Herald*, 20 September 1920; for attacks on Halifax as a ship repair port, see *Citizen and Evening Chronicle*, 8 May 1884, a long rebuttal of Boston attempts to discredit Halifax; and for merchant criticisms of labour for raising the price of ship repairs, see the remarks of George E. Boak in *Citizen and Evening Chronicle*, 9 May 1884; Dalhousie University Archives, MS 9 48 (microfilm), Business Book of the Caulkers' Association of Halifax & Dartmouth 1882-1895 (hereafter Caulkers' Minutes), Minutes of 11 October 1886.

12.   See *Steel's Elements of Mastmaking, Sailmaking and Rigging* (New York, 1932 [1794]), Part One; *RCRCL, Evidence – Nova Scotia*, p. 229, for comments by a Halifax rigger.

13.   Franklin E. Coyne, *The Development of the Cooperage Industry in the United States, 1620-1940* (Chicago, 1940); Herbert Gutman, "La politique ouvrière de la grande enterprise américaine de 'L'âge du clinquant': le case de Standard Oil Company," *Le mouvement social*, 102 (janvier-mars 1978), pp. 67-99. For the Canadian industry, see the interesting discussion in James Delebaugh, *History of The Lumber Industry of America* (Chicago, 1906), Chapter VII; *RCRCL, Evidence – Nova Scotia*, pp. 11, 53.

14.   Report from Local No. 140, Halifax, in the *Coopers' International Journal*, IX (September, 1903), p. 411.

15.   Crowell, *Novascotiaman*, pp. 286-87. One such well-worn kit, belonging to a sailmaker who travelled up and down the Atlantic seaboard, is preserved in the Dartmouth Heritage Museum. On the artisanal character of sailmaking, see Mark G. Hirsch, "Sailmakers: The maintenance of craft tradition in the age of steam," in Royden Harrison and Jonathan Zeitlin, eds., *Divisions of Labour: Skilled Workers and Technological Change in Nineteenth Century Britain* (Chicago, 1985), p. 92; and Samuel Sadler, *The Art and Science of Sailmaking* (London, 1906).

16.   An important distinction was drawn between ship joiners and ship carpenters. The ship carpenters erected the structure and their work could not be removed without affecting the strength of the structure; the work of the joiners was not intended to add to structural strength and could therefore be removed without affecting it. The ship carpenter worked with heavy materials, seldom devoting much time to the finish of surfaces; the joiner worked with light material and had constantly to bear in mind the finish and appearance of work when it was completed. In Halifax, the

term "shipwright" encompassed both aspects of the work, but "joinery" was far less practised in a port devoted to ship repair than was "ship carpentry."

17.   See, for example, the discussion in Sir Wescott Abell, *The Shipwright's Trade* (Cambridge, 1948), p. 77.

18.   Lloyd's Register of Shipping, *Rules and Regulations for the Construction and Classification of Wood Vessels* (London, 1917), p. 61; R.D. Culler, *Skiffs and Schoners* (Camden, Maine, 1974), p. 9. I am indebted to Niels Jaanash of the Maritime Museum of the Atlantic for this reference.

19.   According to the *Census of Canada*, the number of artisans in these trades actually rose from 163 in 1871 to 207 in 1891, but this statistic is complicated by the emergence of many black, rural coopers in the community of Hammonds Plains, who made casks for fish at well under the costs of production in Halifax. (In 1891 we find in Halifax County no fewer than eighty-seven cooperages employing only 124 men.) Of the major trades listed in 1891, 153 were coopers, thirty-two were in ship construction, and twenty-two were sailmakers. The census data underestimate considerably the number of shipwrights and caulkers.

20.   Of the sixty-four cooperages operating in Halifax from 1872 to 1920, the average life span was 6.9 years: because of extremely low barriers to entry, the trade was chronically overcrowded and bankruptcies common. Locational factors – the need to locate right on very expensive and scarce waterfront property – probably accounted for the much greater stability of sailmaking and ship repair: two of the seven shipbuilding/repairing firms lasted throughout the period, while the average life span for the nineteen sail-lofts was 11.5 years. See *McAlpine's City Directory for 1871-72* (Halifax), continuing to *McAlpine's City Directory for 1920-21*.

21.   *Evening Express*, 15 April 1874.

22.   For this mass exodus of rural craftsmen, see Alan Brookes, "Out-Migration from the Maritime Provinces, 1860-1900: Some Preliminary Considerations," in P.A. Buckner and David Frank, eds., *Atlantic Canada After Confederation* (Fredericton, 1985), pp. 34-63.

23.   *Evening Express*, 1 December 1874.

24.   Public Archives of Canada, RG 27, Vol. 32, File 1 (A-K), Special investigation in regard to the tendency of the Rates of Wages and Hours of Labour in Canada – The Building Trades.

25.   *Supplementary Rules of the Shipwrights' and Caulkers' Association* (n.p. [Halifax], n.d. [1867]), p. 13; Carpenters Hall, Halifax, Records of Local 83, United Brotherhood of Carpenters and Joiners of America, Minutes of 18 July 1899.

26.   Caulkers' Records, Minutes for 16 January 1882.

27.   *Ibid.*, Minutes of 23 January 1882, 11 May 1885. This motion was later overturned, perhaps because it was impracticable.

28.   Webb, *Industrial Democracy*, pp. 73, 517; E.J. Hobsbawm, "National Unions on the Waterside," in *Labouring Men: Studies in the History of Labour* (London, 1974 [1964]), p. 205.

29.   *Supplementary Rules*, p. 15.

30.   *RCRCL, Evidence – Nova Scotia*, pp. 144, 184; *Acadian Recorder*, 15 May 1895; Minutes of Local 83, 16 July 1895; Caulkers' Minutes, 14 May 1883, 14 January 1884, 27 April 1885.

31.   Caulkers' Minutes, 11 November 1884.

32.   *Acadian Recorder*, 27, 29 January 1886; *Morning Chronicle*, 28, 30 January, 2 February 1886; Caulkers' Minutes, 2 March 1886.

33.   PANS, RG 5, Series P, Vol. 126, No. 102, Petition of Shipwrights and Caulkers of the City of Halifax and Dartmouth, 15 February 1864.

34.   *Supplementary Rules*, p. 13.

35.   *Evening Express*, 1 March 1865.

36.   *Debates and Proceedings of the House of Assembly, Nova Scotia*, 1866, p. 15; *RCRCL, Evidence – Nova Scotia*, p. 107; for the emigration of ship-wrights and caulkers, under the direction of H.I. Crandall and James Lyle, to Honolulu, see the Crandall Papers, Dartmouth Heritage Museum, and *Dartmouth Times*, 16 February 1884.

37.   *Citizen and Evening Chronicle*, 9 May 1884.

38.   Caulkers' Minutes, 12, 17 July 1886; the Graving Dock Company subsequently opposed the union's control over oakum (Caulkers' Minutes, 7 April 1890), but evidently without success. For Toronto parallels, see Gregory S. Kealey, " 'The Honest Workingman' and Workers' Control: The Experience of Toronto Skilled Workers, 1860-1892," *Labour/Le Travailleur*, 1 (1976), pp. 32-68.

39.   *Morning Chronicle*, 4 June 1864; *Daily Reporter and Times*, 14 June 1870; *Morning Chronicle*, 1, 2 May 1872; *RCRCL, Evidence – Nova Scotia*, pp. 107, 228.

40.   Probate Court (Halifax), Inventory of the Estate of Michael O'Brien, 1912. The O'Brien estate was appraised at $9,425; *Morning Chronicle*, 15 July 1912; *Herald*, 15 July 1912; *Acadian Recorder*, 15 July 1912. The same family names – Regan, Moseley, Devan, Hunt – reoccur again and again in the executive lists of the Caulkers' Association as well.

41.   The only evidence of the association's existence after 1910 I have is mention of the union's floral wreath sent for the funeral of Michael O'Brien in 1912 (*Acadian Recorder*, 17 July 1912).

42.   *Souvenir Booklet, Twenty-Fourth Convention of the Trades and Labor Congress of Canada* (Halifax, 1908).

43.   See J.I. Cooper, "The Quebec Ship Labourers' Benevolent Society," *Canadian Historical Review*, XXX, 3 (1949), pp. 336-43; James Richard Rice, "A History of Organized Labour in Saint John, New Brunswick, 1813-1890" (M.A. thesis, University of New Brunswick, 1968), pp. 19-52; Judith Fingard, "The Decline of the Ship Labourer in 19th Century Timber Ports," *Labour/Le Travailleur*, 2 (1977), pp. 35-53.

44.   *Morning News* (Saint John), 29 August 1842.

45.   *RCRCL, Evidence – Nova Scotia*, p. 95; *Herald*, 12 May 1884; *Acadian Recorder*, 12 May 1884; *Herald*, 2 November 1880.

46. *RCRCL, Evidence – Nova Scotia*, pp. 116, 121; *Acadian Recorder*, 24 January 1885.

47. *Citizen and Evening Chronicle*, 10 May 1884; *Morning Chronicle*, 28 October 1856.

48. *Herald*, 7, 9 May 1884.

49. *Morning Chronicle*, 29, 31 May 1873; *Citizen*, 7 June 1873; *Evening Express*, 20 June 1873; *Acadian Recorder*, 10 May 1880.

50. For interesting details on international working-class resistance to these innovations, including machine-smashing, see Peter N. Stearns, *Lives of Labour: Work in a Maturing Industrial Society* (London, 1975), pp. 126-27.

51. See *RCRCL, Evidence – New Brunswick*, pp. 65, 235.

52. Gareth Stedman Jones, *Outcast London: A Study in the Relationship Between Classes in Victorian Society* (Oxford, 1971), p. 121.

53. *Acadian Recorder*, 8, 14 April, 9 June, 13 July, 21 August 1882; 7, 19 April 1883; *Citizen and Evening Chronicle*, 1 November 1882; PANS, Vertical File, "Labour Unions – 1883" [Manuscript of "An Act to Incorporate Laborers' Union"]; *Statutes of Nova Scotia*, 46 Vic., Cap. 77, 1883, pp. 188-89; *Journals* of the House of Assembly, 1883, p. 127; PANS, RG 7, Vol. 366, No. 24, Constitution of the Laborers' Union.

54. *Acadian Recorder*, 8 October 1919; Probate Court, Estate of John A. Mackasey.

55. PAC, Microfilm, Reel C-1700, 143667-143692, John A. Macdonald Papers, John A. Mackasey to Macdonald, 23 July 1883.

56. He would later be licence inspector for the city of Halifax while leading the Laborers' Union. See *RCRCL, Evidence – Nova Scotia*, pp. 110-12, for his comments on the Halifax liquor trade.

57. *Citizen and Evening Chronicle*, 10 May 1884.

58. *Herald*, 7, 10 May 1884.

59. *Acadian Recorder*, 30 April, 6, 10 May 1884; *Herald*, 2, 9, 10 May 1884.

60. *Acadian Recorder*, 13, 15, 17, 19 May 1884; *Herald*, 13, 16 May 1884.

61. *Acadian Recorder*, 27 May, 9 July 1884; 15 July 1886.

62. *Acadian Recorder*, 6 April 1889, 4 May 1894, 10 June 1899.

63. *Herald*, 2, 3, 4, 8, 12 April 1902.

64. *Evening Mail*, 15 March 1902; *Herald*, 3 April 1902.

65. Peter DeLottinville, "Joe Beef of Montreal: Working Class Culture and the Tavern, 1869-1889," *Labour/Le Travailleur*, 8-9 (1981-1982), pp. 9-40, studies "waterfront culture" in Montreal and brings out the rifts between skilled workers and casual longshore labourers.

66. See Bryan Palmer, "Most Uncommon Common Men: Craft and Culture in Historical Perspective," *Labour/Le Travailleur*, 1 (1976), pp. 5-31; Palmer, *A Culture in Conflict: Skilled Workers and Industrial Capitalism in Hamilton, Ontario, 1860-1914* (Montreal, 1979), Chapter III; Gregory S. Kealey, *Toronto Workers Respond to Industrial Capitalism, 1867-1892* (Toronto, 1980), Chapters 3-6.

67.   For the subsequent history of the Halifax longshoremen, see Catherine Ann Waite. "The Longshoremen of Halifax 1900-1930: their living and working conditions" (M.A. thesis, Dalhousie University, 1977).

68.   For studies of the social impact of merchant capital in the region, see Gary Hughes, *Two Islands, Miscou and Lamèque and their State of Bondage 1846-1861* (Saint John, [c. 1980]); Rosemary Ommer, " 'All the Fish of the post': property, resource rights and development in a nineteenth century inshore fishery," *Acadiensis*, X, 2 (Spring, 1981), pp. 107-23; Graham Wynn, *Timber Colony* (Toronto, 1981); I.R. Robertson, "Highlanders, Irishmen and the land question in nineteenth-century Prince Edward Island," in C.M. Cullen and T.C. Smout, eds., *Comparative Aspects of Scottish and Irish Economic and Social History, 1600-1900* (Edinburgh, 1977); David Sutherland, "The Stanyan ropeworks of Halifax, Nova Scotia: glimpses of a pre-industrial manufactory," *Labour/Le Travailleur*, 6 (1980), pp. 149-58; and Judith Fingard, *Jack in Port: Sailortowns of Eastern Canada* (Toronto, 1982). For a general interpretation of merchant capital as a conservative force, see Elizabeth Fox-Genovese and Eugene Genovese, *Fruits of Merchant Capital: Slavery and Bourgeois Property in the Rise and Expansion of Capitalism* (Oxford, 1983).

Kealey and Palmer, The Knights of Labor

1.   Gustavus Myers, *A History of Canadian Wealth* (Toronto, 1972); H.C. Pentland, "The Development of a Capitalistic Labour Market in Canada," *Canadian Journal of Economics and Political Science*, 25 (November, 1959), pp. 450-61; Pentland, "Labor and the Development of Industrial Capitalism in Canada" (Ph.D. dissertation, University of Toronto, 1960); Stanley B. Ryerson, *Unequal Union: Roots of Crisis in the Canadas, 1815-1873* (Toronto, 1968); Gordon W. Bertram, "Historical Statistics on Growth and Structure of Manufacturing in Canada, 1870-1957," in J. Henripin and A. Asimakopulos, eds., *C.P.S.A. Conference on Statistics, 1962 and 1963* (Toronto, 1964), pp. 93-146; Bryan D. Palmer, *A Culture in Conflict: Skilled Workers and Industrial Capitalism in Hamilton, Ontario, 1860-1914* (Montreal, 1979), pp. 3-31; Gregory S. Kealey, *Toronto Workers Respond to Industrial Capitalism, 1867-1892* (Toronto, 1980), pp. 1-34; *People's Journal* (Hamilton), 1 April 1871, cited in Steven Langdon, *The Emergence of the Canadian Working Class Movement* (Toronto, 1975), p. 3; *Journal of the Board of Arts and Manufactures for Upper Canada*, 7 (1867), p. 220.

2.   See, for instance, Terry Copp, *The Anatomy of Poverty: The Condition of the Working Class in Montreal, 1897-1929* (Toronto, 1974); Michael J. Piva, *The Condition of the Working Class in Toronto, 1900-1921* (Ottawa, 1979); David Millar, "A Study of Real Wages: The Construction, Use and Accuracy Check of a Constant-Dollar Plotter," unpublished research paper, University of Winnipeg, 1980.

3.   Jacques Ferland, "The Problem of Change in the Rate of Surplus Value

Studied Through the Evolution of the 'Social Cost of Labour' in Canada, 1870-1910" (M.A. research paper, McGill University, 1980).

4.   Terence V. Powderly, *The Path I Trod: The Autobiography of Terence V. Powderly* (New York, 1940), pp. 3-4, 102.

5.   All organizational data throughout are based on our own calculations. We should note, however, a debt of gratitude to two pieces of pioneering research on the Knights that were of inestimable value to us. Eugene Forsey's massive compilation of materials on organized labour in Canada before 1902 includes much on the Knights and a helpful attempt at a local-by-local reconstruction. See Eugene Forsey, *Trade Unions in Canada, 1812-1902* (Toronto, 1982). Jonathan Garlock, *Knights of Labor Data Bank* (Ann Arbor, 1973), and Garlock, "A Structural Analysis of the Knights of Labor" (Ph.D. dissertation, University of Rochester, 1974), have been of considerable help. For a description of the data bank, see Garlock, "The Knights of Labor Data Bank," *Historical Methods Newsletter*, 6 (1973), pp. 149-60. Our corrections to the data bank will be incorporated into the computer file at Ann Arbor. These corrections are based on the labour and local press of Ontario, on the Ontario Bureau of Industry, *Annual Reports*, on various trade union minutes and proceedings, and on the extensive Ontario correspondence scattered throughout the Powderly Papers, recently indexed at the PAC by Russell Hann. The population data are from the 1881 and 1891 censuses.

6.   The original version of this article contained more evidence and argument. This drew a critical response and our subsequent reply. See Michael Piva, "The Bonds of Unity: A Comment," and Kealey and Palmer, "The Bonds of Unity: Some Further Reflections," *Histoire sociale/Social History*, XVI (May, 1983), pp. 169-90.

7.   Ezra Cook, ed., *Knights of Labor Illustrated: Adelphon Kruptos: The Full Illustrated Ritual Including the 'Unwritten Work' and an Historical Sketch of the Order* (Chicago, 1886); Catholic University of America, Washington, D.C., Powderly Papers, "The Great Seal of Knighthood" and "Secret Circular: Explanation of the Signs and Symbols of the Order"; Carroll D. Wright, "An Historical Sketch of the Knights of Labor," *Quarterly Journal of Economics*, I (January, 1887), pp. 142-43; Powderly, *The Path I Trod*, pp. 434-35.

8.   *Gananoque Reporter*, 25 August 1887.

9.   Note the comments in Russell Hann, "Brainworkers and the Knights of Labor: E.E. Sheppard, Phillips Thompson, and the Toronto *News*, 1883-1887," in Gregory S. Kealey and Peter Warrian, eds., *Essays in Canadian Working Class History* (Toronto, 1976), p. 57; Lawrence Goodwyn, *Democratic Promise: The Populist Movement in America* (New York, 1976).

10.   *Palladium of Labor* (Hamilton), 5 September 1885; Powderly Papers, O'Neill to Powderly, 13 January 1885; *Statistics as Collected by Headlight Assembly No. 4069, K. of L., for Its Exclusive Use* (St. Thomas, 1885), p. 3.

11.   *Journal of Commerce*, 13 March 1891; *Labor Union*, 13 January 1883.

12.   Ontario Bureau of Industry, *Annual Report* (Toronto, 1888); *St. Thomas Times*, 21 April 1886; *Journal of United Labor* (Philadelphia), March, 1883.

13.   G. Weston Wrigley, "Socialism in Canada," *International Socialist Review*, I (1 May 1901), p. 686; F.W. Watt, "The National Policy, the Workingman and Proletarian Ideas in Victorian Canada," *Canadian Historical Review*, XL (March, 1959), pp. 1-26.

14.   See, for instance, *Journal of United Labor*, 25 March 1886.

15.   Powderly Papers, Cross to Powderly and G.E.B., 9 June 1887; *Gananoque Reporter*, 3 December 1887.

16.   See, especially, Leon Fink, *Workingmen's Democracy: The Knights of Labor and American Politics* (Urbana, Ill., 1983).

17.   *Brantford Expositor*, 16 July 1886; *London Advertiser*, 29, 30 October 1886; Susan Levine, "The Best Men in the Order: Women in the Knights of Labor," paper presented to the Canadian Historical Association, London, 1978; and Levine, "The Knights of Labor and Romantic Ideology," paper presented to the Centennial Conference, Newberry Library, Chicago, May 17-19, 1979.

18.   *Palladium of Labor*, 26 December 1885.

19.   Sir John A. Macdonald to Sir Charles Tupper, 21 June 1886, in Sir Joseph Pope, ed., *The Correspondence of Sir John A. Macdonald* (Toronto, 1921), p. 382.

20.   On the Knights and the Irish, see Eric Foner, "Class, Ethnicity, and Radicalism in the Gilded Age: The Land League and Irish America," *Marxist Perspectives*, 1 (Summer, 1978), pp. 6-55; on Home Rule, see Kealey, *Toronto Workers*, Ch. 14.

21.   Powderly Papers, George Havens to Powderly, 4 January 1883.

22.   Kealey, *Toronto Workers*, Ch. 11.

23.   *Labor Union*, 3, 10 February, 3 March 1883; Powderly Papers, Gibson to Powderly, 7 February 1883, and Powderly to Gibson, 9 February 1883.

24.   *Trade Union Advocate* (Toronto), 11, 18, 25 January, 1, 8, 15 February 1883; Public Archives of Canada (PAC), Toronto Trades and Labor Council, Minutes, 19 January, 2 February 1883; *Globe* (Toronto), 5, 8 February 1883.

25.   Powderly Papers, D.B. Skelly to Powderly, 15 December 1884; PAC, Macdonald Papers, Small to Macdonald, 10 April 1883.

26.   *Palladium of Labor*, 25 August, 28 September, 13, 20 October, 24 November 1883, 12 January, 31 May, 5 December 1884, 8, 15 May, 4 July, 28 November, 5 December 1885.

27.   Kealey, *Toronto Workers*, Ch. 11.

28.   *Globe*, 14 October 1884.

29.   PAC, Macdonald Papers, Boultbee to Macdonald, 12 September, 29, 30 December 1884; Macpherson to Macdonald, 27 December 1884.

30.   PAC, Toronto Trades and Labor Council, Minutes, 4, 14, 18, 29 December 1885; *News* (Toronto), 4 January 1886; *Palladium of Labor*, 5 December 1885; Powderly Papers, O'Donoghue to Powderly, 29 March 1886.

31.   PAC, Macdonald Papers, Piper to Macdonald, 2, 3 February 1886; *Toronto World*, 13, 16 March 1886; Kealey, *Toronto Workers*, Chs. 6, 11; Powderly Papers, O'Donoghue to Powderly, 29 March 1886.

32.   Greg Kealey, ed., *Canada Investigates Industrialism* (Toronto, 1973), pp. ix-xxvii; Fernand Harvey, *Révolution industrielle et travailleurs* (Montréal, 1978).

33.   *St. Thomas Daily Times*, February-December, 1886; *Canada Labor Courier* (St. Thomas), 29 July, 30 December 1886. See also Barbara A. McKenna, "The Decline of the Liberal Party in Elgin County," paper presented to the Canadian Historical Association, London, 1978.

34.   Powderly Papers, William Garson to Powderly, 21 March 1884 and 22 October 1885.

35.   *London Advertiser*, 21 December 1886; *Sarnia Observer*, 10 September 1886, 7 January 1887; *Canadian Labor Reformer* (Toronto) 18 December 1886; *Toronto World*, 2 December 1886; *Globe*, 8 December 1886; *News*, 22 December 1886.

36.   *London Advertiser*, 24 November, 7, 9, 10, 11, 16, 17, 18, 29, 30 December 1886, 7, 11 January 1887; *Palladium of Labor*, 27 November, 11 December 1886; *Canada Labor Courier*, 30 December 1886; Powderly Papers, Hewit to Powderly, 13 December 1886.

37.   Kealey, *Toronto Workers*, Ch. 12.

38.   Powderly Papers, Freed to Powderly, 2 December 1886; *Palladium of Labor*, 4, 7, 11, 18 December 1886; *Hamilton Spectator*, 4, 7, 8, 14, 22 December 1886.

39.   *Ibid.*, 13 January, 24 February 1887.

40.   Kealey, *Toronto Workers*, Chs. 12-13.

41.   *Courier* (Brantford), 4 January, 15 April, 28 December 1886; *Brantford Expositor*, 16 April, 20 August, 24 September, 17, 31 December 1886; *Canada Labor Courier*, 30 December 1886, 13 January 1887; *Brockville Recorder*, 1887-88; *Ottawa Citizen*, 1890-91.

42.   *Brockville Recorder*, 4 January 1888; *Cornwall Freeholder*, 3, 10 January, 7 February 1890. These newspaper discussions are somewhat confusing, as various candidates denied formal connections with the Order. Yet, in the aftermath, the *Cornwall Freeholder*, 7 February 1890, argued that one loser "had arranged against him the workingmen, which is no mean factor in election contests in Cornwall these days." Cf. Kealey, *Toronto Workers*, Ch. 12.

43.   Kealey, *Toronto Workers*, Chs. 3, 10; Palmer, *A Culture in Conflict*, Ch. 6; Eugene Forsey, "The Telegraphers' Strike of 1883," *Transactions of the Royal Society of Canada*, Series 4, 9 (1971), pp. 245-59; *Iron Molders Journal* (Cincinnati) (hereafter *IMJ*), 31 August 1883; *Palladium of Labor*, 18, 25 August 1883.

44.   For Toronto, see Kealey, *Toronto Workers*, Ch. 10; for Chatham, see *Canada Labor Courier*, 30 December 1886, 13 January 1887; for cotton and lumber, see below.

45.   Kealey, *Toronto Workers*, Ch. 10; Palmer, *A Culture in Conflict*, Ch. 6.

46.   For background on the Iron Molders, see C.B. Williams, "Canadian-American Trade Union Relations: A Case Study of the Development of Bi-National Unionism" (Ph.D. dissertation, Cornell University, 1964); Palmer, *A Culture in Conflict*; Kealey, *Toronto Workers*, Ch. 5. The following is also based on the *IMJ* and the International's convention proceedings.

47.   David Montgomery, *Workers' Control in America* (New York, 1979), Ch. 1 and *passim*; Kealey, *Toronto Workers*, Ch. 5; Palmer, *A Culture in Conflict*, Ch. 3; Wayne Roberts, "Studies in the Toronto Labour Movement, 1896-1914" (Ph.D. dissertation, University of Toronto, 1978), Ch. 3.

48.   Strike data are drawn from *IMJ*; Iron Molders International Union (hereafter IMIU), *Proceedings*, 1860-1895; and Ontario Bureau of Industry, *Annual Reports*.

49.   Kealey, *Toronto Workers*, Ch. 5; Palmer, *A Culture in Conflict*, Ch. 3.

50.   Dale Chisamore *et al.*, *Brockville: A Social History* (Brockville, 1975), Ch. 4.

51.   *Ibid.*, Ch. 5; *IMJ*, 1868-92; IMIU, *Proceedings*.

52.   Chisamore *et al.*, *Brockville*, Ch. 5.

53.   Daniel Walkowitz, *Worker, City, Company Town* (Champaign, Ill., 1978), pp. 211, 213, 239-40; and a review of Walkowitz by Bryan Palmer, *Labour/La Travailleur*, 4 (1979), pp. 261-67.

54.   *Brockville Recorder*, 12, 13, 14 June, 25 July, 17 November 1883.

55.   *Ibid.*, 5, 6, 10 March 1884; Knights of Labor, General Assembly, *Proceedings*, 1884, p. 652.

56.   Powderly Papers, James R. Brown to Powderly, 29 September 1882; *Palladium of Labor*, 18, 25 August 1883; *IMJ*, 31 August 1883; Nancy Stunden, "Oshawa Knights of Labor Demonstration Medal," *Canadian Labour History, Newsletter of the Committee on Canadian Labour History*, 4 (1974), pp. 1-2.

57.   *Palladium of Labor*, 20 October, 8, 15, 22 December 1883; *IMJ*, 31 August 1890.

58.   Powderly Papers, Lewis Allchin to Powderly, 20, 25 October 1884.

59.   *News*, 23 February, 6, 9, 15 March 1886; *IMJ*, 30 September 1890.

60.   *Labor Record* (Toronto), 14 May 1886; Trent University Archives, Gainey Collection, IMIU Local 191, Minutes, 1886.

61.   *British Daily Whig* (Kingston), 13, 14, 16, 18, 19, 23 May 1887; *Gananoque Reporter*, 21 May 1887; Ontario Bureau of Industry, *Annual Report* (Toronto, 1887), p. 42.

62.   IMIU, *Proceedings*, 1882 and 1886; *IMJ*, 31 May 1890.

63.   IMIU, *Proceedings*, 1890 and 1895; *IMJ*, August, 1889.

64.   *IMJ*, 31 January 1891.

65.   Bryan Palmer, " 'Give us the road and we will run it': The Social and Cultural Matrix of an Emerging Labour Movement," in Kealey and Warrian, eds., *Essays in Canadian Working Class History*, pp. 106-24; *IMJ*, 31 October 1890, 31 July 1886.

66.   IMIU, *Proceedings*, 1886; *IMJ*, 31 October 1890.

67. IMIU, *Proceedings*, 1888; Richard Oestreicher, "Solidarity and Fragmentation: Working People and Class Consciousness in Detroit, 1877-1895" (Ph.D. dissertation, Michigan State University, 1979), Ch. 7.

68. Ontario Bureau of Industry, *Annual Reports*, 1886, 1889, 1890; Peter DeLottinville, "The St. Croix Manufacturing Company and its influence on the St. Croix Community, 1880-1892" (M.A. thesis, Dalhousie University, 1979).

69. Ontario Bureau of Industry, *Annual Report*, 1887; *Brockville Recorder*, 12 July 1887.

70. Ontario Bureau of Industry, *Annual Report*, 1888; *Cornwall Standard*, 28 January, 2 February 1888; *Montreal Gazettee*, 14 February 1888. Our thanks to Peter DeLottinville for these newspaper references. See also *Gananoque Reporter*, 4, 11, 18 February 1888.

71. Ontario Bureau of Industry, *Annual Report*, 1889; *Gananoque Reporter*, 16 March 1889.

72. This draws on: Powderly Papers, R.R. Elliot to Powderly, 12, 19 July 1888, William Hogan to Powderly, 21 September, 5 November 1888, Archy Sloan to Powderly, 3 September 1888, Powderly to William Sloan, 10 September 1888; *Journal of United Labor*, 12 July 1888. See also Powderly Papers, D.J. O'Donoghue to Powderly, 9 August 1888; *Globe*, 25 July, 10 August 1888.

73. The following draws on: Edward McKenna, "Unorganized Labour versus Management: The Strike at the Chaudière Lumber Mills, 1891," *Histoire sociale/Social History*, 10 (1972), pp. 186-211; Forsey, *Trade Unions*, Ch. 7; Peter Gillis, "E.H. Bronson and Corporate Capitalism" (M.A. thesis, Queen's University, 1975), pp. 72-81; Ontario Bureau of Industry, *Annual Report*, 1892; and *Ottawa Citizen* and *Ottawa Journal*, September-October, 1891.

Heron, Hamilton Steelworkers

1. *Spectator* (Hamilton), 31 December 1895; W.A. Child, "Iron Trade Built By Determined Men," *ibid.*, 15 July 1926; William Kilbourn, *The Elements Combined: A History of the Steel Company of Canada* (Toronto, 1960).

2. William T. Hogan, *Economic History of the Iron and Steel Industry in the United States* (Lexington, Mass., 1971), vol. 1, pp. 343-57; David Brody, *Steelworkers in America: The Nonunion Era* (New York, 1960), pp. 1-26.

3. James J. Davis, *The Iron Puddler: My Life in the Rolling Mills and What Came of It* (Indianapolis, 1922), pp. 85-113; *Iron Age* (New York), 4 July 1895, p. 25; 30 April 1899, p. 29; 5 April 1900, p. 11; Canad , Department of Trade and Commerce, *Report* (Ottawa), 1908, Part I, pp. 796-97. The first serious student of the Canadian steel industry, W.J.A. Donald, noted just before World War I: "Wrought iron and puddled bars have practically passed from the iron and steel vocabulary." *The Canadian Iron and Steel Industry: A Study in the Economic History of A Protected Industry* (Boston, 1915), p. 212.

214   THE CHARACTER OF CLASS STRUGGLE

4. Child, "Iron Trade"; Hogan, *Iron and Steel Industry*, pp. 38-50; John A. Fitch, *The Steel Workers* (New York, 1910), pp. 45-56.

5. Brody, *Steelworkers*, pp. 50-79; Palmer, *A Culture in Conflict: Skilled Workers and Industrial Capitalism in Hamilton, Ontario, 1860-1914* (Montreal, 1979), pp. 83-85. In 1899 the AFL's local organizer, John Flett, claimed to have organized the city's rolling-mill hands, but, if he did, the local must have died soon afterward. Many of the Hamilton Steel and Iron Company's new steel plant employees apparently came from the United States with union experience, but no lodge was formed in these early years. The company nonetheless agreed to pay them according to the Amalgamated wage scale. *Labour Gazette* (hereafter *LG*), I, no. 9 (May, 1901), p. 471.

6. Child, "Iron Trade"; *Stelco Flashes*, XIV, 6 (June, 1950), p. 7.

7. F.H. Bell, "Lifting and Conveying Material in the Foundry," *Canadian Foundryman* (hereafter *CF*), XII, 3 (March, 1921), p. 19; *Times*, 6 April 1907; Bryce M. Stewart, "The Housing of Our Immigrant Workers," Canadian Political Science Association, *Papers and Proceedings* (Ottawa, 1913), p. 98.

8. See, for example, *Herald* (Hamilton), 16 April 1910, 19 September 1912, 12 August 1916, 5 July 1917, 7 September 1918.

9. See, for example, G.W. Austen, "Excessive Labour Turnover and Its Remedies," *Industrial Canada*, XXI, 5 (May, 1920), pp. 74-75; "Cost of 'Labour Turnover,' " *LG*, XX, 11 (November, 1911), p. 1419; A.O. Dawson, "The Relations of Capital and Labour," *Social Welfare*, II, 7 (1 April 1920), pp. 171-72; Paul F. Brissenden and Emil Frankel, *Labor Turnover in Industry: A Statistical Analysis* (New York, 1922).

10. Donald, *The Canadian Iron and Steel Industry*, p. 209.

11. Donald Eldon, "American Influence in the Canadian Iron and Steel Industry" (Ph.D. thesis, Harvard University, 1952), p. 304.

12. Steel Company of Canada, *Annual Report* (Hamilton, 1912).

13. *Canadian Engineer* (hereafter *CE*), V, 2 (August, 1897), p. 120; *Stelco Flashes*, XIV, 6 (June, 1950), p. 7; Gillies-Guy Company Archives (Hamilton), H.W. Robinson Typescript, 14 November 1952.

14. *Canadian Mining Review*, XV, 2 (February, 1896), p. 39; *CE*, III, 7 (January, 1896), pp. 248-49; *Spectator*, 10 February 1896; Charles Reitell, *Machinery and its Benefits to Labor in the Crude Iron and Steel Industries* (Menasha, Wisc., 1917), pp. 9-10; Ontario, Inspectors of Factories, *Report* (Toronto, 1896), p. 11; *Stelco Flashes*, XIV, 6 (June, 1950), p. 6; A.R.R. Jones, "A Gigantic Automaton," *Iron and Steel of Canada*, VII, 4 (April, 1924), pp. 63-64.

15. *Spectator*, 10 February 1896; see also Fitch, *Steel Workers*, p. 27; and Lady Bell, *At the Works: A Study of a Manufacturing Town* (London, 1907), pp. 35-42. This task provided F.W. Taylor, the celebrated theorist of scientific management, with one of his most famous experiments, involving Schmidt, the Dutch labourer. F.W. Taylor, *The Principles of Scientific Management* (New York, 1967), pp. 41-47

16. Ontario, Bureau of Mines, *Report* (Toronto, 1908), pp. 301-02; Canada, Department of Mines, Mines Branch, *Report on the Mining and Metallurgical Industries of Canada, 1907-8* (Ottawa, 1908), p. 337.

17. Bureau of Mines, *Report*, 1908, p. 304; Steel Company of Canada, *Annual Report*, 1920; E.G. Brock, "Making Pig Iron at Hamilton," *CF*, XIX, 2 (February, 1928), pp. 7-10; Jones, "Gigantic Automaton," p. 63; and Appendix I in the original published version of this article: CHA *Papers* (1982), p. 128.

18. *CE*, VIII, 1 (July, 1900), pp. 46-47; *Iron Age*, 5 July 1900, p. 7; Bureau of Mines, *Report*, 1908, p. 303; Reitell, *Machinery*, pp. 23-24, 29; Frank Popplewell, *Some Modern Conditions and Recent Developments in Iron and Steel Production in America* (Manchester, 1906), p. 96; Steel Company of Canada, *Annual Reports*, 1912-13; *Canadian Mining Journal*, XXXIV, 5 (1 August 1913), pp. 488-89; *Canadian Machinery* (hereafter *CM*), IX, 1 (2 January 1913), p. 56; *CF*, VI, 12 (December, 1915), p. 217; Fitch, *Steel Workers*, p. 46; and Appendix II in the original published version of this article: CHA *Papers* (1982), p. 129.

19. Child "Iron Trade"; *Hamilton: The Birmingham of Canada* (Hamilton, 1892); Bureau of Mines, *Report*, 1908, pp. 307-08; American Iron and Steel Institute, *Directory* (New York, 1916), p. 307.

20. Fitch, *Steel Workers*, p. 51. A 1906 photograph of a group of Hamilton Steel and Iron Company rolling-mill hands reveals both the muscles required and the tongs still used in their work. See Craig Heron, Shea Hoffmitz, Wayne Roberts, and Robert Storey, *All That Our Hands Have Done: A Pictorial History of the Hamilton Workers* (Oakville, 1981), p. 42.

21. *Stelco Flashes*, XIV, 6 (June, 1950), p. 9.

22. Kilbourn, *Elements Combined*, p. 93; *CF*, IV, 9 (September, 1913), pp. 142-44; *Canadian Mining Journal*, XXIV, 5 (1 August 1913), p. 489; American Iron and Steel Institute, *Yearbook* (New York, 1919), p. 414.

23. Inspectors of Factories, *Report*, 1916, pp. 15, 48.

24. Cf. Stephen Meyer III, *The Five Dollar Day: Labor Management and Social Control in the Ford Motor Company, 1908-1921* (Albany, 1981).

25. *LG*, 1, 5 (January, 1901), p. 223; *Spectator*, 3 March 1919.

26. *Times* (Hamilton), 10, 11, 14 April 1902; *Spectator*, 11 April 1902, 18 October 1905; Kilbourn, *Elements Combined*, pp. 121, 124; Public Archives of Canada (hereafter PAC), RG 27, vol. 299, file 3475.

27. Because Stelco has consistently denied researchers access to its archives, it has not been possible either to determine the ethnic distribution of workers among the various departments or to compute detailed tables of wage rates or earnings. Fragmentary data drawn from scattered press accounts and government sources indicate that the basic hourly wage rate for labourers in the steel plants hovered in the fifteen- to seventeen-cent range between 1902 and 1915 – well below the twenty cents per hour the Department of Labour estimated to be the average wage for factory labourers in Hamilton in 1915, or the twenty-five cents per hour earned by the civic labourers. In contrast, the cost of food in the city had risen

by 53.7 per cent between 1900 and 1913. Wage rates chased soaring living costs during the war, reaching 37½ cents per hour in 1919, but falling again in the early 1920's. Wages and prices seem to have remained relatively stable in the 1920's. *Spectator*, 8 April 1907, 15 February 1919; PAC, RG 27, vol. 294, File: "Reports – Employment Offices (B-N)," Hamilton; *Census of Canada*, 1921, II, p. 456; IV, p. 401; *LG*, XVI, 5 (November, 1915), p. 620; XXI, 3 (March, 1921), p. 472; XXX, 12 (December, 1930), p. 468; Canada, Board of Inquiry into Cost of Living, *Report* (Ottawa, 1915), II, p. 142; *Herald*, 18 February 1919; Canada, Department of Labour, *Wages and Hours of Labour in Canada, 1920-1929* (Ottawa, 1930), p. 38.

28.   The condition of the southern and eastern European peasant in this period is discussed in Robert F. Foerster, *The Italian Emigration of Our Times* (New York, 1919), pp. 64-105; Robert F. Harney, "Men Without Women: Italian Migrants in Canada, 1885-1930," *Canadian Ethnic Studies*, XI, 1 (1979), pp. 29-47; Antonio Pucci, "The Italian Community in Fort William's East End in the Early Twentieth Century" (M.A. thesis, Lakehead University, 1977), pp. 1-60; Virginia Yans-McLaughlin, *Family and Community: Italian Immigrants in Buffalo, 1880-1930* (Ithaca, 1977), pp. 25-36; William I. Thomas and Florian Znaniecki, *The Polish Peasant in Europe and America*, 5 vols. (New York, 1918-20), I, pp. 87-302; Joseph J. Barton, *Peasants and Strangers: Italians, Rumanians, and Slovaks in an American City, 1890-1950* (Cambridge, Mass., 1975), pp. 27-47; Caroline Golab, *Immigrant Destinations* (Philadelphia, 1977), pp. 43-100; Frank H. Serene, "Immigrant Steelworkers in the Monongahela Valley: Their Communities and the Development of a Labor Class Consciousness" (Ph.D. thesis, University of Pittsburgh, 1979), pp. 26-51.

29.   Robert F. Harney, "The Commerce of Migration," *Canadian Ethnic Studies*, IX, 1 (1977), pp. 42-53; Harney, "Montreal's King of Italian Labour: A Case Study of Padronism," *Labour/Le Travailleur*, IV (1979), pp. 57-84; Jane Synge, "Immigrant Communities – British and Continental Europeans – in Early Twentieth Century Hamilton, Canada," *Oral History*, IV, 2 (Autumn, 1976), pp. 38-51; Matthew James Foster, "Ethnic Settlement in the Barton Street Region of Hamilton, 1921 to 1961" (M.A. thesis, McMaster University, 1977); *Herald*, 31 August 1912; *Labor News*, 30 October 1914.

30.   *Census of Canada*, 1911, II, p. 427; 1931, II, p. 746; *Special Report on the Foreign-Born Population* (Ottawa, 1915), pp. 46-47; *Spectator*, 17 June 1904, 18 October 1905, 27 October 1906; *Herald*, 5 June 1911, 31 August 1912; "The Housing Situation in Hamilton," *Canadian Municipal Journal*, VIII, 7 (July, 1912), pp. 255-56; Methodist Church, Department of Temperance and Moral Reform, and Presbyterian Church, Board of Social Service and Evangelism, *Report of a Preliminary and General Social Survey of Hamilton* (n.p., [1913]), p. 39; Bryce M. Stewart, "The Housing of Our Immigrant Workers," Canadian Political Science Association, *Papers and*

Proceedings (1913), p. 107; Robert F. Harney, "Boarding and Belonging," *Urban History Review*, 2-78 (October, 1978), pp. 8-37.

31.   Thomas and Znaniecki, *Polish Peasants*, 1, p. 199. See also David Montgomery, *Workers' Control in America: Studies in the History of Work, Technology, and Labor Struggles* (Cambridge, 1979), p. 37.

32.   PAC, RG 27, vol. 297, file 3231; Labour Canada Library (Hull), Canada, Royal Commission on Industrial Relations, "Evidence" (typescript), III, p. 2316. See also Wayne Roberts, ed., *Baptism of a Union: The Stelco Strike of 1946* (Hamilton, 1981), pp. 12-15; Diana Brandino, "The Italians of Hamilton, 1921-1945" (M.A. thesis, McMaster University, 1977), pp. 69-70; Robert Henry Storey, "Workers, Unions and Steel: The Shaping of the Hamilton Working Class, 1935-1948" (Ph.D. thesis, University of Toronto, 1981), pp. 208-11.

33.   *Spectator*, 1 April 1910, 11 February 1919; PAC, RG 27, vol. 299, file 3475; *Herald*, 4, 16 April 1910.

34.   Canada, Royal Commission on the Relations of Capital and Labour, *Report: Evidence – Ontario* (Ottawa, 1889), p. 821; Ontario, Inspector of Insurance and Registrar of Friendly Societies, *Report* (Toronto, 1902), C130; *Herald*, 28 April 1911, 16 January 1912, 10 January 1916; *LG*, XIV, 2 (August, 1913), p. 117; XXIX, 6 (June, 1929), p. 649; Royal Commission on Industrial Relations, "Evidence," III, pp. 2289, 2299; *Spectator*, 4 October 1928; *CF*, XVI, 1 (January, 1925), p. 31. All the men interviewed for Stelco's commemorative publication in 1950 had risen modestly on the company's job ladders. See *Stelco Flashes*, XIV, 6 (June, 1950). On this phenomenon of an internal labour market, see Fitch, *Steel Workers*, pp. 141-42; Brody, *Steelworkers*, pp. 85-87; Katherine Stone, "The Origins of the Job Structures in the Steel Industry," *Radical America*, VII, 6 (November-December, 1973), pp. 40-43; Richard Edwards, *Contested Terrain: The Transformation of the Workplace in the Twentieth Century* (New York, 1979), p. 131; Michael Burawoy, *Manufacturing Consent: Changes in the Labor Process under Monopoly Capitalism* (Chicago, 1979).

35.   Roberts, *Baptism of a Union*, pp. 12-15.

36.   *Spectator*, 16 October 1912; Charles Rumford Walker, *Steel: The Diary of a Furnace Worker* (Boston, 1922), pp. 21-26, 46-47, 52-53, 70, 84; Jones, "Gigantic Automaton," p. 103; *Stelco Flashes*, XIV, 6 (June, 1950), p. 7; Popplewell, *Modern Conditions*, p. 103; Kilbourn, *Elements Combined*, p. 119.

37.   University of British Columbia Library, Special Collections, James Robertson Papers, Box 5, File 1, "Notes from Conversations with Officers of the Steel Company of Canada, Hamilton, Ontario, Dec. 21/23."

38.   PAC, RG 27, vol. 305, file 16 (37). Without access to company records it is difficult to date the company's adoption of these job ladders, but, according to the local press, the resolution of a major strike in 1910 involved investigations of wage structures in the United States and the introduction of several new gradations in wage rates. *Times*, 2 April 1910; *Herald*, 13 April 1910.

39.   In their experiences in American steel plants at the end of World War I, Charles Rumford Walker and Whiting Williams saw some of this attitude among "pit men" in the open-hearth department who eyed the slightly better paid jobs of helpers on the "floor" in front of the furnace. Walker, *Steel*, pp. 30-31; Williams, *What's On the Worker's Mind, By One Who Put On Overalls to Find Out* (New York, 1921), p. 21. See also Stone, "Job Structures," pp. 40-43; Edwards, *Contested Terrain*, p. 131.

40.   *Western Clarion*, 30 June 1906.

41.   *Herald*, 29 September 1916; *Spectator*, 8 August 1916.

42.   PAC, Sir Joseph Flavelle Papers, MG 30, A 16, vol. 2, file 11, Department of Labour, R. Hobson to J.W. Flavelle, 8 July 1916; Royal Commission on Industrial Relations, "Evidence," III, p. 2429.

43.   Cf. Craig Heron, "The Crisis of the Craftsman: Hamilton's Metal Workers in the Early Twentieth Century," *Labour/Le Travailleur*, 6 (Autumn, 1980), pp. 7-48.

44.   The following account of the 1910 strike is based on reports in the *Herald, Spectator*, and *Times* for 1-5 and 12-13 April 1910 and on PAC, RG 27, vol. 297, file 3231.

45.   *Spectator*, 1 April 1910. This division along ethnic lines contrasts with the dramatic strike at Pennsylvania's Bethlehem Steel Company, which had begun in February, 1910, but there the skilled machinists initiated and led the strike. See Robert Hessen, "The Bethlehem Steel Strike of 1910," *Labor History*, XV (Winter, 1974), pp. 3-18.

46.   *Spectator*, 1 April 1910; Brody, *Steelworkers*, pp. 132-140; Hessen, "Bethlehem Steel Strike."

47.   *Herald*, 1-2 April 1910; *Times*, 2 April 1910.

48.   It is perhaps significant that the city's first ethnic fraternal society, the First Italian Society of Hamilton, was organized on June 30, 1910, in the wake of the great strike. The Poles organized two years later into the Society of St. Stanislaus Kostka, in 1913 into a "nest" of the Polish Falcons Alliance, and in 1915 into a branch of the Sons of Poland. In 1911 a Hamilton edition of a Buffalo Polish newspaper and in 1912-13 a local Italian paper, *L'Italia Di Hamilton*, circulated in the city; unfortunately, no copies have survived. Ontario, Inspector of Insurance, *Report* (Toronto, 1911), C248; William Boleslaus Makowski, *History and Integration of Poles in Canada* (Lindsay, 1967), pp. 75-76; Joseph A. Wyrtwal, *Behold! The Polish Americans* (Detroit, 1977), pp. 102-03, 161; *Spectator*, 12 December 1910; *Herald*, 20 September 1913; *Labor News*, 6 March 1914; *City of Hamilton Directory* (Hamilton, 1914), p. 799.

49.   Jesse E. Robinson, *The Amalgamated Association of Iron, Steel, and Tin Workers* (Baltimore, 1920); Brody, *Steelworkers*, pp. 214-46; David Brody, *Labor in Crisis: The Steel Strike of 1919* (Philadelphia, 1965); *Amalgamated Journal*, XXI, 5 (16 October 1919), pp. 3, 31; *Spectator*, 24, 29 September 1919.

50.   *Amalgamated Journal*, XXI, 13 (11 December 1919), p. 8; XXI, 44 (15 July 1920), p. 24; XXII, 17 (17 February 1921), p. 20; *Labor News*, 20

February, 25 June, 30 September, 9 December 1920; M.T. Montgomery, "Stelco Story," United Steelworkers of America, *Information* (August-September, 1954), p. 5; McMaster University Archives, M.T. Montgomery Papers, Interview; Steel Company of Canada, *Annual Report*, 1919; Canada, Department of Labour, *Labour Organization in Canada* (Ottawa, 1924), p. 250; (1925), p. 254; Robertson Papers, "Notes from Conversations."

51. See Storey, "Workers, Unions, and Steel," pp. 297-418.

52. See W. Craig Heron, "Working-Class Hamilton, 1895-1930" (Ph.D. thesis, Dalhousie University, 1981), pp. 619-49; *Herald*, 8, 11 January, 25 April, 30 July 1917; *Labor News*, 30 September 1920; Storey, "Workers, Unions, and Steel."

53. Steel Company of Canada Ltd., *The Twenty Fifth Milestone, 1910-1935: A Brief History of Stelco* (Hamilton, 1935), p. 54.

54. See Bernard Elbaum and Frank Wilkinson, "Industrial Relations and Uneven Development: A Comparative Study of the American and British Steel Industries," *Cambridge Journal of Economics*, 3 (1979), pp. 293-302.

Kealey, 1919: The Canadian Labour Revolt

1. Royal Commission on Industrial Relations, Evidence, Victoria, B.C., 26 April 1919, pp. 242-43. (Henceforth cited as Mathers Commission.) One SPC view of the commission is *Causes of Industrial Unrest* (Winnipeg, 1919), a pamphlet published by SPC Local No. 3.

2. Mathers Commission, Evidence, Edmonton, 6 May 1919, pp. 987-90.

3. *Ibid.*, Moose Jaw, 9 May 1919, pp. 1330-42.

4. *Ibid.*, Sudbury, 17 May 1919, pp. 1968-72.

5. *Ibid.*, Toronto, 28 May 1919, pp. 2940-44.

6. *Ibid.*, Hamilton, 21 May 1919, pp. 2261-81.

7. *Ibid.*, Montreal, 29 May 1919, pp. 3255-60.

8. For a partial reconstruction of this evidence from newspaper sources, see Nolan Reilly, "The General Strike in Amherst, Nova Scotia, 1919," *Acadiensis*, IX (1980), pp. 56-77; see also *Eastern Federationist*, 14 June 1919.

9. Mathers Commission, Evidence, New Glasgow, N.S., 5 June 1919, pp. 3533-55.

10. *Ibid.*, Halifax, 4 June 1919, pp. 4355-59. On Dane, see Clifford Rose, *Four Years with the Demon Rum* (Fredericton, 1980), pp. 5-9, 83.

11. Mathers Commission, Evidence, Calgary, 3 May 1919, p. 786.

12. *Ibid.*, Regina, 8 May 1919, p. 1191.

13. *Ibid.*, Montreal, 29 May 1919, p. 3163.

14. See Russell Hann's excellent introduction to Daphne Read, comp., *The Great War and Canadian Society* (Toronto, 1978), pp. 9-38.

15. All strike data in this paper are drawn from recalculations for the Historical Atlas of Canada, volume III. These recalculations are based on the addition of Maritime provinces material compiled from local sources by Ian McKay of Dalhousie University and on a careful re-examination of all the "incomplete" files available in the PAC, Department of Labour, Strikes

and Lockouts files. This work commenced by Peter DeLottinville has been carried through to completion by Douglas Cruikshank. These data currently being compiled for publication in the Atlas provide an entirely new data series for Canadian strike activity. For a report on McKay's work, see his "Strikes in the Maritimes, 1900-1914," *Acadiensis*, XIII (1983), pp. 3-46.

16.   David Bercuson, *Confrontation at Winnipeg: Labour, Industrial Relations, and the General Strike* (Montreal, 1974); Reilly, "The General Strike"; Craig Heron and Bryan D. Palmer, "Through the Prism of the Strike: Industrial Conflict in Southern Ontario, 1901-14," *Canadian Historical Review*, LVIII (1977), pp. 423-58.

17.   Unless other sources are cited this account draws on PAC, Department of Labour, Strikes and Lockouts files as well as on the original published version, *Labour Gazette*, 20 (1920), pp. 267-94.

18.   For a brief account, see Terry Copp, *Anatomy of Poverty* (Toronto, 1974), pp. 134-35.

19.   *Gazette* (Montreal), 28 May, 6 June 1919.

20.   *Ibid.*, 20 June 1919. For a brief reminiscence of the emerging Montreal Red world, see Catherine Vance, *Not by Gods, But by People: The Story of Bella Hall Gould* (Toronto, 1968), pp. 19-44. On the Vickers strike, see *Ontario Labor News* (Toronto), 1 July 1919.

21.   On Cobalt, see Brian F. Hogan, *Cobalt: Year of the Strike,1919* (Cobalt, 1978); on Kirkland Lake, see Laurel Sefton MacDowell, *"Remember Kirkland Lake": The Gold Miners' Strike of 1941-42* (Toronto, 1983), pp. 58-60, and Wayne Roberts, ed., *Miner's Life: Bob Miner and Union Organizing in Timmins, Kirkland Lake and Sudbury* (Hamilton, 1979), pp. 1-2.

22.   J.T. Montague, "Trade Unionism in the Canadian Meat Packing Industry" (Ph.D. thesis, University of Toronto, 1950), pp. 31-38; George Sayers Bain, "The United Packinghouse, Food and Allied Workers" (M.A. thesis, University of Manitoba, 1964), pp. 35-67.

23.   *Machinists Monthly Journal*, 31 (April, 1919), p. 330, cited in Donald Wright, "Belshazzar, the Medes, and the Persians: The Rise and Fall of the Metal Trades Strike in Toronto, 1919," unpublished paper, Dalhousie University, 1979. Planning for 1919 took place at the second provincial convention of the IAM in late November, 1918. See *Labour Gazette*, 19 (1919), pp. 51-52. See also *Ontario Labor News*, 1 May-1 July 1919.

24.   For details, see David Jay Bercuson, ed., *Alberta's Coal Industry 1919* (Calgary, 1978); Bercuson, *Fools and Wise Men: The Rise and Fall of the One Big Union* (Toronto, 1978), pp. 196-214; Allen Seager, "Socialists and Workingmen: The Western Canadian Coal Miners' Movement, 1900-1920," paper presented at American Historical Association meetings, December, 1982.

25.   Nolan Reilly, "The General Strike," his "Notes on the Amherst General Strike and the One Big Union," *Bulletin of the Committee on Canadian Labour History*, 3 (Spring, 1977), pp. 5-8, and his "The Emergence of

Class Consciousness in Industrial Nova Scotia: A Study of Amherst, 1891-1925" (Ph.D. thesis, Dalhousie University, 1982). See also *Eastern Federationist*, 24 May-21 June 1919.

26. Borden Papers, PAC, MG 26 H vol. 113 pt. 1 and pt. 2, file OC 564 (henceforth Borden Papers). See, for example, N.W. Rowell to White, Toronto, 26 May 1919; White to Rowell, Ottawa, 26 May 1919; T.L. Church to Borden, Toronto, 27 May 1919; Church to Borden, 31 May 1919; Church to Borden, 2 June 1919.

27. The literature on the munitions industry, the IMB, and labour unrest is growing, but for contrasting views, see: D.J. Bercuson, "Organized Labour and the Imperial Munitions Board," *Relations Industrielles*, 28 (1974), pp. 602-16; Peter Rider, "The Imperial Munitions Board and its Relationship to Government, Business, and Labour, 1914-1920" (Ph.D. thesis, University of Toronto, 1974), esp. Ch. 9; Michael Bliss, *A Canadian Millionaire: The Life and Business Times of Sir Joseph Flavelle, Bart., 1858-1939* (Toronto, 1978), esp. pp. 270-72, 280-84, 320-25, 378-81; Myer Siemiatycki, "Munitions and Labour Militancy: The 1916 Hamilton Machinists' Strike," *Labour/Le Travailleur*, 3 (1978), pp. 131-51; Craig Heron, "The Crisis of the Craftsman: Hamilton's Metal Workers in the Early Twentieth Century," *Labour/Le Travailleur*, 6 (1980), pp. 7-48; and, for Toronto metal trades background, Wayne Roberts, "Toronto Metal Workers and the Second Industrial Revolution, 1889-1914," *Labour/Le Travailleur*, 6 (1980), pp. 49-72.

28. TTLC, *Minutes*, 2, 16 March, 6, 20 April 1916, including correspondence from Draper and Watters of the TLC.

29. *Ibid.*, 1, 13, 15 May 1919; *Ontario Labor News*, 15 May 1919.

30. Borden Papers, Rowell to White, 26 May 1919, and White to Rowell, 26 May 1919. Statistics from *Ontario Labor News*, 1 June 1919.

31. *Ibid.*, Borden to R.O. Hawtrey, 2 June 1919.

32. Low estimate is Department of Labour; high estimate is given by Major Church in letter to Borden, 2 June 1919. The *Globe* decided on 8,000. See *Globe*, 30 May-7 June 1919.

33. Data on additional Saskatchewan locations from W.J.C. Cherwinski, "Organized Labour in Saskatchewan: The TLC Years, 1905-45" (Ph.D. thesis, University of Alberta, 1972), Chapter 2, and his "Saskatchewan Organized Labour and the Winnipeg General Strike, 1919," unpublished paper, Memorial University of Newfoundland, 1976; for Prince Rupert, see *B.C. Federationist*, 30 May 1919; for Radville through Souris, see Walter Scott Ryder, "Canada's Industrial Crisis of 1919" (M.A. thesis, University of British Columbia, 1920), p. 36. How reliable this last list of whistlestops (literally) is, isn't clear. Ryder, however, was writing in the immediate aftermath of the event and most of these are railway junction towns where there were probably significant groups of shopcraft workers.

34. On Brandon, see A.E. Smith, *All My Life* (Toronto, 1949), Chs. 3-6; Kathleen O'Gorman Wormsbecker, "The Rise and Fall of the Labour Political Movement in Manitoba, 1919-1927" (M.A. thesis, Queen's University,

1977), esp. Ch. 2; Brandon Trades and Labor Council, *Strike Bulletin*, 21-31 May 1919; *Western Labor News* (Winnipeg), 7, 9 June 1919. On the earlier Brandon strike, see *Confederate* (Brandon), 4 April 1919, and *Western Labor News*, 25 April, 7 May 1919.

35.   On Saskatchewan, see Cherwinski, "Organized Labour," Ch. 2, and his "Organized Labour and the Winnipeg General Strike."

36.   For the Edmonton strike, see William R. Askin, "Labour Unrest in Edmonton and District and its Coverage by the Edmonton Press, 1918-19" (M.A. thesis, University of Alberta, 1973); Carl Betke, "Influence and Community: The Ambiguity of Labour Organization in Edmonton, 1906-1921," paper presented at the Canadian-American Urban Development Conference, University of Guelph, August, 1982. See also *The One Big Union Bulletin* (Edmonton), 25 March 1919; *Edmonton Strike Bulletin*, 5, 11 June 1919; *Edmonton Free Press*, 12 April-12 July 1919.

37.   For Calgary, see Elizabeth Ann Taraska, "The Calgary Craft Union Movement, 1900-29" (M.A. thesis, University of Calgary, 1975), quotation at p. 46; and *Calgary Strike Bulletin*, 30 May-24 June 1919; *Labour Gazette*, 18 (1918), pp. 615, 759, 857, 1005, 820, 974-75.

38.   *B.C. Federationist*, 16 May 1919; Vancouver Trades and Labor Council, Executive Minutes, 15 May 1919. See also Paul Phillips, *No Power Greater* (Vancouver, 1976), pp. 80-81; *Strike Bulletin* (Vancouver), 9-26 June 1919; *The Camp Worker* (Vancouver), 2 June 1919; *The Vancouver Citizen*, 16 June-3 July 1919; *The Critic*, 26 April-12 July 1919.

39.   *B.C. Federationist*, 23 May 1919; Borden Papers, G.H. Deane to Borden, Vancouver, 27 May 1919, J. Kavanagh, Secretary VTLC, to Borden, 27 May 1919; and VTLC, Executive Minutes, 22, 27, 28 May 1919.

40.   *B.C. Federationist*, 30 May 1919.

41.   For list of unions supporting the strike, see *ibid.*, 6 June 1919. On women, see *Strike Bulletin*, 16 June 1919. It is worth noting the *Citizen*, the viciously anti-union publication of the Citizens' Committee, propagandized actively for women's support. See, for only two examples, "To the Women," 20 June 1919, and "Women! With Whom?" 21 June 1919.

42.   *B.C. Federationist*, 27 June, 4 July 1919; for another brief account of the Vancouver strike, see Elaine Bernard, "Vancouver 1919," *Democrat*, 20 (June-July, 1980).

43.   Phillips, *No Power Greater*, pp. 80-81. See also the short memoir by machinist Arthur J. Turner, *Somewhere – A Perfect Place* (Vancouver, 1981), pp. 22-26, for a brief memory of the Victoria sympathy strike. See also *Semi-Weekly Tribune* (Victoria), 14 April-30 June 1919, and Victoria Trades and Labor Council, Minutes, esp. 9 June 1919.

44.   Antonio Gramsci, *Selections from Political Writings (1910-1920)* (New York, 1977), p. 61; Nan Milton, ed., *John MacLean: In the Rapids of Revolution* (London, 1978), pp. 190, 137.

45.   On Newfoundland, see Melvin Baker, Robert Cuff, Bill Gillespie, *Workingmen's St. John's: Aspects of Social History in the Early 1900s* (St. John's, 1982). Also Robert Cuff, "The Quill and the Hammer: Labour Activism

in Newfoundland and Nova Scotia, 1917-1925" (Honours B.A. thesis, Department of History, Memorial University of Newfoundland, 1980); Bill Gillespie, "A History of the Newfoundland Federation of Labour, 1936-63" (M.A. thesis, Memorial University of Newfoundland, 1980); John Joy, "The Growth and Development of Trades and Manufacturing in St. John's, 1870-1914" (M.A. thesis, Memorial University of Newfoundland, 1977); and Ian McDonald, "W.F. Coaker and the Fishermen's Protective Union in Newfoundland Politics, 1909-1925" (Ph.D. thesis, University of London, 1971).

46.   Larry Peterson, "The One Big Union in International Perspective: Revolutionary Industrial Unionism 1900-1925," *Labour/Le Travailleur*, 7 (1981), pp. 41-66; James E. Cronin, "Labor Insurgency and Class Formation: Comparative Perspectives on the Crisis of 1917-1920 in Europe," *Social Science History*, 4 (1980), pp. 125-52.

47.   *B.C. Federationist*, 4 July 1919.

48.   Trades and Labour Congress of Canada, *Proceedings*, 1917, pp. 141-55. For a good example of similar fights in the U.S., see Cecelia F. Bucki, "Dilution and Craft Tradition: Bridgeport, Connecticut, Munition Workers, 1915-1919," *Social Science History*, 4 (1980), pp. 105-24. Also see John Laslett, *Labor and the Left* (New York, 1970).

49.   TLCC, *Proceedings*, 1918, pp. 138-39. Note that my count is slightly at variance with Gerald Friesen, " 'Yours in Revolt': Regionalism, Socialism, and the Western Canadian Labour Movement," *Labour/Le Travailleur*, 1 (1976), p. 141. The point, of course, remains the same. His count, however, is 29 west and 51 east vs. 3 west and 81 east.

50.   TLCC, *Proceedings*, 1919, pp. 156-57, 165-66, 190-92; David Frank, "The Cape Breton Coal Miners, 1917-1926" (Ph.D. thesis, Dalhousie University, 1979), pp. 315-19; on the IAM, see *Proceedings*, 1920, especially pp.129-40, 559-62, 248-56, 187-98, 380. See also *Bulletin* (Winnipeg), April-August, 1919.

51.   The syndicalist "accusation," ironically, has come from both ends of the ideological spectrum over time. Gideon Robertson, for example, simply, and I believe sincerely, equated the OBU with the IWW. Later Communist historians, refusing to forgive Bob Russell's refusal to join the CPC, have made the same charge. More recently some historians have repeated the error, while not necessarily sharing either Robertson's or the CPC's political position. See, for example, *Canada's Party of Socialism* (Toronto, 1982), pp. 32-33; James Foy, "Gideon Robertson: Conservative Minister of Labour, 1917-1921" (M.A. thesis, University of Ottawa, 1972); Bercuson, *Confrontation at Winnipeg*, p. 89; Bercuson, *Fools and Wise Men*; A. Ross McCormack, *Reformers, Rebels, and Revolutionaries: The Western Canadian Radical Movement 1899-1919* (Toronto, 1977), pp. 98, 112-13, 143ff.; Martin Robin, *Radical Politics and Canadian Labour 1880-1930* (Kingston, 1968), pp. 50-51, 171-77, 275. This argument is not unique to this paper, of course. See Peterson, "One Big Union," pp. 53-58, and Friesen, " 'Yours in Revolt,' " pp. 139-40, for similar interpretations.

52.   *The Soviet* (Edmonton), 1, 13 (20 June 1919).

53.   *Red Flag* (Vancouver), 1, 9 (22 March 1919); also *The Soviet*, 1, 18 (24 May 1919).

54.   *B.C. Federationist*, 23, 30 May 1919.

55.   Gloria Montero, *We Stood Together: First Hand Accounts of Dramatic Events in Canada's Labour Past* (Toronto, 1979), p. 14. Also, of course, the source of Bercuson's title.

56.   Borden Papers, A.R. Mosher to Borden, 29 May 1919; Department of National Defence, RG 24, vol. 3985, N-S-C 1055-2-21, *Secret*, "Memorandum on Revolutionary Tendencies in Western Canada," prepared by Assistant Comptroller, RNWMP.

57.   E.J. Hobsbawm, *Labouring Men* (London, 1964), p. 144; Michelle Perrot, *Les Ouvriers en grève, France 1871-90*, Tome 1 (Paris, 1974), p. 64.

58.   The new literature on ethnic workers is already too voluminous to list, but note especially Varpu Lindstrom-Best's work on the Finns and Orest T. Martynowych's essays on Ukrainian socialism. See, also, the special issue of *Canadian Ethnic Studies*, 10 (1978), on ethnic radicalism. For additional Winnipeg evidence, see Donald Avery, "The Radical Alien and the Winnipeg General Strike of 1919," in Carl Berger and Ramsay Cook, eds., *The West and the Nation* (Toronto, 1976), pp. 209-31, and his "Ethnic Loyalties and the Proleterian Revolution," in Jorgen Dahlie and Tissa Fernando, eds., *Ethnicity, Power, and Politics in Canada* (Toronto, 1981), pp. 68-93.

59.   On Vancouver telephone operators and the General Strike, see Elaine Bernard, *The Long Distance Feeling: A History of the Telecommunications Workers Union* (Vancouver, 1982), pp. 50-65.

60.   Robert Morris, "Skilled Workers and the Politics of the 'Red' Clyde," unpublished paper, University of Edinburgh, 1981. As Morris notes, his echo of Edward Thompson's "moral economy" is intentional.

61.   On the war economy in general, see R.T. Naylor, "The Canadian State, the Accumulation of Capital, and the Great War," *Revue d'études canadiennes*, 16, 3-4 (1981), pp. 26-55. On inflation specifically, see: Terry Copp, *Anatomy of Poverty*, for Montreal; Michael J. Piva, *The Condition of the Working Class in Toronto*; Harry Sutcliffe and Paul Phillips, "Real Wages and the Winnipeg General Strike: An Empirical Investigation," unpublished paper, University of Manitoba, 1973; Gordon Bertram and Michael Percy, "Real Wage Trends in Canada 1900-26," *Canadian Journal of Economics*, 12 (1979), pp. 299-312; and Eleanor Bartlett, "Real Wages and the Standard of Living in Vancouver, 1901-1929," *B.C. Studies*, 51 (1981), pp. 3-62. For a slightly later period, see Michael J. Piva, "Urban Working-Class Incomes and Real Incomes in 1921: A Comparative Analysis," *Histoire sociale/Social History*, 31 (1983), pp. 143-65. See also, for a U.S. comparison, Frank Stricker, "The Wages of Inflation: Workers' Earnings in the World War One Era," *Mid-America*, 63 (1981), pp. 93-105. For the general U.S. economic context, see David M. Gordon, Richard Edwards, Michael Reich, *Segmented Work, Divided Workers: The Historical*

Transformation of Labor in the United States (New York, 1982), pp. 127-64.

62.   Cronin, "Labour Insurgency and Class Conflict." See also his *Industrial Conflict in Modern Britain* (London, 1979), pp. 109-20.

63.   Much of this has been chronicled elsewhere. For an apologetic but detailed description of the creation of the RCMP, see S.W. Horrall, "The Royal North-West Mounted Police and Labour Unrest in Western Canada, 1919," *Canadian Historical Review*, LXI (1980), pp. 169-90. On victimization, especially of postal workers, see Borden Papers, various letters June to September, 1919, pp. 62179-257. On one particularly unseemly aspect of TLC behaviour, see Tom Traves, " 'The Story that Couldn't be Told': Big Business Buys the TLC," *Ontario Report*, 1, 6 (September, 1976), pp. 27-29.

64.   A.B. Perry, "Draft Memorandum," 1 September 1919, Royal Canadian Mounted Police Papers, volume 1003, PAC.

65.   Yves Lequin, "Social Structures and Shared Beliefs: Four Worker Communities in the Second Industrialization," *International Labor and Working-Class History*, 22 (1982), pp. 1-17.

66.   On Councils in Canada, see Bruce Scott, " 'A Place in the Sun': The Industrial Council at Massey-Harris, 1919-1929," *Labour/Le Travailleur*, 1 (1976), pp. 158-92; Tom Traves, *The State and Enterprise: Canadian Manufacturers and the Federal Government 1917-1931* (Toronto, 1979), pp. 86-94; and Foy, "Gideon Robertson." For U.S. comparisons, see Stuart D. Brandes, *American Welfare Capitalism, 1880-1940* (Chicago, 1976), esp. pp. 119-48.

67.   *Socialist Bulletin* (Winnipeg), 1, 7 (July, 1919).

68.   *Red Flag*, 1, 22 (21 June 1919). For an academic echo of labour's educational gains from the strike, see D.G. Cook, "Western Radicalism and the Winnipeg Strike" (M.A. thesis, McMaster University, 1921), p. 62, where it is argued, on the basis of interviews with Winnipeg strikers, that: "The gains of the strike were many for the labour group. The six-week's strike was like a college course in Economics. Papers were read, issues discussed, and many addresses were given by the leaders. Many of the labour men became enlightened as to the real struggle. There grew a strong spirit of solidarity in the rank and file of labour."

Brandt, Women's Work in the Quebec Cotton Industry

1.   Pat Armstrong, *Labour Pains* (Toronto, 1984), p. 39.

2.   *Canadian Textile Journal*, June, 1920, pp. 80-82; Province of Quebec, Provincial Secretary's Department, Bureau of Statistics, *Statistical Year Book* (Quebec, 1921), p. 371.

3.   *Census of Canada*, 1891, vol. 3, Table 1, p. 120; *ibid.*, 1951, vol. 4, Table 19, pp. 19-79, 19-89. Since women were overwhelmingly employed in the mills rather than converting plants, this analysis will focus only on their role in the production of grey cloth.

4. Labour costs normally accounted for about 50 per cent of the values and, except for the price of raw cotton, were by far the most important factor in determining the total cost of operations. See, for example, the annual reports of Dominion Textile Company Limited reprinted in the *Annual Financial Review of Canada*, 1920-1951.
5. This situation is reflected in return on shareholder's equity calculated from annual financial reports.

Return on Shareholders' Equity (%)

	Dominion Textile	Montreal Cottons	Wabasso
1919	18.6	11.5	5.3
1920	12.0	10.1	14.3
1921	11.1	6.7	11.1
1922	9.6	6.5	9.1
1923	n/a	6.4	7.4
1924	4.8	5.8	5.0
1925	5.9	6.7	5.5
1926	7.0	6.4	6.2
1927	7.8	5.9	7.7
1928	6.8	5.4	4.4
1929	6.1	2.4	nil

6. *The Canadian Journal of Fabrics*, XV (May, 1898), p. 149.
7. Herbert J. Lahne, *The Cotton Mill Worker* (New York, 1944), p. 175.
8. Melvin T. Copeland, *The Cotton Manufacturing Industry of the United States* (New York, 1966), p. 70.
9. *Canadian Textile Journal*, 12 June 1922, p. 519.
10. *Ibid.*, December, 1913, p. 361.
11. *Ibid.*, 4 July 1922, p. 267; Copeland, *Cotton Manufacturing*, p. 75.
12. Copeland, *Cotton Manufacturing*, p. 85.
13. *Canadian Textile Journal*, 30 December 1924, p. 1177.
14. *Census of Canada*, 1911, vol. 3, Table V, p. 216-17.
15. PAC, RG 33/20, vol. 50, Royal Commission of Enquiry into the Textile Industry (1936), "Memoire," p. 137.
16. "Florida," Magog worker, 1916-1966.
17. Dominion Textile Company Limited, *Magog. A busy town of happy homes situated in a district noted for its beauty* (Montreal, 1917), p. 6.
18. For a summary of women's employment in the nascent American cotton industry, see Elizabeth Faulkner Baker, *Technology and Women's Work* (New York, 1964), pp. 8-15.
19. "Marie," Valleyfield worker, 1918-1919. Cf. William F. Ryan, *The Clergy and Economic Growth in Quebec (1896-1914)* (Quebec, 1966), p. 78.
20. Royal Commission of Enquiry into the Textile Industry, "Memoire," pp. 64-65.
21. Note the comments in Veronica Beechey, "The Sexual Division of Labour and the Labour Process: A Critical Assessment of Braverman," in Stephen Wood, ed., *The Degradation of Work? Skill, Deskilling and the Labour Process* (London, 1982), pp. 63-64.

22. Roger Penn, "Skilled manual workers in the labour process, 1856-1964," in Wood, ed., *The Degradation of Work*, pp. 100-06; Tony Elger, "Braverman, capital accumulation and deskilling," *ibid.*, pp. 34-40.

23. Magog Branch, Dominion Textile Company Records, *Les Moulins des Cantons de l'Est*, 1947-1951.

24. Interviews with former cotton workers of both sexes stressed the extent to which the cleaner, more skilled jobs, especially in finishing, were the preserve of anglophone workers. At Magog, the grey cotton mill and the print works, although located side by side, were striking symbols of the "two solitudes," with French Canadians concentrated in the former and English Canadians in the latter.

25. See, for instance, Copeland, *Cotton Manufacturing*, p. 134.

26. *Canadian Textile Journal*, 22 August 1947.

27. Copeland, *Cotton Manufacturing*, p. 82.

28. PAC, Department of Labour, Strikes and Lockouts, RG 27, vol. 331, file 52.

29. Eighty-seven interviews were conducted with former cotton workers in Valleyfield and Magog.

30. PAC, Strikes and Lockouts, RG 27, vol. 299, file 3423; vol. 321, file 160.

31. *Census of Canada*, 1911, vol. 3, Table V, pp. 216-17; *ibid.*, 1931, vol. 7, Table 56, pp. 696-97; *ibid.*, 1941, vol. 7, Table 18, p. 578.

32. *Report of the Royal Commission of Enquiry into the Textile Industry* (Ottawa, 1938), p. 148; "Luzina," Magog worker, 1923-1933; "Nicole," Valleyfield worker, 1935-1949; "Mathilde," Magog worker, 1926-1934. In the realm of influential ideas, note the writings of Henri Bourassa and Abbe Groulx. See Susan Mann Trofimenkoff, *The Dream of Nation, A Social and Intellectual History of Quebec* (Toronto, 1983), pp. 184-99, 218-32.

33. "Alphonsine," Magog worker, 1923-1968.

34. Canadian and Catholic Confederation of Labour, *Annual Proceedings* (1939), p. 147. For a fuller discussion of the CCCL's attitudes toward female workers, see M.-J. Gagnon, "Les femmes dans le mouvement syndical québécois," in Marie Lavigne and Yolande Pinard, eds., *Les Femmes dans la société québécoise: aspects historiques* (Montréal, 1977), pp. 145-68.

35. "Memoire," p. 25.

36. *Ibid.*, p. 124.

37. "Adele," Magog worker, 1924-1934.

38. "Memoire," p. 126.

39. *Ibid.*, p. 125; "Pierrette," Magog worker, 1932-1979.

40. Leonard Marsh, *Employment Research* (Toronto, 1935), p. 201.

41. Turgeon Commission, Testimony, 16 March 1936, pp. 233-40.

42. *Census of Canada*, 1931, vol. 7, pp. 110-11; *ibid.*, 1941, vol. 7, pp. 694-95.

43. *Canadian Textile Journal*, 3 November 1944, advertisement by Aberfoyle yarns; PAC, RG 36/4, National War Labour Board, United Textile Workers of America Appeal re: Wage Increases, 23 September 1943, p. 24; and the Webber article in this volume.

44.   *Canadian Textile Journal*, 22 May 1942, p. 16; PAC, RG 28A, vol. 26, Department of Munitions and Supplies, "History of the Textile Division," p. 21; *Annual Financial Review of Canada*, Dominion Textile Financial Statement, 1942.

45.   See Francine Barry, *Le Travail de la Femme au Québec. L'Evolution de 1940 à 1970* (Montréal, 1977), pp. 43-50; *Annual Financial Review*, Dominion Textile Financial Statement, 1943.

46.   "History of Textile Industry," p. 21; *Canadian Textile Journal*, 26 January 1943, 23 March 1945.

47.   PAC, "Strikes and Lockouts," RG 27, vol. 404, file 16; vol. 424, file 5.

48.   PAC, Rowley-Parent Collection, vol. 5, file 27.

Webber, The Malaise of Compulsory Conciliation

1.   SC 1907, c. 20; revised with amendments, RSC 1927, c. 112. Throughout this paper, I use the words "mediation" and "conciliation" interchangeably, treating them as synonymous.

2.   All of the orders-in-council referred to in this paper were passed under the authority of the War Measures Act, RSC 1927, c. 206.

3.   National Labor Relations (Wagner) Act, ch. 372, 49 Stat. 449 (1935).

4.   The government's practice often differed considerably from its profession. For a thoughtful discussion of the trustworthiness of official pronouncements, see Paul Craven, *'An Impartial Umpire': Industrial Relations and the Canadian State 1900-1911* (Toronto, 1980), pp. 222-30. In this paper, I have relied principally on the confidential records of the Department of Labour and, in the case of the Kirkland Lake dispute, on MacDowell's useful monograph (see below, note 8) for the details of intervention. For the reader's convenience, I have cited publicized board reports to the *Labour Gazette*, although the versions originally submitted by board members were also examined.

5.   RSC 1927, c. 112, s. 26. This paragraph of the paper summarizes the regime established by the IDIA. I shall only give references for direct quotations from that statute.

6.   See Irving Martin Abella, *Nationalism, Communism, and Canadian Labour: the CIO, the Communist Party, and the Canadian Congress of Labour 1935-1956* (Toronto, 1973). For simplicity's sake, I will use the initials CIO to refer to the Canadian movement allied to the American Congress of Industrial Organizations. In 1940, the Canadian movement founded its own federation: the Canadian Congress of Labour (CCL).

7.   A provision forbidding discrimination against employees for union activities was placed in the Criminal Code by SC 1939, c. 30, s. 11, but because of the criminal burden of proof and the need to use the ordinary courts, this was very difficult to enforce. Similar prohibitions are found in: The Strikes and Lockouts Prevention Act, SM 1937, c. 40, s. 46; The Freedom of Trade Union Association Act, 1938, SS 1938, c. 87; Trade Union Act, SNS 1937, c. 6; Industrial Conciliation and Arbitration Act, SBC, 1937, c. 31; and The Industrial Conciliation and Arbitration Act, SA 1938, c.

57. The latter three statutes also imposed a duty to bargain, but without the supervision of labour relations boards or the possibility of certification.

8.   J.L. Cohen, *Collective Bargaining in Canada* (Toronto, 1941), p. 15, quoted in Laurel Sefton MacDowell, *"Remember Kirkland Lake": The History and Effects of the Kirkland Lake Gold Miners' Strike* (Toronto, 1983), p. 31.

9.   The definitions contained in PC 3495 were later amended by PC 1708 (10 March 1941).

10.   RSC 1927, c. 110.

11.   PAC, RG 27, vol. 255, file 750.5. All citations of PAC material refer to the Department of Labour Records unless otherwise indicated.

12.   "Memorandum to the Prime Minister on Co-operation in War Time Activities," PAC, RG 27, vol. 254, file 721.021:1. The Trades and Labor Congress of Canada (TLC) unions still contributed their share to the wartime strike statistics, however. In 1940, they accounted for 79,306 days lost, as opposed to 86,775 for CCL unions, 65,450 for the Confederation of Catholic Workers of Canada, and 16,032 for the Canadian Federation of Labour: "Strikes in Canada, 1940," PAC, RG 27, vol. 254, file 721.02:1.

13.   PC 1743 (11 July 1918). Compulsory arbitration was established by PC 2525 (11 October 1918). For the relationship between PC 1743 and PC 2685, including a table of concordance, see the memorandum of the Assistant Deputy Minister of Labour, Ottawa, 5 March 1940, PAC, RG 27, vol. 254, file 721.02:1.

14.   MacDowell mentions that in 1941 in the National Steel Car plant in Hamilton, Ontario, a government-appointed controller at first refused to meet at all with representatives of a union supported by a majority of the employees, and then consented to bargain only with a non-union committee of employees: MacDowell, *Kirkland Lake*, pp. 32-33.

15.   PC 7440 (16 December 1940); PC 8253 (24 October 1941).

16.   PC 7307 (16 September 1941), s. 3 and s. 4; "Labour Law by Order-in-Council," *Canadian Forum*, 21 (1941), p. 239, quoted in MacDowell, *Kirkland Lake*, pp. 112-13; PC 8821 (13 November 1941); PC 6893 (1 September 1944).

17.   In 1941, for example, of the disputes giving rise to applications under the IDIA, forty-four concerned recognition alone, forty-five concerned recognition and other issues, and fifty-four dealt only with issues other than recognition: Memorandum, Assistant Deputy Minister of Labour to Minister of Labour, Ottawa, 1 April 1942, PAC, RG 27, vol. 254, file 721.02:1. (The number in the last category would under-represent somewhat the total number of disputes caused by non-recognition matters because after 15 November 1941, wage matters alone would have been referred to War Labour Boards.) It should be noted that although PC 1003 did do away with disputes *expressly* concerned with recognition, many unions still had great difficulty securing first collective agreements.

18.   PC 10802 (1 December 1942); S.O. 1943, c. 4.

19.   All facts here presented concerning the Kirkland Lake dispute, other than the contents of the reports of the IDI Commission and conciliation board, are taken from MacDowell, *Kirkland Lake*.

20. Case No. 19, Report of the IDI Commission, Kirkland Lake, 12 August 1941, PAC, RG 27, vol. 144, file 611.04:21.

21. The quotation is from the minority report in the Electro-Metallurgical dispute, *Labour Gazette*, 45 (1945), pp. 50-51. See also the minority reports in the Page-Hersey Tubes and John Inglis disputes: *Labour Gazette*, 45 (1945), pp. 45-47, and *Labour Gazette*, 44 (1944), pp. 1501-05.

22. Majority report in the Kirkland Lake dispute, *Labour Gazette*, 41 (1941), p. 1351 (emphasis in the original).

23. MacDowell, *Kirkland Lake*, p. 120.

24. The facts of these disputes are taken from the documents contained in PAC, RG 27, vol. 1764, file 755:11, and vol. 1763, file 755:8, respectively.

25. See quotation accompanying note 21, and *Labour Gazette*, 45 (1945), p. 47.

26. E.L. Deitch to C.R. Sullivan, Welland, Ontario, 19 January 1945, PAC, RG 27, vol. 1764, file 755:11.

27. Memorandum, O'Connor to Maclean, Ottawa, 30 June 1944, PAC, RG 27, vol. 1763, file 755:8.

28. Memorandum, MacNamara to Maclean, Ottawa, 25 November 1944, PAC, RG 27, vol. 1763, file 755:8; *Labour Gazette*, 45 (1945), p. 491.

29. "Conciliation Proceedings under Wartime Labour Relations Regulations as of July 1, 1945," PAC, RG 27, vol. 254, file 721.02:1. That conciliation, and not adjudication, was the primary role of IDIA boards in the early years of the policy has been noted by Ben M. Selekman, *Postponing Strikes* (New York, 1927), pp. 102-13; James J. Atherton, "The Department of Labour and Industrial Relations, 1900-1911" (M.A. thesis, Carleton University, 1972), p. 220; and Craven, *'An Impartial Umpire,'* pp. 299-301.

30. See, for example, IDIA, RSC 1927, c. 112, s. 14; SC 1940-41, c. 20. In the Swift Canadian dispute, the employer nominee withdrew when the department said that the company could not make up his loss in pay for attending the conciliation board proceedings: PAC, RG 27, vol. 1764, file 755:17.

31. See below. Also, see the union brief in the Canadian Oil Companies case, PAC, RG 27, vol. 1764, file 755:12, the chairman's request for precedents and the union brief in the John Inglis case, PAC, RG 27, vol. 1764, file 755:14, and the majority report in the Sun Publishing case, *Labour Gazette*, 44 (1944), p. 1495.

32. See the minority reports in the Canadian Oil Companies case, *Labour Gazette*, 44 (1944), p. 1355, and in the Upper Canada Mines case, *Labour Gazette*, 45, (1945), pp. 328-31.

33. See below and the Sun Publishing case, PAC, RG 27, vol. 1764, file 755:13.

34. Exchange of memoranda, Maclean to MacNamara, Ottawa, 28-29 July 1944, PAC, RG 27, vol. 1764, file 755:12.

35. The facts of this dispute are primarily taken from documents in PAC, RG 27, vol. 1765, files 755:24 and 755:24 part 2.

36. *Labour Gazette*, 45 (1945), p. 170; Clement to Maclean, Vancouver, B.C., 19 January 1945, PAC, RG 27, vol. 1765, file 755:24. B.G. Webber has told me that he was not informed of Clement's letter (interview, 30 March

1983). I presume that Haskins, who had signed the majority report with Clement, was not informed.

37.   G.S. Pearson to Mitchell, Victoria, 27 February 1945, PAC, RG 27, vol. 1756, file 755:24. Webber says that O'Brien had earlier criticized him for being too willing to compromise (interview, 30 March 1983). A letter in his possession (O'Brien to Webber, 27 March 1945) indicates that Webber had been conciliatory: "I am also glad to know that you tried your best to get the members to agree to an adjournment so that the parties might have been got together, and something definite arrived at before the board was finally adjourned." That O'Brien had at least publicly opposed compromise is evident from his comment before the Board: "I do ask you to bear in mind and to see our point that Maintenance of Membership would be a useless thing – no use to us at all. We should have to refuse to accept it, even if the employer offerred it to us without a Board, because it does nothing, in our opinion, in an industry such as this, but day-nurse a minority. . . ." *Labour Gazette*, 45 (1945), p. 172.

38.   Reported at 1 CCH Can. Lab. L. Rep., para. 2150.

39.   *Labour Gazette*, 45 (1945), p. 325.

40.   *Labour Gazette*, 44 (1944), p. 1500.

41.   *Labour Gazette*, 44 (1944), p. 1359. In this instance, the employees' nominee was Bora Laskin, later Chief Justice of Canada.

42.   *Labour Gazette*, 45 (1945), p. 48. See the employer's nominee's vigorous response, quotation accompanying note 21 above.

Maroney, Feminism at Work

1.   Much of the material for this piece was gathered from interviews with trade union feminists. Since some of them wish to remain anonymous, I have not attributed any statements.

2.   Interview, December, 1982. For a similar statement from U.S. women, which points to equal pay as a feminist issue, stresses the difficulties of media-distorted "feminist jargon," and points to unions as "the main tool that women have, that workers have," see District 6, "Union Women on Feminism," *Heresies*, 9 (1980), p. 85.

3.   Julie White, *Women and Unions* (Ottawa, 1981): 27 per cent of the female work force is unionized in comparison with 43 per cent of the male labour force and over 60 per cent of the female membership are in public-sector unions. In the decade following 1966, female membership increased 160 per cent in comparison with 40 per cent for men.

4.   Public health nurses, Toronto, and hospital workers, Winnipeg, demanded equal pay for work of equal value, as have hospital and clerical workers, nurses, and teachers in Quebec's Common Front. For historical material, see Judi Coburn, " 'I See and Am Silent': A Short History of Nursing in Ontario," and Elizabeth Graham, "School Marms and Early Teaching in Ontario," both in J. Acton, ed., *Women at Work: Ontario 1850-1930* (Toronto, 1974).

5.   Dorothy Gillmeister, "The Equal Opportunity Fantasy: A Hard Look at Voluntary Affirmative Action," *Status of Women*, 6, 2 (1980).

6.   For example, with steelworkers, at Stelco in Hamilton. The list includes a joint campaign by machinists and local women in St. Thomas, a Women into Rail campaign, and the integration of the sawmills in B.C.

7.   The major reports to conventions of the *centrales* include CSN, "La lutte des femmes: combat de tous les travailleurs" (1976) and "La lutte des femmes: pour le droit au travail social" (1978); CEQ, "Condition féminine" (1974); and Fédération des Travailleurs du Québec, "Femmes et syndiqués" (1973).

8.   Mona-Josée Gagnon, "Les femmes dans le movement syndical québécois," *Sociologie et Société*, 6, 2 (1974).

9.   Special issue, *Resources for Feminist Research*, 10, 2 (1981). Henceforth *RFR*.

10. Debbie Field, "Women's Committees in Unions," *RFR*, 10, 2 (1981), pp. 8-9.

11. Women's struggles against exclusion from the auto industry in the U.S. met with at least an ambivalent response from their union. Nancy Gabin, "'They Have Placed a Penalty on Womanhood': The Protest Actions of Women Auto Workers in Detroit Area UAW locals, 1945-47," *Feminist Studies*, 8, 2 (1982). It is likely that similar exclusions occurred in Canada.

12. Unionization, of course, benefits women and men economically; cf. Morley Gunderson, "Male-female Wage Differentials and the Impact of Equal Pay Legislation," *Review of Economics and Statistics*, 57 (1975); White, *Women and Unions*, p. 57. Nevertheless, higher-paid skilled workers have refused to bargain for across-the-board increases that effectively erode their own income, particularly with respect to peers, in an inflationary period.

13. René Geoffroy and Paule Ste-Marie, "Le travailleur syndiqué face au travail rémunéré de la femme," *Études pour la commission royale d'enquête sur la situation de la femme au Canada*, no. 9, Ottawa.

14. Recently, however, benefits for women have been strike issues in the context of a pro-natalist policy. The Quebec public-sector Common Front obtained the best maternity/parental leave provisions in the country – twenty weeks full pay (instead of fifteen weeks at 60 per cent with an obligatory loss of two weeks' salary provided by federal insurance benefits) with up to two years' job security – while the Canadian Union of Postal workers struck unsuccessfully for maternity benefits among other issues; in 1980 CAIMAW (affiliated to the mainly B.C.-based Congress of Canadian Unions – membership about 40,000 – which has a good record on women's issues) held out for seven months in a strike for equal pay for work of equal value for seven female data processors; equal pay became an issue in a strike by Vancouver Municipal workers later in 1981.

15. Janet Routledge, "Women and Social Unionism," *RFR*, 10, 2 (1981).

16. Grace Hartman, "Women and the Unions," in G. Matheson, ed., *Women in the Canadian Mosaic* (Toronto, 1976); Peter Warrian, "Patriarchy and the Trade Unions," paper presented at the Committee on Socialist Studies, Ottawa, June, 1981; Lynn Frogett, "Feminism and the Italian Trade Unions," *Feminist Review*, 8 (1981).

17. Micki McCune, "Fighting for Our Rights: The CLC Women's Conference," *RFR*, 10, 2 (1981).

18. Jackie Ainsworth *et al.* document earlier attempts by UBC clerical workers to organize with CLC public sector (Canadian Union of Public Employees) and private sector (Office and Professional Employees International Union/ Office and Technical Employees Union) in "Getting Organized: In the Feminist Unions," in M. Fitzgerald *et al.*, eds., *Still Ain't Satisfied: Canadian Feminism Today* (Toronto, 1982).

19. The Bank Book Collective, *An Account to Settle* (Vancouver, 1979).

20. Henry Radecki, *One Year Later: The 1978-79 Strike at INCO: The Effects on Families* (Sudbury, 1979).

21. Meg Luxton, "The Home: A Contested Terrain," in Fitzgerald *et al.*, eds. *Still Ain't Satisfied*.

22. In Montreal, IWD celebrations were held by the unions as a *fête populaire* with little political content in 1973 and 1974; in 1975, women from the inter-central *commission féminine* along with those from abortion and health work, day care, and the far left held a teach-in that led to several co-operative demonstrations. In 1978, drawing on the Montreal example, women in the Revolutionary Marxist Group – now defunct – promoted IWD celebrations/demonstrations to link up with union women across English Canada. Some centres, notably Vancouver, had already begun to mark IWD.

23. The typology of harassment is taken from Catherine A. MacKinnon, *Sexual Harassment of Working Women: A Case of Sex Discrimination* (New Haven, 1979). Quotation from Women's Rights Committee, "Sexual Harassment in the Workplace," discussion paper, B.C. Federation of Labour, March, 1980. For a useful report on union practice, see Marlene Kadar, "Sexual Harassment as a Form of Social Control," in Fitzgerald *et al.*, eds., *Still Ain't Satisfied*.

24. Jane Humphries, "The Working-Class Family, Women's Liberation, and the Class Struggle: The Case of Nineteenth-Century British History," *Review of Radical Political Economics*, 9 (1977); see also Meg Luxton, *More Than A Labour of Love: Three Generations of Women's Work in the Home* (Toronto, 1980).

25. Barbara Ehrenreich, "A Funny Thing Happened on the Way to Socialist Feminism," *Heresies*, 9 (1980), p. 5.

26. Official unemployment rates were already about 12 per cent in May, 1980. On micro-technology, see Heather Menzies, *Women and the Chip* (Montreal, 1981).

27. Pat Armstrong and Hugh Armstrong, "Job Creation and Unemployment for Canadian Women," paper presented at the NATO Symposium, "Women and the World of Work," Portugal, 1982.

28. It is appropriate to discuss André Gorz's *Farewell to the Working Class* (Boston, 1982) because it was one of the key texts discussed by top union leadership at the CLC winter school in 1983.

Palmer, The Rise and Fall of British Columbia's Solidarity

1. See Bryan Palmer, "Building the House of Labor," *Solidarity Times*, 30 November 1983; Paul Phillips, *No Power Greater: A Century of Labour in B.C.* (Vancouver, 1967).

2. Mike Kramer interview, 10 June 1985; Ian Mulgrew, "No one laughs about class war," *Globe & Mail*, 21 March 1984.

3. "130 Days," *Sun*, 14 November 1983. Nor was such a comment a product of purely local concern. See *Financial Post*, 16 July 1983; Alan Bayless, "British Columbia Bracing For Labour Strife," *Wall Street Journal*, 21 August 1983.

4. This paper, written for this collection, is an abbreviated and politically subdued version of a more extensive analysis: Palmer, "Reformism and the Fight Against the Right: British Columbia's Solidarity," forthcoming 1986.

5. Evert Hoogers interview, 7 June 1985. For some pertinent comment on the ossification of trade union leadership, see Rosa Luxemburg, *The Mass Strike, the Political Party, and the Trade Union* (Detroit, 1925), esp. pp. 79, 88, 93.

6. Marx, "The Eighteenth Brumaire of Louis Bonaparte," in Marx and Engels, *Selected Works* (Moscow, 1968), p. 97.

7. The most thorough treatment of this period of anti-communism in the British Columbia labour movement is Jerry Lembcke, and William Tattam, *One Union in Wood: A Political History of the International Woodworkers of America* (Madeira Park, B.C., 1984).

8. On labour, see Laurel Sefton MacDowell, "The Formation of the Canadian Industrial Relations System During World War II," *Labour/Le Travailleur*, 3 (1978), pp. 175-96; and the Webber article in this volume. On social security, see Denis Guest, *The Emergence of Social Security in Canada* (Vancouver, 1980), esp. pp. 101-38. A fascinating argument about the links between labour and welfare is Peter Warrian, "The Rise and Fall of Industrial Pluralism," presented to the Harry Crowe lecture series, 18 January 1985.

9. See Leo Panitch and Donald Swartz, "Towards Permanent Exceptionalism: Coercion and Consent in Canadian Industrial Relations," *Labour/Le Travail*, 13 (Spring, 1984), pp. 144-64; Nelson Lichtenstein, *Labor's War at Home: The CIO in World War II* (New York, 1982), pp. 178-202; Bill Freeman, *1005: Political Life in a Union Local* (Toronto, 1982); K. Klare, "Juridical Deradicalization of the Wagner Act and the Origins of Modern Legal Consciousness, 1937-1974," *Minnesota Law Review*, 62 (1978), pp. 265-339.

10. Wayne Roberts, "Lots of 'Ums: Collective Bargaining and Industrial Democracy," unpublished paper, 1985.

11. Howard White, *A Hard Man to Beat: The Story of Bill White, Labour Leader, Historian, Shipyard Worker, Raconteur* (Vancouver, 1983), p. 210.

12. See Alan F.J. Artbise, "'A Worthy if Unlikely Enterprise': The Labour Relations Board and the Evolution of Labour Policy and Practice in British Columbia, 1973-1980," *B.C. Studies*, 56 (Winter, 1982-83), pp. 3-43.

13.   Note Philip Resnick, "Social Democracy in Power: The Case of British Columbia," *B.C. Studies*, 34 (Summer, 1977), pp. 3-20.

14.   See Patricia Marchak, "The New Economic Reality: Substance and Rhetoric," in Warren Magnusson *et al.*, *The New Reality: The Politics of Restraint in British Columbia* (Vancouver, 1984), pp. 22-40.

15.   Note Glen Williams, *Not For Export: Toward a Political Economy of Canada's Arrested Industrialization* (Toronto, 1983).

16.   See Duncan Cameron and Francois Houle, eds., *Canada and the New International Division of Labour* (Ottawa, 1985).

17.   Leo Panitch, *Workers, Wages, and Controls: The Anti-Inflation Programme and its Implications for Canadian Workers* (Toronto, 1976).

18.   David Wolfe, "The Rise and Demise of the Keynesian Era in Canada," in Michael S. Cross and Gregory S. Kealey, eds., *Modern Canada, 1930-1980* (Toronto, 1984), pp. 48-78.

19.   Panitch and Swartz, "Permanent Exceptionalism."

20.   Note the essays in Magnusson *et al.*, *The New Reality*.

21.   Panitch and Swartz, "Permanent Exceptionalism," p. 134.

22.   Bob Dylan, "Union Sundown," *Infidels* (Columbia Records, 1983).

23.   White, *A Hard Man to Beat*, p. 212.

24.   On Social Credit in B.C. in the 1970's and early 1980's, see Stan Persky, *Son of Socred* (Vancouver, 1979); Persky, *Bennett II: The Decline and Stumbling of Social Credit Government in British Columbia* (Vancouver, 1983); Bill Tieleman, "The Socred Blues Again," *Canadian Dimension*, 17 (September, 1983), pp. 3-4.

25.   On the marketing of the Socreds, see Peter Cameron, "The Kinsella Tapes," *New Directions*, I (June-July, 1985), pp. 8-14, 18.

26.   See Magnusson *et al.*, *The New Reality*, pp. 192-208.

27.   See Cliff Stainsby and John Malcolmson, *The Fraser Institute, the Government, and a Corporate Free Lunch* (Vancouver, 1983); Ben Swankey, *The Fraser Institute: A Socialist Analysis of the Corporate Drive to the Right* (Vancouver, 1983); Sid Tafler, "Pushing the 'Right' Ideas," *Globe & Mail*, 10 December 1983.

28.   This represents only the most visible and obnoxious tip of the legislative iceberg. For a full listing of the bills, see Magnusson *et al.*, *The New Reality*, pp. 281-85; Operation Solidarity Leaflet, "What Does the Legislation Mean to You?" Solidarity Coalition Files, Vancouver. Response to the budget was immediate. See Serge Joyal, Secretary of State to Hon. R. H. McClelland, Minister of Labour, Solidarity Coalition Files, Vancouver; Dan Smith, "Where BC's bitter budget bites hardest," *Toronto Star*, 14 July 1983; "Behind the Figures are the tears," *Sun*, 8 July 1983; *Pacific Tribune*, 15 July 1983; "Big Lie Budget Sledge Hammer Legislation," *Research Notes* (NDP Caucus), July, 1983; Larry Kuehn Papers, Special Collections, University of British Columbia, Vancouver, Box 4, File 6 (July, 1983), hereafter Kuehn Papers.

29.   I am thus arguing against the liberal Keynesianism of many budget critics, who seem to be claiming that there was no crisis necessitating the budget. But in terms of *capital's* priorities the budget made sense, even if it may

THE CHARACTER OF CLASS STRUGGLE

have been perceived as too excessive in its attempt to resolve all of the issues with one devastating sledgehammer blow. Note the liberal Keynesianism of the economists writing in Magnusson *et al.*, *The New Reality*, pp. 41-74, and comparable views in Rod Mickleburgh, "Operation Solidarity: How it was," in *British Columbia's Solidarity: What we can learn* (Ottawa, 1984), p. 12; Mickleburgh, "Chilling concise logic," Vancouver *Province*, 14 September 1983. Such views are challenged in Michael Lebowitz, "Review of *The New Reality*," forthcoming *Labour/Le Travail* (1986).

30.   See Norman Ruff, "Social Credit as Employer," in Magnusson *et al.*, *The New Reality*, pp. 152-64.

31.   *Sun*, 9 July 1983. Walker's words appeared in his weekly *Province* column and are quoted in Palmer, "The Opposition in British Columbia," *Speaking Out*, 2 (1983), p. 2.

32.   It is important to stress, against the "official" accounts of Solidarity, the extent to which early mobilization took place outside of the British Columbia Federation of Labour. While this is noted in William Carroll, "Solidarity Coalition," in Magnusson *et al.*, *The New Reality*, pp. 96-97, it is understated. In Art Kube, Rod Mickleburgh, and Meyer Brownstone, *British Columbia's Operation Solidarity*, and in the Operation Solidarity-sponsored video "Common Cause," 1984, it is ignored.

33.   "Coalition Against Budget Launched," *Pacific Tribune*, 15 July 1983; Evert Hoogers interview, 7 June 1985; Women Against the Budget interview (Gail Meredyth, Marion Pollock, Jackie Larkin), 12 June 1985; "Thousands join call to battle Socred Budget," *Province*, 24 July 1983; "Withdraw all the Legislation," *Pacific Tribune*, 29 July 1983; Ian Mulgrew, "Thousands protest Restraint in BC," *Globe & Mail*, 25 July 1983.

34.   On the worker occupation of an extended-care facility for the mentally handicapped in Kamloops, see *Province*, 20 September 1983; *Pacific Tribune*, 29 July 1983.

35.   Art Kube interview, 11 June 1985; David Cadman interview, 13 June 1985; Bob Buzza to Kuehn *et al.*, "Operation Solidarity: BC Federation of Labor Meeting, 15 July 1983," 19 July 1983, Kuehn Papers, Box 5, File 9; *Globe & Mail*, 16 July 1983; *Pacific Tribune*, 15 July 1983.

36.   Ian Mulgrew, "20,000 join protest against BC cuts," *Globe & Mail*, 28 July 1983; *Sun*, 28 July 1983; *Pacific Tribune*, 29 July 1983; "Operation Solidarity Reports," Kuehn Papers, Box 4, File 6; Evert Hoogers interview, 7 June 1985.

37.   Kramer interview, 10 June 1985; *Pacific Tribune*, 29 July 1983; Jacquie Boyer to Marie Kootnikoff, "Lower Mainland Budget Coalition Meeting," 25 July 1983, Kuehn Papers, Box 4, File 9.

38.   Novakowski to Kuehn *et al.*, "Solidarity," 8 August 1983; "Minutes of 3 August meeting"; "BC Fed Budget and Resource Allocation for Solidarity Coalition," all in Kuehn Papers, Box 5, File 9; Renate Shearer interview, 4 June 1985; Jean Swanson interview, 6 June 1985; Women Against the Budget interview, 12 June 1985.

39.   "50,000 jam Empire Stadium as mass budget protests sweep province," *Pacific Tribune*, 19 August 1983; *Globe & Mail*, 15 August 1983; *Province*,

11 August 1983; Hoogers interview, 7 June 1985; Denny Boyd, "Lonely voice delivers a message for Bill Bennett," *Sun*, 11 August 1983.

40. Women Against the Budget interview, 12 June 1985. In my lengthier discussion of Solidarity ("Reformism and the Fight Against the Right") I have tried to outline the role played by the Stalinist Communist Party of Canada. In essence it delivered the original Budget Coalition to Kube and the B.C. Federation of Labour bureaucracy, an outcome that was predictable given the CP's conception of its place in the labour movement. On the degeneration of Stalinism as a political tendency, see Ian Angus, *Canadian Bolsheviks: The Early Years of the Communist Party of Canada* (Montreal, 1981).

41. Women Against the Budget interview, 12 June 1985; Art Kube interview, 11 June 1985.

42. George Dobie, "A New Shape for Labor," *Sun*, 3 November 1976; Mike Bocking, "Rallying to the Cause Grows Difficult," *Sun*, 17 August 1983.

43. "Report on Operation Solidarity Think-Tank," Kuehn Papers, Box 5, File 9; Fred Wilson, "Phase II: Pressure on Government Must Escalate," *Pacific Tribune*, 19 August 1983.

44. Swanson interview, 6 June 1985; "Solidarity Coalition 8-Week Action Proposal," Kuehn Papers, Box 4, File 7; Carroll, "Solidarity Coalition," p. 99; *Pacific Tribune*, 19 August 1983; "Petition Blitz of Province Set by Solidarity Coalition," 2 September 1983. An example of the petition is in Kuehn Papers, Box 5, File 9.

45. *Province*, 25 August 1983.

46. Women Against the Budget interview, 12 June 1985; Renate Shearer interview, 4 June 1985; Art Kube interview, 11 June 1985; Evert Hoogers interview, 7 June 1985; "Office occupation signals renewed pressure on gov't," *Pacific Tribune*, 21 September 1983; Doug Ward, "Coalition tries to sell a showdown," *Sun*, 28 September 1983; *Globe & Mail*, 19 September 1983.

47. Allen Garr, "Solidarity – impressive coalition with no future," *Province*, 27 September 1983.

48. Cadman interview, 13 June 1985; Kube interview, 11 June 1985; Shearer interview, 4 June 1985; Swanson interview, 6 June 1985; David Yorke to Larry Kuehn, 28 September 1983, Kuehn Papers, Box 4, File 8; Undated clipping, Vancouver *Sun*, Solidarity Coalition Files (October, 1983); *Pacific Tribune*, 19 October 1983; *Globe & Mail*, 17 October 1983; *Sun*, 17 October 1983; *Province*, 15 October 1983.

49. On this aspect of the struggle, note Jeremy Wilson, "The Legislature Under Siege," in Magnusson *et al.*, *The New Reality*, pp. 114-130; Sharon Yandle, "The NDP in BC: Observing Their Friends on the Move," *Canadian Dimension*, 18 (March, 1984), pp. 5, 8; *Globe & Mail*, 11 August 1983; *Sun*, 11 August 1983; "The NDP and Solidarity," *Labour Focus*, 7 (January, 1984), pp. 7-8; Art Kube, "Operation Solidarity/Solidarity Coalition: Common Cause," in Kube *et al.*, *British Columbia's Operation Solidarity*, p. 8.

50. *Province*, 22 September 1983; *Sun*, 2 September 1983; Doug Ward,

"Coalition tries to sell a shutdown," *Sun*, 28 September 1983; *Sun*, 6 October 1983; "Vancouver Island Zone Meeting Report," 27 September 1983, and *Socialist Challenge*, "No Time to Back Down!" 29 September 1983, Box 4, File 8; "Solidarity Coalition, Delegated Conference Resolutions from Local Coalitions/Groups," Box 5, File 10, all in Kuehn Papers; Shearer interview, 4 June 1985; Swanson interview, 6 June 1985; "Coalition Promises Continued Struggle," *Pacific Tribune*, 26 October 1983; *Sun*, 19 October 1983.

51. Kramer interview, 10 June 1985; Kube interview, 11 June 1985; Shearer interview, 4 June 1985.

52. Kube interview, 11 June 1985; Kuehn interview, 10 June 1985; Rod Mickleburgh, "Strategy key to general strike," *Province*, 19 October 1983; "General Strike Real, Kube Warns," *Sun*, 28 October 1983; "Five Communications Principles," and "Public Sector Co-ordinating Meeting," 25 October 1983, Box 5, File 9, and "BCTV Newshour Final 83-10-25," and Kuehn to BCTF, 11 October 1983, Box 4, File 9, all in Kuehn Papers.

53. *Sun*, 28, 29, 31 October, 1 November 1983; *Province*, 1 November 1983; Operation Solidarity Press Release, 3 November 1983, and "Provincial Assembly Meeting Minutes," 3 November 1983, in Kuehn Papers, Box 4, File 10, Box 5, File 10.

54. *Globe & Mail*, 1-4 November 1983; *Sun*, 2 November 1983; *Solidarity Times*, 9 November 1983; *Pacific Tribune*, 9 November 1983; Kube interview, 11 June 1985; Larry Kuehn, "BC Teachers Strengthen the Labour Movement," *Canadian Dimension*, 18 (March, 1984), p. 10; "Teachers Weak Link in Chain," *Kamloops News*, 4 November 1983.

55. *Globe & Mail*, 9 November 1983; *Solidarity Times*, 9 November 1983; *Sun*, 8 November 1983; Kuehn, "Teachers Strengthen Movement," pp. 9-10; Cadman interview, 13 June 1985; "Injunction Situation," Kuehn Papers, Box 5, File 19. Many of the injunctions were granted precisely because the escalating Operation Solidarity public-sector job actions were widely perceived to be sympathetic strikes in support of the BCGEU rather than, as many Solidarity activists conceived, a broad protest against the legislation. Leo McGrady, a Vancouver labour lawyer who was acting on behalf of many education-sector unions at the Labor Relations Board, noted that this ended up being quite a problem for the education sector and pointed out that the injunctions were just the kind of state repression that was supposed to trigger an unlimited general strike. But in his words, the injunctions elicited "a certain amount of relief" among some labour leaders; "certainly there was no escalation." Leo McGrady interview, 7 June 1985. I have dealt with this aspect of Solidarity's history in far more detail in "Reformism and the Fight Against the Right." Kramer admitted in February, 1984, that many in the labour movement thought "the teachers would fold." My notes from a Solidarity panel, Simon Fraser University, but see as well, Doug Ward, "Sell-Out of Solidarity Debated," *Sun*, 8 February 1984.

56. *Globe & Mail*, 10 November 1983; *Province*, 9 November 1983; *Sun*, 12

November 1983; Kramer interview, 10 June 1985; Colin Kelly interview, 10 June 1985.

57.   For a fuller account of all of this, see my "Reformism and the Fight Against the Right." Note, as well, George Mason, "Weekend in Kelowna," *Vancouver Magazine*, 17 (June, 1984), pp. 20-23; *Sun*, 10 November 1983.

58.   See "Memo Lists Secret Labor Offer," *Sun*, 12 November 1983; Kramer interview, 10 June 1985; Kube interview, 11 June 1985; Kuehn interview, 10 June 1985.

59.   Shearer interview, 4 June 1985.

60.   Women Against the Budget interview, 12 June 1985; Susan Cross (Tele-communications Workers' Union member and Provincial Solidarity Steering Committee member) interview, 16 June 1985; Cadman interview, 13 June 1985.

61.   *Sun*, 14 November 1983.

62.   Kramer interview, 10 June 1985.

63.   Kramer interview, 10 June 1985; Kube interview, 11 June 1985; Cadman interview, 13 June 1985; "Back to Work!" *Sun*, 14 November 1983; *Sun*, 15 November 1983; *Solidarity Times*, 16 November 1983.

64.   Shearer interview, 4 June 1985; Kramer interview, 10 June 1985; Terry Glavin, "Kube booed at meeting," *Sun*, 15 November 1983; *Solidarity Times*, 16 November 1983.

65.   Province of British Columbia, *Restraint and Recovery: The Next Steps* (Victoria, 1983), p. 1; *Globe & Mail*, 19 November 1983; *Sun*, 16-18 November 1983.

66.   Kuehn Papers, Box 4, File 10 (November, 1983), esp. "Notes From Meeting with Heinrich, 21 November 1983," and "Letter from Island Teachers," 23 November 1983; also "Nanaimo Situation," Box 4, File 11. For personal attacks on Kuehn, see "Partial Transcript, Bennett interview, BCTV, Webster Show, 83-11-18," Kuehn Papers, Box 4, File 10, and *Caribou Observer* (Quesnel), 6 December 1983. Also Kuehn interview, 10 June 1985; "The Deal that Came Unstuck," *BCTF Action Update*, 23 November 1983; Allen Garr, "Munro Perhaps Feeling Abused," *Province*, 20 November 1983; *Sun*, 6 December 1983; Doug Ward, "Socred Stand Pushing Labor to Strike Edge," *Sun*, 3 December 1983.

67.   *The People's Report* (Vancouver, 1985); Shearer interview, 4 June 1985; Kuehn interview, 10 June 1985; Kube interview, 11 June 1985; Croll interview, 16 June 1985; Kelly interview, 10 June 1985; *Sun*, 1, 7 December 1983; Hoogers interview, 7 June 1985; Evert Hoogers, "BC's Solidarity Movement: Revival Hits a Snag," remarks to *Labor Notes* Conference, Detroit, June, 1984; Stuart Rush, "The Solidarity Movement in British Columbia: It's Still the Only (People's) Game in Town," remarks to a Panel on Solidarity at the Colleges – Institutes Educators' Association, Vancouver, 25 May 1984; Dan Smith, "Bennett vs. Labor Turning into a Rout," *Toronto Star*, 21 April 1984; Karl Marx, "The Eighteenth Brumaire of Louis Bonaparte," p. 97.

THE CANADIAN SOCIAL HISTORY SERIES

Terry Copp,
The Anatomy of Poverty:
The Condition of the Working Class in Montreal 1897-1929, 1974.
Gregory S. Kealey and Peter Warrian, Editors,
Essays in Canadian Working Class History, 1976.
Alison Prentice,
The School Promoters: Education and Social Class in Mid-Nineteenth Century
Upper Canada, 1977.
Susan Mann Trofimenkoff and Alison Prentice, Editors,
The Neglected Majority: Essays in Canadian Women's History, 1977.
John Herd Thompson,
The Harvests of War: Prairie West, 1914-1918, 1978.
Donald Avery,
"Dangerous Foreigners": European Immigrant Workers and Labour Radicalism
in Canada, 1896-1932, 1979.
Joy Parr, Editor,
Childhood and Family in Canadian History, 1982.
Howard Palmer,
Patterns of Prejudice: A History of Nativism in Alberta, 1982.
Tom Traves, Editor,
Essays in Canadian Business History, 1984.
Alison Prentice and Susan Mann Trofimenkoff, Editors,
The Neglected Majority: Essays in Canadian Women's History, Volume 2, 1985.
Ruth Roach Pierson,
"They're Still Women After All": The Second World War and Canadian
Womanhood, 1986.
Bryan D. Palmer, Editor,
The Character of Class Struggle: Essays in Canadian Working-Class History,
1850-1985, 1986.
Angus McLaren and Arlene Tigar McLaren,
The Bedroom and the State: The Changing Practices and Politics of
Contraception and Abortion in Canada, 1880-1980, 1986.
Alan Metcalfe,
Canada Learns to Play: The Emergence of Organized Sport, 1807-1914, 1986.
Marta Danylewycz,
Taking the Veil: An Alternative to Marriage, Motherhood, and Spinsterhood in
Quebec, 1840-1920, 1987.
Craig Heron,
Working in Steel: The Early Years in Canada, 1883-1935, 1988.
Wendy Mitchinson and Janice Dickin McGinnis, Editors,
Essays in the History of Canadian Medicine, 1988.
Joan Sangster,
Dreams of Equality: Women on the Canadian Left,
1920-1950, 1989.